Liturgies and Trials

The Secularization of Religious Language

Liturgies and Trials

The Secularization
of Religious Language

Richard K. Fenn

The Pilgrim Press
New York

First published 1982
Basil Blackwell Publisher Limited
108 Cowley Road, Oxford OX4 1JF, England

Library of Congress Cataloging in Publication Data

Fenn, Richard K.
  Liturgies and trials.

  Bibliography: p. 207
    1. Religion and language.   2. Liturgics.
  3. Secularism.   I. Title.
  [BL65.L2F46 1981b]   200'.14   81-19250
  ISBN 0-8298-0495-1   AACR2

*The Pilgrim Press, 132 West 31 Street,
New York, NY 10001*

Printed and bound in Great Britain

Contents

vi

Acknowledgments

This book developed from the encouragement and example of far too many friends and colleagues to be mentioned here. Bryan Wilson has given the manuscript a careful reading and continues to make me question whether religion is of more than residual importance in modern societies. If religious language is a survival of primitive forms of speaking, as he suggests, its future diminishes as religious communities abandon magic and the millennium in order to fit into secularized societies. He has been very charitable as well as helpful in his criticisms. To David Martin I owe an appreciation for the continued force and ambiguity of religious language in secular societies. In fact, it was a conversation with David Martin that first led me to explore my understanding of the liturgy, an exploration that resulted in chapter 2 of this book and in my continuing interest in liturgical change. To David Martin also I am indebted for a careful reading of this manuscript. Many of my ideas took shape during long conversations with my colleagues at Maine, James Gallagher and Burton Hatlen. Much of the work on chapters 6 and 7 was initiated during a summer term at Columbia University, for which I wish to thank Amitai Etzioni. At that time also, assistant US attorney Thomas Engle in New York City offered me the hospitality of his office and access to his files on the Cueto–Nemikin case. I wish to thank them all.

Some of the work in this book has appeared elsewhere. I wish to thank the editors of the *Annual Review of the Social Sciences of Religion* for permission to reprint portions for chapters 4 and 5. The Conférence Internationale de Sociologie

Religieuse granted permission to reprint material comprising most of chapter 1, and the editors of *PN Review* (Manchester) granted their permission to reprint what is largely chapter 2. I am most grateful to each of them. In addition, I wish to thank the editors of Heinemann for permission to quote sections of Alan Davies (ed.), *Problems of Language and Learning* (London, 1975) and Beacon Press for permission to quote from Daniel Berrigan, *The Trial of the Catonsville Nine* (Boston, 1970). Other publishers whose permission to quote I gratefully acknowledge are Argo Books Inc. for extracts from Eugen Rosenstock-Huessy's *Speech and Reality* (Norwich, Vt, 1970); the *Columbia Journal of Law and Social Problems* for extracts from volume 12 (1976); Fortress Press for a passage from Norman Perrin's *Jesus and the Language of the Kingdom* (Philadelphia, Pa, 1976); Alfred A. Knopf, Inc. for an extract from Richard Sennet and Jonathan Cobb's *The Hidden Injuries of Class* (New York, 1972); Pantheon Books, a division of Random House, Inc. for an extract from Michel Foucault's *The Archaeology of Knowledge* (New York, 1974), translated by A.M. Sheridan Smith; and Rudolf Steiner Press for an extract from Owen Barfield's *Speaker's Meaning* (London, 1967). In typing successive drafts of this book, Eva Meyn and Sue McLaughlin have been indefatigable and helpful far beyond what I could have asked of them.

I have dedicated the book to my family as a way of thanking each of them for our life together. My love and gratitude go to Caroline, my wife, and our children Kimball, Caroline and Thomas.

Introduction

The world used to give relatively few choices. The choice of a name was solemnized in the ritual of baptism, as those who spoke for the individual gave the new baby a name in the family of God. The choice of a spouse, again one of the few great choices made by individuals in a less complex society than ours, was solemnized in the ritual of the church or synagogue in order to leave no doubt in anyone's mind that promises had been made and that private passions were being lent to such public purposes as the raising of children. But in more complex societies individuals enjoy a wide range of choices, many of them fateful but few actually solemnized. They choose whether or not to work, and they choose when to retire. They choose whether or not to fight in the armed forces, and they choose when to die. Each of these decisions, and many lesser ones in everyday life, are choices on the side of life or on the side of death. Like birth and marriage, they are worthy of being celebrated in religious liturgies, because they bind individuals to one another in the service of life itself. But the vast array of life-and-death decisions go largely unsolemnized, although they may nevertheless be taken on religious grounds. The lack of liturgical settings that announce such decisions and make them binding for ever and ever is one measure of the process that we have come to name "secularization."

When decisions are made in a liturgical context, no doubt is allowed to remain concerning what is intended and who is responsible for the outcome. The solemnization of marriage vows leaves no doubt that unconditional promises are being made, until death supplies the only remaining contingency capable of ending the marriage. The same liturgy makes all those responsible who are present and prohibits any future tampering with a union formed by the presence of God. But decisions in secular contexts are seldom so clearly made. Children are notoriously too certain as to when a promise has been made, and adults are chronically uncertain about promises. Intentions are often implicit or suspect in everyday life, and the authority of one speaker to make a statement or promise encounters challenges from spouses, students, citizens, and others who have earned the right to ask, "Are you sure?" Outside the liturgy, speaking is always problematical, but the problems ramify in societies that give choices and responsibilities on limited grounds to an increasingly diverse array of groups and individuals.

Of course, there is ancient precedent for these uncertainties. In the Garden of Eden story the myth of the Fall suggests that the most profound human uncertainty concerns even the intentions of God. Intentions are not always expressed, of course, and when they are expressed, they are still liable to misinterpretation. The Eden myth suggests that the origin of evil lies in the serpent's inquiry, "Did God say . . .?", an early reminder that man is in trouble when testimony on the intentions of God becomes unreliable hearsay in the court of human discourse. But even when God's intentions are explicit, the force of God's speech is open to misinterpretation. Was the word of God to Adam (Man) a wish, a command, a threat, or a promise? The myth of the Fall claims that uncertainty about the content and the force of expressed or implied intentions is at the root of all evil, and the Western religious tradition accords this type of uncertainty a very high place indeed in its catalogue of human dilemmas.

Simple situations are seldom simple, and in the light of subsequent tragedy they may become extremely problematical. Take, for instance, the conversations between a young woman and her family about her wishes for terminal care should she ever become fatally ill. Karen Ann Quinlan apparently expressed her wishes to her family under seemingly straightforward circumstances. The circumstances entailed the hopeless illness of a relative and of a friend. Her stated wishes were simple enough: to avoid protracted, costly, and futile medical care. But under later circumstances, when Karen Ann lay comatose as a result of a mixture of toxic substances in her bloodstream, her family's testimony as to her wishes was subject to serious cross-examination and challenge in a secular court of law. "Did Karen say . . .?" became one question that preoccupied the court in this matter, and the question concerned life, death, the sanctity and authority of the family, and religious freedom. In chapter 6 we will see that later tragedy made the earlier statements seem incomplete or irrelevant in the eyes of the court. While to the family they were a crucial source of guidance, the court required more authoritative and reliable testimony on which to base a decision.

Religion is traditionally the court of last resort for the problems of authority posed by the ambiguities of human speech. Oaths, sacraments, and signs are liturgical expressions of speech that have become unambiguous, serious, and binding both on those who speak and on those who listen. But in the case of Karen Ann Quinlan there were no liturgical guarantees for her words, which were unambiguous, serious, and binding only within the context of the family. The Quinlans therefore sought to claim that the family stands for a sacred community whose obligations, given and received in good faith, must be honored before other tribunals. In the trial court, however, cross-examination raised significant doubts as to the relevance and force of Karen's words under present circumstances. The serpent's question is still effective ("Did . . . say?"), since it undermines certainty regarding what the speaker (Karen) originally meant, uttered, and intended. Apart from the structure of a liturgy, in which legitimate doubts about meaning and intention are suspended, human speech is unlikely to stand the test of later questioning and unforeseen circumstances. Least of all can such speech compete with the credibility of "expert" testimony or with the authority of the official speech of the state through the judiciary. I will develop this point in later chapters not only on the Quinlan case, but on the trials of the Catonsville Nine and others who have challenged secular authority with the force of religious convictions and testimony.

The Eden myth expresses the ancient human obsession with language on two levels. The first concerns the theological notion of sin: to question God's motives and to reinterpret the meaning of divine speech. The serpent begins with an exaggeration implied in the question, "Did God say, 'You shall not eat of *any* tree in the garden?' " The exaggeration permits Eve to interpret God's speech when she reminds the serpent that God intended to refer only to the "tree in the midst of the Garden." Gerhard Von Rad, whose analysis of the Fall I have been following here, states:

...man's ancient folly is in thinking he can understand God better from his freely assumed standpoint and from his notion of God than he would if he would subject himself to his Word. (1961: 86)

On a more mundane level, however, the Eden myth concerns the human condition in which speech is always open to challenge and reinterpretation. Interpretation is itself an act that estranges man from a paradise in which words are serious, unambiguous, and have the force of deeds.

Take the act of speech that constitutes a promise. "The promises of God are sure," states the prophet, but certainly not the promises of humans. Students of acts of speech note that a "full-blown" promise is difficult to find in ordinary human conversation. Some promises sound more like threats or predictions: "I shall return" being perhaps the most famous military promise of this mixed variety. A genuine promise satisfies too many conditions to be readily found in everyday speech: a set of conditions that is itself a matter of debate among linguistic philosophers. To be a promise an act of speech will, at the very least, be serious and should be taken literally; otherwise the one who promises can easily be disregarded or misinterpreted (Wootton 1975: 49). A promise, to be a genuine promise, also commits the speaker to doing something that the speaker can do, intends to do, and will do: something that the speaker would not otherwise do unless by promising the speaker becomes obligated to do so (ibid: 49–50). But a promise is not a promise unless the speaker and the hearer live in a community where these are, in fact, the rules governing promises. Only then will they know that the rules are being followed and invoked by the very act of promising. Full-blown human promises require fidelity to the rules in the speaker and, in the one who hears, faith that the rules are being followed.

No wonder that such promises are rare in human conversation. When they occur, they are given and received with signs and symbols that something out of the ordinary is occurring. I am thinking specifically of wedding ceremonies in which extraordinary care is taken that all the conditions are fulfilled that make full-blown promises possible for mere humans. Announcements of intention to marry and a final pronouncement begin and conclude a process in which both persons promise that only death will part them. There can be no mistake about the seriousness of this promise, and its seriousness is guaranteed by those who watch with "the eyes of God" as rings are exchanged, hands clasped, and solemn steps taken. Even those who know of conditions that would prevent a full-blown promise from taking place are told to speak (now) or keep silent forever. The liturgical language of religion is therefore the last human defense against the slipperiness, ambiguity, and uncertainty of all human acts of speech; and even these liturgical guarantees are widely known to fail.

The Eden myth claims that there once was a context in which there was little room for ambiguity and misunderstanding in language. To hear the word of God was to understand; to understand was also to obey. But outside the gates of paradise language becomes ambiguous and problematical in all respects. After the Fall, so to speak, the connection between the word and the context in which the word is spoken becomes tenuous. The child's outraged reminder to the parent, "But you promised!" signifies that the child understood a parent's word to be good for all times, whereas the parent knows that the promise depends on the circumstances of context. The child may also not distinguish between a pious wish, a statement of intention, and an actual promise and may misjudge the degree to which the speaker is serious. The ultimate criterion for seriousness in speech, of course, is action. Every parent and politician knows that promises can only be "redeemed" by appropriate deeds. Otherwise the one who promises must engage in a secondary set of speech-acts that provide reasons, excuses, justifications, and motives for the original promise and for subsequent default. But students of speech-acts seem also to disagree on what constitutes an adequate or correct excuse, explanation, or statement of motive: a disagreement that fairly reflects the problematical nature of language in general and of these speech-acts in particular. "That's no excuse" is as frequently heard from outraged children as "But you promised!" Outside the gates of God there is ample room for misunderstanding the conditions for a genuine promise or an adequate excuse. The myth does say, after all, that the first failure to provide an adequate excuse was the sign that the linguistic tie between God and man had been broken.

The seriousness of a promise depends not only on the context but also on the relationship of the speaker to the hearer. In the Eden myth God appears to have promised to provide for human wants so long as humankind avoids a particular tree. But the guarantee of the promise is the relationship between God and humans: a relationship of faith, which in the Old Testament is indistinguishable from trust in the divine Word and obedience to it. The Word of God is "solid," whereas all other words are slippery at best and may be downright empty or misleading. But one only knows the word as solid if one is in a solid relationship to the author: a relationship of trust and obedience. That relationship authenticates the promises of God; it is the proof that eludes philosophical syllogisms and a search for empirical results. Only those in the proper relationship of God therefore understand the nature of the proof itself. Outside that relationship there is ample room for speculation concerning the seriousness of God's promises and whether they are to be taken literally as threats, or as empty words intended to keep the hearer at a safe distance from divine knowledge and power. Enter the serpent as a sign that the proper relationship is in danger.

The myth of Eden, then, carries the secular understanding that language has become problematical in every respect regardless of the myth's theological motif. A promise can *be* a promise only when the context is clearly established; and a promise can be *taken* as a promise only when there is a community of speech with rules for actors and actions that are widely understood and obeyed. But these connections are what some students of language call "defeasible," and indeed the connections can easily be loosened or severed altogether. That is why, I will argue, religious language goes to such lengths to re-establish the problematic connections between word, context, and motive, as well as the links between the speakers and hearers. In the first three chapters, I will argue that those connections become clearest, of course, in the liturgy itself.

The liturgy is as close as humans ordinarily come to re-entering the closed linguistic garden of paradise. It is no accident, of course, that the entrance to many churches is like a great gate. The openings and passages within the church signify that words can be solemnized only when individuals pass through them. The gate to the sanctuary itself signifies the entrance to a place where words spoken in memory of God's words recreate God's deeds. The liturgy literally "opens the gates of heaven to man below."

The liturgy supplies the symbolic context, just as the church supplies the setting, in which words can be taken seriously because only those are allowed to speak who are utterly serious about what they are saying. The proper relationship of speaker to hearer is guaranteed through a variety of liturgical connections. Some speakers are *ordained* to speak, and others are *chosen*, while in the liturgical solemnization of marriage vows the speakers are *permitted* to speak by those in ecclesiastical authority. The words of the speakers, even in marriage ceremonies, are usually prescribed, although in some cases a couple are permitted to write their own vows if the words are authorized by the local clergy. The proper relationship of speaker to hearer is further guaranteed by the prescribed responses: "Amen," "I will," "I do." No room is left for words that are not serious, and there is no space in the liturgical context for words that are not properly received. The liturgy is the opposite of the tower of Babel. Babel, which means the "gate of God," is man's attempt to open the gate to the place where truer words were never spoken, but according to the myth only confusion results.

Myths concerning the "gates of Eden" or "the gates of God" may be the most suggestive metaphors for that period in the life of the individual in which words were once closely rooted in a specific context and were understood through the specific relationship of the speaker to the hearer. That period is clearly childhood, regardless of wherever else in the history of the race such a context was initially experienced. To the child the verbal act of promising has power because the child knows the voice of the speaker, the speaker's intentions and capacities, the obligation undertaken by the one who promises, and the certain outcome of that verbal act in specific deeds. These are the powerful connections between words and deeds, between people, and between people and situations that make the promises of childhood sure and that create an elemental faith or trust in the child. The liturgy attempts to re-establish such powerful connections by guaranteeing the intentions and the sincerity of the speakers, by determining the meaning of words and how they will be understood (by those) in the liturgical context, and by certifying the capacity and obligations of those who promise to turn their words into deeds. The liturgy recreates the paradise of childhood in order to create faith.

Like the promises of childhood, the promises and other verbal actions of the liturgy are never wholly guaranteed against misinterpretation and default. Every marriage ceremony is conducted with the knowledge of all participants that even these solemn words may be spoken in vain. The intentions of one or both partners may not be wholly in accord with their words even when neither person lacks sincerity. Sincerity itself cannot always be guaranteed: let alone the capacity always to act on one's stated intentions of lifelong fidelity. The myth of the Fall is not wholly suspended during the liturgy but hangs over each occasion like a watchful serpent in a tree, who waits for an opportunity to arouse doubt concerning the meaning of the words, the motives of the speaker, and the relationship of certain words to certain deeds.

Despite these failings, the liturgy is still the primary human strategy for recreating a stage in early childhood in which speech was first learned and experienced as powerful. A child often may be heard repeating the words of the adult. In this way parental promises or commands become internal rather than merely external guarantees or forces: "Mommy will return," "I will return," "Don't be afraid." By repeating these promises the child makes them personal and effective in later contexts. Note, then, how in the liturgy the adult repeats the words of the clergy: "I . . . take thee to be my wedded husband . . . till death us do part." Here again the speech originates outside in the form of an authoritative speaker and becomes personal only through repetition. In the act of repetition the words become personal and effective. But, as with the child, the liturgical acts are only the beginning of a process in which "inner speech," to use Luria's apt phrase, takes over the function of regulation and the promises of fidelity come true.

Like a mythical paradise or one's own childhood, however, liturgical settings for serious speech can seem long distant even in the relatively recent past. They appear to be in another time and another place, where words seem unconditional and speakers always true. But in everyday life, as in the course of personal development, the impact of serious speech on human behavior comes under subtle influences. Words that were once meant unconditionally take on a metaphoric meaning. According to the myth, "You shall die" becomes "You shall be as gods." The intentions even of authoritative speakers become doubtful, and their promises and commands, once taken at face value, are retrieved again for analytical inspection and reinterpretation. As I will argue in the opening three chapters, many settings in modern societies, especially the court and the classroom, specialize in raising doubts about the trustworthiness, credibility, and authority of serious speech.

The Eden myth also suggests another memory of powerful speech-acts: the act of calling. God, walking in the Garden, calls Adam by name: "Adam, where are you?" The use of his name calls Adam out of hiding into a new relationship that is marked by ambivalence: ambivalent combination of fear and trust of the human toward God. God calls, and humans reveal themselves almost against their own will. Humans call, and in responding the divine voice reveals the whereabouts and will of God. The myth recovers the power of the initial memory of being called upon by name, which in childhood is the act of being called into being through a relationship to the parent. To be called by name, however, is also to receive a calling: to be given a duty and a promise. Underlying the power of acts of speech such as promising, then, is the act of calling: calling by name, calling upon, calling for, and calling to. No wonder that a doctrine of vocation expresses in Western religion the notion of a divine calling that is inherited by every person who accepts and receives the promises of God. Certainly to be called by name places the child in every family in a position of being called upon and called to respond to new duties and opportunities that are most promising. To be so called upon places a burden of responsibility on all whose behavior is "uncalled for." And to be called on gives every child, including one as comatose and mute as Karen Ann Quinlan, the right to call upon her parents for protection. Childhood in the family therefore is a period in which scenes are enacted that in retrospect take on sacred significance. The very basis of faith and trust is laid in the speech of family members to one another. Children come to understand the nature of full-blown promises and legitimate excuses in their conversations with other members of the family; and, as their faith is inevitably disappointed, they may come to imagine that there was once a paradise in which words wholly expressed intentions and promises always come true. The search for such a context animates those who turn to religious movements that claim to be "the one true family." Certainly the churches have held the family sacred and have sought to give religious guarantees to the promises that constitute the family in the solemnization of holy matrimony. The law also acknowledges that:

Marriage is a coming together *for better or for worse*, hopefully enduring, and intimate to the degree of being sacred. (*Griswold* vs. *Connecticut*, 381 US 486 [1965] [emphasis added])

These words of Justice Douglas, in which a well-known phrase from the liturgy takes on the force of law, support the claim of Joseph Quinlan that he and his family should be allowed by the court to make the final decision regarding the termination of extraordinary measures for their hopelessly brain-damaged daughter, Karen Ann. There were other "sacred" rights also on trial in the Quinlan case, such as the right to privacy, the right to life, and the right to the free exercise of religious beliefs. But in a secular society there is no clear priority of one sacred sphere over another, especially when the state and the family or church disagree concerning matters of life and death (see Appendix I for a summary of Karen Ann Quinlan's case).

At the heart of the Quinlans' plea is the assertion that on several occasions Karen Ann Quinlan had told the members of her family that she would not like to have her life prolonged by "extraordinary measures should any terminal illness or accident arise." Although other occasions are discussed by her mother and sisters during the trial itself, the plaintiff's brief refers to two such occasions in particular. Karen Ann Quinlan had previously expressed her wishes with regard to the proposed action.

(1) In February of 1974, the father of a friend of Karen Ann Quinlan was dying of cancer. Karen, in discussions with her mother, Julia Quinlan, her sister, Mary Ellen, and her friend, Laurie Gaffney, made statements

to the effect that if she were suffering from a terminal illness, she would not wish her life to be prolonged through the futile use of extraordinary medical measures.
(2) In March of 1975, a friend of the family died of cancer. His wish before dying was to return to his own home and die there. In discussions with her mother, Julia Quinlan, and her sister, Mary Ellen, Karen made statements to the effect that if she were in similar circumstances, she would not want anyone to prolong her illness and suffering through the futile use of extraordinary medical measures. (In the Superior Court of New Jersey, Chancery Div., Morris County, Docket no. C–201–75; *in the Matter of Karen Ann Quinlan, an Alleged Incompetent* – trial brief of the plaintiff, p. 35)

Unfortunately for the Quinlans' case, these statements suffered from the same erosion of force and meaning that afflict all human utterances. They lacked the formal protection of the liturgy, and in retrospect the legal serpent could always raise questions concerning Karen's meaning and intent. Indeed, before the mother and sister of Karen Ann Quinlan could testify as to what they remembered Karen to have said and what she meant, several lawyers raised strong objections concerning the admissibility of such testimony. In summarizing these objections, Judge Muir said:

The preciseness of the [Karen Ann's] state of mind is suggested to be the thing that must be in issue, and it's suggested that this is too remote; that there's no continuity of intent; and that there are different fact situations making it something that is not in issue. (*In the Matter of Karen Ann Quinlan* I: 431)

The same objections, as I have suggested earlier, can be raised to any speech-act such as a promise or a threat. What did the speaker mean to say? Does that meaning reflect only the context of the original act of speech? Are we bound today by those original words?

Certainly Karen Ann's state of mind (her wishes and intentions) are at issue here, because in the light of her later tragedy those wishes took on a moral force even more binding than when she first spoke. In effect, the family had "promised" to honor her will if an occasion for using "extraordinary" measures should arise. The deputy attorney general for the state of New Jersey saw this quite clearly, when he said:

Really, what plaintiff is seeking here is the judicial honoring of a living will. Now I think that's somewhat absurd, absent legislation. (*ibid.*: 430)

In a living will, of course, the individual states a preference for removing extraordinary measures when they become futile, and those receiving the will sign it in token of their promise to honor that preference. In this case the Quinlans stated that their obligations took on the force of a sacred promise.

The commitments were sacred for two reasons. First, they arose from the intimate context of the family, whose members have obligations to one another that are sacred in the eyes of God if not always before the law. Second, the commitments have the force of the sacred because they were made "in harmony with" the religious culture of the Roman Catholic Church. "Harmony" here simply supplies a larger sacred context of meaning that gives weight to the family's commitments. But in cross-examination lawyers attempted to show that the commitments, like the family's decision to ask the court for permission to terminate extraordinary measures, were not caused, controlled, commanded, or celebrated by the Catholic Church. The promises, implied or explicit, lacked liturgical force. Indeed the lawyers sought to demonstrate that the family's decision was made *prior* to consultations on the matter with the local clergy and that a decision to *continue* extraordinary measures could also have been made in harmony with the church's teaching. The state's lawyers attempted to introduce a serpentine uncertainty into the family's claim that their understandings, their commitments to Karen, and their final decision to terminate extraordinary measures should be held sacred. The family's lawyer rejoined:

. . . it is in fact the right of the entire Quinlan family, including Ann, Karen Ann, that we set forth, for it is the love, faith, and courage unique to a father and mother, a sister and brother, *the love, faith, and*

courage unique to the Quinlan family, that brings us here today. (ibid.
II: 211; emphasis added)

While, in the opinion of one lawyer, it may have been
"absurd" in this trial to seek "judicial honoring of a living
will," Karen's religious beliefs did form one line of argument
and defense before the law. In the opinion of Daniel Coburn,
the court-appointed guardian of Karen Ann Quinlan, the case
was "tried primarily on the father's right as a Catholic to
exercise the religious beliefs of his daughter" (*Columbia
Journal of Law and Social Problems* [*CJLSP*] 12(1976):489).
But these beliefs, and their relevance to Karen's attitudes
towards being kept alive in hopeless circumstances by medical
machinery, could only be ascertained by admitting them as
heresay evidence. To admit them would have been a clearly
inadmissible procedure in most cases and one to which every
lawyer in this case objected except for the two lawyers with
the most serious responsibilities on opposing sides of the case:
Coburn, acting as the guardian, and Armstrong, who filed for
the plaintiff, Mr Quinlan.

In admitting the mother's testimony concerning what her
daughter Karen had once said in very different circumstances
and with intentions now too remote to be ascertained, the
court on one occasion did open itself to the force of implicit
promises and personal convictions too sacred to be ignored
even in a secular judicial context. As Coburn put it, "It was
very dramatic hearing the mother repeat the statements as to
what Karen had said" (*CJLSP* 12: 489). Her statements were,
from a legal point of view, mere representations of the mother's
memory "as to what Karen had said." As such, the representations were "somewhat questionable," since her mother put
into Karen's mouth phrases that had achieved currency only
some years later and then only in medical parlance, for
example, "artificial means of life maintaining devices" (*CJLSP*
12: 489). But the key word in Coburn's account is "dramatic,"
since it reveals the force of testimony that recreates the initial
acts of speech, their seriousness, and their later solemnization
by tragic events.

Although the family's explicit promises might not be proven to be in accordance with Karen Ann's personal wishes, let alone with the teachings of the Catholic Church, the family itself took on the aura of the sacred. Coburn's conclusion is compelling enough on this point (see Appendix II for more on Coburn's testimony):

Basically the case was tried — totally absent any medical issues — was tried on the family's right of privacy which they prevailed on by the way. The overtones of the case were religious all the way through . . . (*CJLSP* 12: 521, emphasis added)

Coburn means by "religious" not so much the family's exercise of one of its options within the Catholic faith as he means the right of the family itself to hold its own understandings as sacred. Indeed the brief for the plaintiff argued this point from the very beginning. Words had been spoken in that family: words whose seriousness and capacity to compel depended on the authority of the sacred context to the family. In the end, religion seems to have provided little in the way of support for the implied promise of the family, little in the way of guarantees for Karen Ann's personal beliefs on life and death, and little defense for the family itself as a sacred community. Instead, religion was reduced to a source of character-witness for the fitness of Joseph Quinlan to be his daughter's guardian.

It is perhaps not surprising that the role of religion in this trial was so drastically reduced. The courts were presented with the accounts of the Quinlan family concerning conversations with Karen Ann in which a tacit promise was made to honor her wishes to be spared futile medical care should the occasion ever arise. The courts heard the family's account of these conversations but failed to conclude that an irrevocable understanding had been reached. Intentions so far removed in time and circumstance are indeed difficult to ascertain and in any event are likely to change with new occasions and circumstances. *Here the courts clearly saw the reported conversations as non-liturgical: unable to remain unequivocal over time and yet to transcend the specific context in which they occurred.*

We see here the problematic character of all conversations, really, but especially those in which promises may have been made. Wootton summarizes the problem very well.

To argue that in our society promising has some central features which constrain interaction in any instance, one must set up such general features and demonstrate in any instance precisely where and how this constraint operates. To do this involves deciding in each case whether or not a promise has been made but . . . this is always ambiguous . . . alternative formulations are always available and often in fact made use of by members themselves in their attempts to justify, excuse, defend, fault and so on. (1975: 105)

In the Quinlan case the courts never decided whether a commitment had been made to Karen, implicitly or otherwise, that would have the force of a sacred obligation in the eyes of the law, although this was the ground on which the original plea of the plaintiff rested. Instead, the court focussed on whether the father of the family was a fit person to be guardian with responsibility for life-and-death decisions in his daughter's care. The court reduced the sacred to a question of good faith on the part of the father by considering whether there were significant faults in his character that would prevent him from making a decision free from ulterior motives or emotional strains that sometimes becloud human judgment. As I will point out in later chapters on the Quinlan and two other trials, the process of secularization results in precisely such a reduction of religion to a guarantee of personal authenticity: of authenticity without credibility or authority in secular contexts.

The sacred, in the absence of liturgical forms for binding words to deeds, is unable to provide a boundary that guarantees the individual, the church, or the family from unwarranted state intrusions. The family had sought a transcendent justice that recognizes as sacred their commitments to one another: especially their commitment to honor the wishes of one member of the family no longer able to speak for herself. Lacking a liturgical form to which they could point for evidence of the binding nature of these commitments or the circumstances under which they were undertaken, the Quinlans could give only their testimony. But religious testimony under the constraints of the law falls on the hard ground of the rules of evidence. The courts did not accept the Quinlans' testimony concerning their conversations with Karen Ann as sufficiently relevant, reliable, or weighty to influence later judicial decisions. I will argue (chapter 7) that the courts do not accept other conversations that might appear to be privileged or protected by the First Amendment even when these conversations are defined by the church as essential to its ministry. In the process of secularization very few words indeed are immune to later scrutiny and reinterpretation.

The sacred commitments of members of a family to one another, implicit or otherwise, withstand only with the greatest difficulty the secularizing force of state power. In the terminology of a brief submitted to the Supreme Court of New Jersey on behalf of the state's attorney general, "appellant can take no solace in the doctrine of substituted judgement" (*In the matter of Karen Ann Quinlan* II: 61). Where, as in this case, that individual is unable to speak or act on her own behalf, the state "acting in the role of *parens patriae* is the ultimate guardian of all incompetents" (ibid. II: 61). To the unborn fetus or the adult nearly returned to fetal state, as well as to adults and children alike who find themselves abused by their families, the state's intervention may be a liberating and saving one. But in this case the ultimate guardian ignores the apparent wishes of the very person whom the state claims to protect.

The logic is worthy of the discussions of God's will in the Eden myth. The attorney general argued that Karen Ann Quinlan's earlier statements about terminal care should now be ignored in her own best interests. Those earlier statements by Karen Ann referred to circumstances ("a lengthy and painful terminal illness") that do not obtain in the present. Besides, she spoke in one set of circumstances and might now have a different set of wishes. Even the family's recollections of the earlier conversations constitute "unreliable hearsay and should not have been admitted at trial" (ibid. II: 61). Their "probative weight," regardless of their reliability, is not great enough,

according to the attorney general, to support a judicial determination of what her present intentions might be should she
be able to speak her mind. In the absence of such certainties,
and in the light of the state's role as ultimate guardian, public
policy matters far more than any hypothetical wishes of a
speechless and thoroughly comatose patient. Public policy, of
course, is what the courts say it is, and one New Jersey court
had already said that no one has the right to "choose to die."

The Quinlan case is instructive because it fits three major
and usually contrasting sociological viewpoints on the process
of secularization. The first viewpoint is uniformly negative in
portraying the state as a secularizing force that rides rough-
shod over the sacred commitments that bind individuals and
family members together in ties of enduring loyalty and faith.
The second is more or less neutral in portraying the state as
relying on rational and legal sources of legitimacy that often
override traditional ties in order to provide uniform and non-
arbitrary treatment for all citizens before the law. Religion is
reduced to an expression of individual probity in the private
sphere rather than as a source of legitimacy to the whole
society and its major institutions. The third viewpoint is more
dialectical in that it contains both the former in a dynamic
process rather than in a linear progression toward the expansion of the state at the expense of everybody and everything.
On the one hand, it finds the individual as the emerging
spokesman of his own rights and responsibilities: the more
serious and authoritative as the individual articulates his or
her convictions in religious terms. The secular state breeds its
own prophets. On the other hand, the secular state cannot
license prophets and so creates the fiction of a popular will
that conforms in certain important respects to the acceptable
prophecy of the individual spokesman. The secular state
imagines a whole that legitimates even its most recalcitrant
individual parts.

First, with regard to the negative views, the New Jersey
Supreme Court determined that Karen Ann's earlier conversations with her family "were remote and impersonal [sic],
lacked sufficient probative weight," and were therefore not

germane to the court's task of deciding the equity of the matter. In the second place, the religious rights and obligations of the family to one of its own members were also found irrelevant in this case, with one major qualification. Thus the Supreme Court apparently recognized no religious protection and support for the internal commitments of the Quinlan family. But the second, more neutral view obtains because the Supreme Court applied a religious test to the character of Joseph Quinlan.

The judge was bound to measure the character and motivations in all respects of Joseph Quinlan as protective guardian; and insofar as these religious matters bore upon them, they were properly scrutinized by the court. (ibid. II: 297)

Any beliefs would do, according to the court: atheistic, agnostic, Buddhist beliefs, so long as they were "formed and viable." The point was simply to determine whether Joseph Quinlan had a suitable character and motives as potential guardian for his own daughter. The functional reduction of religion to a personality assessment along with the court's decision to ignore the family as an autonomous unit with sacred obligations to its own members enabled the court to fill the gap in the civil law with an "ethics committee" which would articulate a majoritarian viewpoint surely to be found in the larger society. This last was an amazing invention. As the court-appointed guardian for Karen Ann Quinlan put it in a later context:

The court made an amazing statement. They concluded that the overwhelming majority of people would make the choice that they were allowing the father to make on behalf of Karen. That conclusion just came out of no place . . . Obviously they cited no authority for that conclusion. They can say what they want. (*CJLSP* 12: 489)

But this cultural fiction serves to legitimate the state's authority to resolve the uncertainty left by gaps in the law and by the ambiguous expressions of intention that characterize everyday speech and language.

The issue here, then, is not *what* wishes should determine the outcome of Karen Ann Quinlan's life, but *whose* wishes shall prevail. The court notes that the majority of Americans undoubtedly have the same wish as the Quinlan family: for a peaceful and humane end to a hopeless condition. But the court establishes a process in which the private understandings of the Quinlans are found inadequate to the new situation, however adequately those understandings and commitments may have expressed the mutual wishes of an earlier occasion. Where God has not apparently solemnized the intentions of two or more parties to an understanding, it is easier for others to sunder those intentions or to mix them with the purposes of other parties and practitioners. That is, after all, one of the primary political functions of the state: to ensure that private agreements are mixed with public ingredients.

We have been examining one case of a secular trend that has exercised the imagination of several generations of sociologists. It is a trend that substitutes political and judicial judgments for traditional loyalties and social bonds that have united families, communities, and churches in the past. Sociological criticism has protested that this trend leaves the individual exposed to the power of the state without the protection of intervening or mediating social units: without the protection, in Karen Ann Quinlan's case, of the church and of the family. In later chapters we will note the effort by the Berrigan brothers and other war protesters to protect helpless individuals by means of sacred, quasi-liturgical words and deeds. Without such interventions the individual is literally at the mercy of an omnipresent state apparatus that limits the right of the person to live or to die according to the beliefs and intentions that the individual may share with smaller, more intimate, and often sacred associations such as the family and the church. The authority of these traditional or "natural" groupings is weighed in the balance with the power of the state and is found wanting (Nisbet 1976: 53). This critical viewpoint resonates with the voice of the Old Testament prophetic literature that similarly charges the state with destroying or ignoring the sacred ties that once united a simpler and more faithful society in its wanderings through the desert and its early settlements.

A more priestly sociological viewpoint celebrates the disinterested and judicious treatment of the individual by a state whose primary commitments are to the preservation of life and to the dignity of each individual citizen. In the Quinlan case, the state carefully scanned the circumstances to determine which of several rights may be at issue here: the right to life, to privacy, to freedom from extraordinary punishment, and the right to the free exercise of religion. In a case involving the Episcopal Church and Puerto Rican terrorists, the state also appeared as the defender of the individual's right to life itself. The state claims to act without the emotional entanglements of close, personal relationships and with a clear sense of its own powers or limitations. The state therefore does not defer to the wishes of a small, traditional unit such as the family or ethnic community, but insists that local associations carry out the legal and moral standards of the larger society. Legitimacy, even for the secular state, derives from the society as a whole.

Against these overriding powers of the secular state, private commitments and sacred duties will not survive unless they are protected by liturgical words: those whom God hath joined together let no man put asunder. Of course, some liturgies are far more exclusive and radical than the services of "Holy Matrimony." The Eucharistic liturgy for instance, used to allow only the faithful to attend and dismissed those who were still being instructed: a practice that falls into disuse whenever the church becomes more hospitable to public purposes and the control of the state. But at the core of the Eucharistic liturgy is an act of remembrance in which those who participate join themselves to one who promised them nothing but trouble at the hands of secular institutions. The liturgy, finally, provides words that are heartfelt and adequate to the occasion. Such words leave little, if anything, unsaid. What is said on liturgical occasions, furthermore, is intended to come true and to hold true, regardless of whatever other pressures may later be brought to bear by outside forces, by professionals and politicians, by other institutions, and by the state itself.

Wishing, intending, and promising: these take the form of speech-acts that establish relationships with a particular future of mutual obligation. To remember these acts of speech, to recall them, is to call them back so that the same acts can again shape the future and renew mutual obligations. The acts of remembering and recalling certain words, such as the words of "institution" which establish the Eucharist, make it possible for individuals to continue to shape their future through common obligations. The same acts would have enabled the Quinlan family to shape their future through their renewed obligation to their daughter and to one another. Without the authority of the liturgy, however, these acts of speech are not likely to be authorized by courts of law. Testimony that remembers and recalls these words of institution is likely to be regarded as hearsay or as lacking probative weight. Liturgical language is never "mere" hearsay and carries great weight even in a secular court. That is why movements that demand freedom for new relationships are likely to find liturgical expression or perish.

In the last analysis, even liturgies are not immune to change. In the last chapter I argue that the process of secularization begins, paradoxically enough, in the attempt to clarify and institutionalize the forceful and ambiguous words of religious prophecy. In making prophecy more instructive, liturgies make prophets less disruptive and relevant to all times and occasions. But the human capacity for perennial and unlimited demands is itself limited; one cannot remain on trial forever. It is the source of the liturgy's profoundest strength that it places the individual once and for all before the court of final appeal and suspends all secular judgments. In a secular world, however, the classroom and the court place the individual in an apparently unending succession of challenges to personal credibility, authority, and authenticity. There are indeed signs in the religious movements that have increasingly attracted new adherents and public attention, that many individuals are seeking a context in which all such challenges come to an end. Whether a secular world is tolerable or will indeed survive remains to be seen.

Before taking up the major ideas in this book in more detail, it would be well to lay my sociological cards on the reader's table. The questions to be asked have been put very well, in fact, in this query from Bryan Wilson (in a personal communication):

Language is clearly not the criterion of the process of social differentiation, which is rooted in structural shifts in social organization. But does this make language epiphenomenal — a derivative of a process that is more substantially located in other phenomena? If so, what is the salience of language? Is it treated here as a facet of an underlying secularization process because it reveals that process in significant ways? Or is the analysis of language important in itself, or because it explains the modern hiatuses between such institutions as courtroom and prayer meeting?

In the following discussion I will assume that language acts both as a bridge and as a boundary between individuals and their societies. As a bridge language enables the private vision or intentions of the individual to make sense to others who may indeed be total strangers. Across this bridge pass the speaker's hopes and fears, intentions and wishes, meanings and beliefs. How much passes depends, of course, not only on the competence of the speaker but on the situation. To strangers who meet under conditions of relative equality in a fluid situation, a wide range of thought and feeling may pass from one to the other. Where the topics and the turns at speaking are rigidly and unevenly divided between speakers, much less of the individual speaker's meaning may get across. Language may therefore also act as a boundary. Some speakers are not permitted the use of Sanskrit, just as some are not entitled to the use of professional or esoteric terminology unless they are properly licensed. Indeed, only a few speakers are entitled to pronounce, to warn and declare, to pass judgment and give blessings. To return to Bryan Wilson's query for a moment, let us simply say that language, to the extent that it is constrained by social rank or institutional boundary, is derivative from forces located beyond the individial speakers. But language also enjoys a certain autonomy: the freedom of the speaker to observe the rules or to break them, to speak plainly or so as to confound the hearer.

The analysis of language is not only important in itself but also because close inspection reveals the linkages and gaps between such institutions as the academy and the court. The answer to Bryan Wilson's question can only be affirmative to both alternatives. No one needs to be reminded that the ambiguous role of religion in modern societies is due in part to the sheer ambiguity of religious language. Every "Hosanna" is both an act of praise and a plea for help. Every image of God that invokes such earthly figures as kings and mothers not only reinforces these earthly authorities but places them in the shadow of a divine judgment. Every symbol that unites believers divides them from others who do not believe. Every text for the laity that makes *common* prayer possible gives an uncommon authority to the prayers and utterances of the clergy. Language, religious language in this example, is important in itself, if one is to examine the degrees of uncertainty and freedom built into the rubrics and rules of any community. But language is also important because it points to the continuity and the separation between religious and secular communities of speech. So many of the terms, let alone the rules of discourse, are common to testimony in the courtroom and the congregation. Many are called to witness in the court as in the church, although few may be chosen to pronounce and absolve, to prophesy and declare, to determine and to dismiss.

Secularization, I will argue, has created powerful linkages between the rules for testifying in both religious and secular settings in modern societies. But each setting limits the semantic range that a speaker may employ, restricts the degrees of openness and ambiguity that a speaker is allowed, defines the force that speakers may give to their utterances, and determines the seriousness with which an audience will take the speakers and their words. I have taken language as the focus here because it not only reveals the ties that bind together apparently dissimilar contexts but because it reveals as well the constraints placed on what one can say and mean in particular contexts. The paradox is simple enough. Religion in the West takes speaking seriously, and in the course of two millennia Western societies have been persuaded to develop rules and procedures for guaranteeing the freedom and the authority, the credibility and the authenticity of speech. But in that same process institutions and occupational groups have placed strict, if still somewhat ambiguous limits on the scope of religious and lay testimony.

Language therefore does reveal the process of secularization "in significant ways." Courtrooms, for instance, that appear to be proceeding within a thoroughly legal linguistic framework find that the framework has been expanded by the introduction of narrative testimony to a speaker's religious commitments. Sometimes the legal framework contracts again, and the verdict restores a somewhat tarnished literal-mindedness to the proceedings; sometimes the framework is broken and the judges find themselves called upon to declare a gap in the law itself; an anomic situation requiring new procedures or understandings. Language may cut both ways, like a two-edged sword.

Sociologists therefore turn to language for insight into what is sometimes called the "middle-range" between individual intentions or deeds and the set patterns of institutions and of the larger society. In the middle range one finds societies changing even as they reassert their rules. There one finds individuals re-writing old roles even while taking them on. New roles come into play in the give-and-take of speaking and hearing, and old roles may take on new meaning as they are rehearsed once again. If sociologists are genuinely to understand what a particular kind of action represents, like the burning of draft cards or the refusal to testify, they must listen carefully to what people say and to whether they speak with force or diffidence, whether with the nuances of an ancient tradition or with unheard-of tongues. In analyzing closely the meaning that is conveyed as speakers translate their religious convictions into secular parlance in the classroom or in the court, sociologists who understand religious speech will be better able to interpret what is gained and lost in these translations without contributing distortions and omissions of their own. It is important, as Weber hinted, to be "musical" with regard to religion, and sociologists have sometimes been thought by theologians to be hard of hearing.

Beyond the tasks of understanding and interpreting the process of secularization, sociologists who focus on language will be better able to explain what passes between societies and individuals. To put it in the abstract formula currently in use, sociologists will find in language a medium by which action reproduces or transforms social systems. Language is also the medium by which social systems constitute the meaning and limits of action. Much depends on whether particular speakers can learn the registers of secular institutions, and much in turn depends on whether particular institutions are susceptible to the force of particular speakers. The authority and credibility of particular speakers, however, in turn depends on the survival of traditional beliefs whose claims can match the authority of medical or judicial theories on matters of life and death. The ability of an individual to challenge effectively the authority of a social system also depends on whether the individual's faith, however traditional or ancient it may be, is spoken with the authority of a particular religious community and not of the person alone. Secular institutions have a way of reducing authoritative declarations to mere assertions of personal opinion in the court or in the classroom. It is clearly not enough for a society to have religious or ethnic communities to protect the individual from the state if one must leave that protection behind in the witness stand. I will therefore be arguing that these communities still have in religious ritual a final guarantee of the authority of speech that cannot later be gainsaid in the classroom or the court. The liturgy provides one boundary remaining between the cities of God and Caesar.

Chapter 1

Signs, Symbols, and Social Integration

In the long course of Western history the notion that individuals and groups are continually tested, whether in small decisions or in critical events that foreshadow the final judgment of God on history, has spread from the circle of the prophets to a wide range of secular contexts such as the courts and classroom, the doctor's office, and academic committees. The individual is perpetually facing judgment by abstract and impersonal criteria that are only partially revealed while always calling into question the individual's own sense of worthiness. As Sennett and Cobb put it in their description of the classroom:

Authority for the teacher is a matter of personal assertion, assertion of his power to do good as opposed to his mere possession of power. Authority appears to the child, however as *passive*, as an audience before whom he must prove himself. The very tolerance of the teacher, the apposition of good to neutral, makes this so. The child feels he is on trial, that he is responsible, like Vinny or Max, for using his ability; the teacher is a judge to him, not a prosecutor. It is not so much when the many are openly scolded that they feel the most pressure from the teacher — at such a time he is showing some real concern about them. It is when the kids are trying to be good that the teacher's power is most felt. (1972: 87)

In the process of spreading beyond the religious community, the theme of the "last judgment" loses its theological framework, and the process of adjudication becomes as endless as it is inescapable. Individuals face challenges to their credibility or seriousness from secular authorities that make their own rules for taking individual testimony seriously. Hopes are occasionally kindled for a millennial judgment to end the experience of being forever on trial. Some prophesy that the end will come with swift and fell divine judgment, while others prophesy, almost with a sense of relief, that when a nuclear holocaust finally comes, all our trials will be over. Pressures build up to put the strengths of East and West to a final test, and individuals themselves seek an end to the experience of being on trial through earning a final degree, through violence, or through any of the kinds of narcotics available in the marketplace. The secularization of the divine lawsuit against mankind leads to desperate measures, strenuous achievements, quiet despair, and occasionally to renewals of religious fervor to obtain divine forgiveness.

The secularization of the heavenly trial has undoubtedly led to the dynamic search for "truth" in modern societies: for reliable and verifiable testimony concerning the universe. The most basic assumptions behind the search for the "truth" in scientific inquiry are very similar, in fact, to those used in trial proceedings. As Luckmann (1973) has observed, scientists since Galileo have assumed that the universe is composed of primary and secondary qualities; some facts, in other words, are more important than others for understanding the cosmos. Scientists, therefore, like lawyers and judges, must weigh the evidence carefully in order to discern what is truly relevant and weighty as opposed to irrelevant and superfluous detail. Scientists also operate with assumptions about appearances: that there is more to the universe than meets the eye. One must therefore probe beneath material surfaces for hidden forces, beneath apparently unrelated or random occurrences for hidden relationships, just as lawyers and judges search for motives and interests beneath the apparently disinterested account of witnesses about particular occurrences. Like lawyers and judges, scientists also search the evidence for inconsistencies and incongruities, for pieces of the puzzle that do not fit, on the assumption that an accurate account of the world's processes will ultimately make sense without missing or incongruous pieces. But therapists also scrutinize a patient's account of feelings and experiences for significant distortions and omissions on the assumption that, beneath the surface and despite the profusion of irrelevant detail, there is an underlying complex of related motives and wishes, of fears and evasions at work in the patient's life. Not only therapists, lawyers, and scientists but social workers and professors place their clients and students "on trial" in taking their testimony or evaluating their writing for inaccurate, irrelevant, distorted, inconsistent, or partial accounts of "the way things are."

The procedures of a classroom or doctor's office are, in fact, very much like those of a court. Wherever individuals speak "for the record," or when they speak in order to create a record, a text develops that can later be perused for inconsistencies or used as a basis for testing the consistency of subsequent words and deeds in the light of the speaker's recorded statements. Witnesses make statements for the record in order to establish the basis, for instance, of an appeal, just as students raise objections in the classroom in order to establish a basis for later appeals against a professor's evaluation of their work. When witnesses in a courtroom describe a set of events leading to some unfortunate offense, their account not only describes "what happened" but also interprets those events as "an honest mistake" or an "error of the mind rather than of the heart," to use two descriptions currently in favor among notable American politicians. Descriptions not only describe and interpret; they also define a situation by allocating responsibility and defending the witness from more serious charges. In fact, careful examination of the accounts of witnesses indicate that these accounts are structured in order to make sense within the context of a court: a structuring at which experienced witnesses, such as policemen making an arrest, are more expert than hapless offenders who lack sophistication in accounting for their conduct in judicial terms and categories (cf. Buckner 1978). Even therapeutic interviews, however, are pre-coded by the patients as well as by the doctors, so that accounts of feelings and dreams take on a quasi-professional phraseology. A prison official, in fact, gave Charles Manson credit for describing his own pathology in nearly professional terms and completeness: a recognition that the prisoner had become sophisticated, if not entirely serious in applying professional labels to his own experience, (Wooden 1976). It is a sophistication known to ethnomethodologists as skill in choosing "strategies for encompassing a situation." In a world that places all individuals frequently on trial, such skills and strategies are necessary for survival. Otherwise one can too easily be discredited or merely ignored.

In this book I am arguing that the secularization of biblical themes lends a seriousness to everyday life: a sense that the individual or the institution is perpetually on trial. But the formal procedures by which academics, doctors, and lawyers obtain evidence, elicit testimonies, and arrive at definitions of the situation for assigning responsibility and blame are not entirely biblical. Indeed, as I suggest in chapter 4, these procedures rely on a more Hellenistic understanding of reality. For New Testament Christians, to witness meant also to commit one's whole life and even to sacrifice oneself, the term "marturion" conveying both the meaning of testifying and of sacrifice. But in Hellenistic terms the words for witness and theory are the same, as O'Neill points out in this telling statement:

Habermas invokes the etymology of Θξωρια in order to trace a development in the concept of theory from the original activity of the representative sent by a polis to witness the sacred festival of another city to the philosopher's μιμησις or representation in the order of his soul of the natural κοσμος. (1978: 202)

In secularized Western societies, then, many individuals are caught in a double-bind. On the one hand, they take seriously the role of the credible witness and seek, on the grounds of their own testimony, to be taken seriously, whether they are reporting what they saw on Mulberry Street or whether they are reporting the results of carefully controlled experiments. But in many secular contexts, their credibility as witnesses depends on their ability to report data "coded" in a fashion that makes sense within the context of the court or within the classroom. Their authority as witnesses, furthermore, depends on their ability to code the data of personal experience or of scientific experiments in terms of a "theory." Some witnesses rely for authority on scientific theories and so receive academic or judicial credit for their testimony. Others, however, rely on religious "theory," as in the case of conscientious objectors or prophetic disturbers of the peace who defend their actions on theological grounds. But in contexts controlled by representatives of scientific or judicial professional groups, religious "theories" or myths do not usually carry weight. Authority in these contexts depends on the ability of the individual to conform his or her testimony to legal or scientific "theories" as to what constitutes, for instance, a breach of the peace, legitimate dissent, the unavoidable constraints of social circumstance, or the relationship between brain waves, respiratory rates, and death itself. Given the long and steady pull of the biblical tradition on the implicit values of the West, it is no wonder that individuals take seriously the opportunity to give credible and authoritative witness. But given as well the professionalization of procedures for reliable and authoritative testimony, most individuals face the likely prospect of being tried and found wanting in the classroom, in the doctor's office, in the employer's office, as well as in the courtroom itself. As Kafka pointed out, a life of continuous trial is potentially dispiriting. Some are only too glad for the trial to be over and for the end to come.

In the sacred liturgies of certain religious traditions, however, the trials of the secular world are brought to a finish in an enactment of the Last Judgment. In the next chapter I will point out the dimensions of the liturgy that place the individual beyond the reach of secular tribunals. The judgment that takes place in the liturgy supersedes all secular judgments. Found acceptable in the liturgical context, the individual need not honor the claims of secular authorities to be taken more seriously than the liturgy itself would warrant. Taken in an ideal-typical sense, *the trial and the liturgy are the poles of sacred and secular authority. The polarity between the liturgy and the trial creates the dynamic tension between sacred and secular authority in modern societies.*

The similarities between the liturgy and a trial are more than superficial. Of course, in both ceremonial contexts individuals testify, perhaps even confess, and find their relative guilt or innocence proclaimed by the prevailing authority. In both contexts, authoritative or expert testimony is given by eye-witnesses, whether eye-witnesses of the acts of God or of man. In both contexts those in attendance are reminded of the letter of the law and called upon to give it an exact or spiritual interpretation, as the case may warrant. Both secular trials and liturgies rely on authoritative interpreters of testimony and of the law. But the differences between liturgies and trials are critically important. Both the liturgy and trial end, but only in secular trials can the parties seek a continuance or appeal. Unlike trials, liturgies may be repeated, whereas trials may be continued, re-opened, and appealed for years at a time. Trials end, but liturgies are finished.

Between the two poles of the liturgy and the trial are various social contexts ranging from the bureaucratic organization of the church, to families, ethnic groups, schools, political parties, and business organizations. I list these contexts in this order to suggest that the peculiar understandings and particular loyalties of the family, for instance, are guaranteed a measure of sacred authority because of the participation of the family in the liturgy. To put it another way: the authority conveyed to familial commitments and understandings by the liturgy places them further beyond the reach of secular tribunals than, for instance, are the contracts and agreements of business organizations. This is not to say that the family is beyond the reach of secular authority or that the family does not at times enlist the state as an ally in protecting its members from religious authorities. Certainly the state can intervene to insist that children of Jehovah's Witnesses, for example, be given blood transfusions, and some families ask the state to intervene in recovering their children from the control of certain religious groups. But the family as a unit, while under the judgment of God, is resistant to the judgment of secular tribunals. Members of families, furthermore, may expect to receive more unqualified forgiveness and acceptance than in secular contexts, where they undergo a continuous process of testing and evaluation and encounter the careful weighing and sifting of their statements for reliability or validity. One is less frequently on trial in the family than in the classroom, although the secularization of the family makes standards of performance and the conditional giving of love increasingly acceptable. Effectiveness-training for spouses and parents, for instance, is all the more necessary in relationships that are intended to be temporary or conditional on satisfactory performance. Divorce makes all marriages "trials" in which the parties may be found wanting, whereas in the context of the liturgy marriages are once and for all, for better and for worse, and in them judgement is forever suspended.

There is in Western civilization a continuing impulse toward the justfication of the self. The impulse originated in Western religious culture: in a biblical tradition that placed an entire people or a specific individual continually on trial. The suspension of that trial may take place in a leap of faith, as Kierkegaard put it, that achieves between mankind and God a suspension of ethical judgments opening the way for genuine solidarity among individuals, between parents and children, indeed among all peoples. This continuing impulse toward justification may take the individual to the public sphere defined by the liturgy, where each individual publicly owns personal failure and lays claim to a merit claimed by a faithful people. In these liturgical acts, individuals participate in a judgment that was given once and for all time. But individuals also take their impulse for justification into every non-liturgical sphere, where they seek to be taken seriously as persons who speak of what they know and have seen. In these secular contexts, however, judgments are never once and for all. New knowledge changes the very "laws" of nature and society and alters the composition of those whose testimony is to be taken especially seriously. New elites emerge as authoritative witnesses and the new laws of nature or society give enhanced credibility to those whose testimony has previously been found irrelevant or lacking in proper weight or validity. The secularization of the religious demand for justification, then, has led to a dynamic process in which elites emerge and decline as laws change and new knowledge becomes authoritative. The same process has transformed virtually every context into a place of potential judgment, where personal or corporate credibility and authority are perpetually problematic.

The concept of religion employed here is a polar conception to a specific meaning of the term "secularity." I will argue, from certain biblical sources, that secular means "temporal" in the sense of *passing away*, finite, epochal. Secular does not mean "worldly" with meanings ranging from instrumental and utilitarian to material, economic, political etc. I also avoid the use here of the term "change" as equivalent to secularity (although some sociologists have considered the terms equivalent), because religion in the biblical sense may express and initiate change: change of a sort that is continuous, fundamental, and therefore not liable to be institutionalized. On one conventional view, the secular represents change and sacralization comes to be the opposite of change. I prefer what appears to me a more biblical view of *religion* as speech that can be relied on: whose meaning will not alter although it may become more apparent. Regardless of whether those meanings become institutionalized, they are established by the word of God; and sometimes they are established within the community of faith. Religious *language* is, of course, established in a number of ways: by being literal, and hence not liable to metaphoric transformations; by being expressed in once and for all liturgical action; by being corporate, "official," and widely shared; and by coming true in the process of being spoken. Religious *speech*, however, is eventful and combines speech-acts with high levels of illocutionary force with simple expressive or representative statements.

The process of secularization dissolves the powerful speech

of the religious community, in which the same words are both sign and symbol, into two distinct vocabularies and rules for speaking. The one, in which words are taken literally, is a vocabulary of symbols that obeys rules of relevance and reliability in secular courts and classrooms. The other is a vocabulary of metaphors that may evoke common loyalties and hopes on private occasion, but publicly these metaphors are either regarded as slippery (however evocative they may be of human emotions), or are seen as outworn and in need of refreshment. Whether it is a literary critic refurbishing a metaphor from a sermon by John Donne or a judge who dispenses with the "mere" metaphors of a devout Christian, religious speech in secular contexts is vulnerable to secular rules for language. It is hardly surprising that religious movements, at least in their most vulnerable periods, have strict rules against casting verbal pearls before swine. The New Testament community was reminded that their founder chose to speak so that outsiders might hear without understanding, while those with faith might hear and also learn to see what was happening in their midst.

In relatively simple or traditional societies, religious language meets the larger society on more or less equal terms: the more so as religious groups effectively speak with one voice, on grounds that are corporate and not merely personal in significance, and in terms that are irreducible to a literal meaning. As modern societies integrate, however, they place all speakers' language on trial and recognize fewer forms of speech as sacred and privileged. The relative frequency of personal usage and of limited symbols increases, as religious language is further confined to a narrower domain of significant speech. Therefore religious language will only encounter the larger society on equal terms in an egalitarian class-system: one in which there are no privileged positions in discourse.

Inequalities in any society license privileged speech. Liturgies are thus privileged in a secular society: they are immune to being interrupted, neutralized, or translated by secular authorities. But the same authorities enjoy privileges of speech in the classroom and the court. (I would therefore define class in terms of the right to restrict significant communication and to monopolize those speech-acts with the highest illocutionary force.) It will be helpful now to examine somewhat more fully the concept of speech-acts before proceeding with the argument. According to Searle (1979: 3ff), there are two kinds of "speech-acts": those that attempt to bring the world into conformity with the spoken word, and those that make the word approximate the world as it is or will be. In the first, more powerful group of speech-acts are "declarations" and "directives" (to use Searles's own choice of descriptive terms). Declarations speak for themselves: a verdict is given, a pronouncement is made, and the word is done. Persons are pronounced married or dead and are henceforth considered by all to be married or dead. Verdicts are given, and from that moment a person is treated as innocent or guilty. Directives are only slightly less forceful, since the speaker must wait for others to comply with certain orders or wishes. Directives range from the most forceful, such as prohibitions and commands, to statements of a milder sort that express a wish or make a suggestion.

Of course, it is not always obvious when a wish is being stated rather than a report being made, as when a child announces that he or she is bored or hungry; just as it is not always obvious that a "Yea" is a "Yea" and not really a "Nay." Indeed it was an early Christian belief that the believer should speak directly and simply, without repetition and guile. But my point is simply that secularization leaves the churches with only the less forceful of directives at their disposal. The churches certainly may suggest and on occasion may exhort, but when does the church ever command? Least of all do the churches engage in declarations beyond the few pronouncements left to them by other occupations and institutions. The courts declare guilt and innocence. The medical professions declare life and death. And the churches share with secular justices the right to pronounce that a marriage has occurred. Unlike the churches' founder or unlike more militant sects in the past, who have tended to pass judgment and give orders in an uncivil manner, the churches have found a more civil tongue better suited for the long haul (Cuddihy 1978).

Earlier I used the distinction between signs and symbols without making the distinction clear. Here I wish drastically to oversimplify the nature of the distinction in order to talk about the social conditions which make the distinction possible (see chapter 8 for a more thorough discussion of the distinction). A *sign* may be a word or a phrase, a gesture or marking, that stands for and elicits a wide range of shared attitudes, feelings, or ideas among those who employ and understand it. The liturgical sign of blood, for instance, stands for life, vitality, the identity of the one who gives his blood, and for sacrifice itself. The blood of the Lamb, the body and blood of Jesus, the blood of Christ in the sacrament of the Eucharist: these representations of blood depend on and call into being a community of shared faith and hope in moments of mutual caring and sacrifice. But blood can also be a symbol: clear, specific, and unique in referring to a certain idea, relationship, or object in the "real world." Blood as a symbol, therefore, simply stands for a mixture of plasma, hemoglobin, and a range of other items that circulate in the body of animals and humans. The same word, then, can be both symbol and sign. It is the substitution of the usage of blood as symbol, for instance, for blood as sign that characterizes the integrative processes of modern societies. The point is not that modern societies avoid speaking of the ideas, attitudes, and feelings once condensed into the term "blood." They simply develop an articulated set of symbols for these aspects of human relationships rather than condense them in signs that are heavily loaded with shared and implicit meanings.

There is little novel in this proposition, as students of Douglas, Bernstein, Labov and Gouldner will readily recognize. Here I will make a brief summary of Bernstein's distinction between "condensed" and "elaborated" codes in order to suggest the extent to which the proposition is indebted to their work. Bernstein's distinction between elaborated and restricted codes parallels Durkheim's typology of two social systems, the organic and the mechanical. In the latter, the speakers share a set of deeply held values and beliefs. They therefore can speak in a more "condensed" style which signals the presence of common assumptions while leaving to nonverbal cues the task of representing the unique or idiosyncratic intentions of the speaker. In so solidary a community, furthermore, speakers "speak to" their shared values and beliefs by using key words or phrases; thus speech in such situations seems conventional and takes on a ritualistic quality. Bloch's study (1975) of "veiled talk" in certain African communities provides a telling instance of such speech, but political rhetoric and after-dinner speech in more "modern" societies may be equally illustrative. My point, however, is that signs are like "passwords" by which individuals justify themselves to each other without having to elaborate. The use of signs makes it unnecessary to put individuals on trial, to cross-examine their testimony, and to render a verdict. With signs, the trial is over.

In less solidary, more highly complex ("organic") communities or societies, however, speakers are required to verbalize their own intentions and special meanings while also taking into account the specific characteristics of their hearers. Speech is tailored more to the situation or the occasion, as in the case of a traveling lecturer who spells out the meaning of terms in his lecture and takes into account the training and orientation of his audience. Bernstein's elaborated code, which "speaks to" the internal variations of a particular community or society, makes alternatives possible by symbolizing the heterogeneity of the society. As the parts of speech become as complex and variable as the parts of a society, the speaker develops a code suitable for abstraction and analysis. Above all, the elaborated code can utilize its linguistic complexity to suggest alternative combinations of ideas and values; it is, as Gouldner (1976) has pointed out, the code which is best suited for social science and political ideologies, since it spells out alternative arrangements in social life or in belief-systems. It is also the code best suited to the court and to the classroom, because it makes possible the judicious weighing of alternative views of reality.

Bernstein notes that the careful awareness and "editing" of the speaker of the elaborated code removes signs and substitutes for them various symbols that can be readily understood in a variety of contexts. Gouldner has very helpfully pointed out that it is *editing* which characterizes the elaborated code: a careful reflection by the speaker on his or her own feelings and intentions, about the meaning of words and their specific application, and about the characteristics of the persons whom the speaker is addressing. Signs that are significant in limited contexts are edited out or translated into symbols. In this sense the elaborated code is a way of speaking which does not depend on a single context and can be spoken in hotels, conventions, professional journals, and indeed wherever relative strangers to one another seek to communicate. It is a language for resident aliens and for speakers who know that what they say *may* be used against them.

When intentions and feelings are not problematical, they can be left to the imagination of the hearer or coded implicitly in signs. But when individuals are on trial and must speak judiciously, they must elaborate on their intentions and even state them at the outset. (For instance, "in this report I intend to summarize the results of my work on conversational patterns between men and women, which I undertook with a view to documenting techniques of sexist suppression.") Again, the meaning of words is problematical when speakers cannot rely on conventions or revelation; the user of the elaborated variant therefore frequently begins a statement or argument by defining problematical terms like "religion" or "integration." The self-conscious editing does not seek to secure agreement on the "real" meaning of the word religion, but only to signal the hearer that the speaker is aware that legitimate differences in usage may exist and to ask for a fair hearing. The speaker is saying that the demonstration of self-conscious editing of his or her own words entitles the speaker to a tolerant hearing without premature judgment. In the elaborated code, semantic differences, although not overlooked, are tolerated for the sake of pursuing the argument. Editing of this sort therefore implicitly takes into account the differences of those who may be listening to or reading the speaker's text and allows for those differences a legitimate but limited role in the process of communicating the speaker's insights.

The use of symbols creates a pragmatic and temporary consensus on usage, on the meaning of words, on the legitimacy of motives, and on the speaker's self-declared intentions. The consensus is temporary at best, because it depends on the mutual, but provisional agreement of the speaker and audience to suspend quarrels on fundamental issues until the terms of the argument have been elaborated, understood, and discussed. As Walter Ong (1970) puts it, the terms of modern discourse are irenic by comparison with the heated and combative rhetoric of the fifteenth and sixteenth centuries. But in place of rhetoric is the judicious speech in which individuals create a record: a testimony that, on further inspection, may be found to have serious errors and omissions.

It is clear that in the process of secularization symbols may substitute for signs; that until the process is complete some symbols may easily appear to be signs; that some symbols take on the function, if not the meaning, of signs; and that the use of symbols to signify shared values is occasionally inauthentic in the absence of those values that could make such usage appropriate. In an interesting study of the decline of religious differences among voters in England over the past century, Wald (1979) argues that prior to the First World War, "two competing systems of belief, derived largely from religious principles, seem to have divided Liberals from Conservatives" (ibid.: 18). A political rhetoric, that combines views of salvation with preferences for government intervention in such moral or social issues as "drink," is a strong indicator of the existence of "condensed" signs: significant symbols that stand for theological or political views widely shared among a specific religious community. Wald argues that "drink" conveyed views of God, human nature, and attitudes toward government intervention along with views about drinking. "Drink" was thus precisely such a condensed *sign*. But with the Third Reform Act of 1870 (specifically the Education Act), denominational control of primary education decreased markedly. Fewer students enrolled in Nonconformist schools over the subsequent generation: a generation that eventually was mobilized more by the secular *symbols* of the Labour Party than by the Liberal Party's astute use of signs that at once conveyed not only political meaning but widely shared religious sentiments (ibid.: 20).

Occasions for the purpose of establishing common, however temporary, understanding will therefore require the deliberate suppression of particular signs that bind together members of sub-communities and present a barrier to societal integration. It is this possibility that has drawn the fire of socio-linguists, such as Labov, who see in Bernstein's argument a slightly veiled attack on non-standard forms of English usage: notably that of the black American community.

William Labov has argued that the language patterns of the black community are fully as capable as the patterns of standard English to serve as symbols of abstract ideas and complex relationships. Labov (1969) is discrediting the claims of other social scientists that black English lacks the capacity to express complicated relationships of cause and effect or to develop logical relationships between ideas. Similar arguments have been made against working-class verbal patterns: that they are too "condensed" to permit meanings to be developed or "elaborated." Gaps in logic or in the understanding of how one factor affects another allegedly therefore do not emerge in working-class patterns of speech: and because the speech apparently fails to open these gaps, the gaps do not come easily to the working-class mind.

What is at issue in this argument is whether to make the working class responsible for its own share of social misery or to place the larger society on trial. The members of that class are condemned by the words which proceed from their own mouths according to the rules of secular discourse. It is all the more important, then, to understand Labov's work as a way of crediting speech that otherwise stands to be discredited by educators and social scientists for being insufficient to convey more complex meanings. He deflates the claims of academic or middle-class Brahmins to be in possession of a Sanskrit which alone can express certain insights into the less obvious aspects of the universe. Modern societies, I suggest, no longer need societal *cohesion* at the expense of minority cultures in order to achieve societal *integration*.

Speech-communities that employ minority "signs" are subject to attack even when they are not officially the object of political repression or excluded from a civil religion. Attacks on minority signs are likely to arise from groups carrying what Bell (1962) has termed "partial" ideologies rather than from the protectors of ideology or the state. I would argue, for instance, that Bernstein's claims for the elaborated code really reflect the ideology of the free-floating intelligentsia. The claims which Bernstein makes for the elaborated code are themselves the typical ideology of intellectuals who claim to enjoy a perspective which transcends particular social contexts: a perspective abstracted from concrete particulars, from which it is possible to make relatively authoritative statements. The "free-floating" intellectual does not need to be a Frenchman to criticize French literature, a sociologist to criticize sociological literature, or a Southerner to comment on Southern literature or race relations. According to the ideology, at the command of the free-floating intellectual are certain universals which provide standards for judging logic, the fairness of social patterns, or the clarity of an individual piece of prose.

This claim for the language in which the more powerful and highly educated express themselves also reflects the self-awareness as well as the self-justifications of a social class which allows some, but by no means all, of a society's members access to truth through a particular language. Not everyone is able to learn it. Those who succeed must undergo changes in their own identity, their relationships, and their views of the world. But the rewards are correspondingly high: access to realms of meaning, freedom to choose one's relationships, and responsibility for one's own way of life. These are clearly the goals of the Western Enlightenment, however little resemblance they bear to everyday life even among intellectuals.

To summarize: It is entirely possible that a society may be highly integrated even in the absence of *any* signs monopolized or merely used by the state, or any other representative institutions. *Integrated societies are not necessarily solidary or cohesive, although the distinction tends to be lost wherever "traditional" societies are used as a model for societal integration.* It is possible for the ideologies of certain groups, such as the intelligentsia, thoroughly to discredit the linguistic, racial, communal, or religious signs of other speech communities in the nation without providing a basis for societal *cohesion* in the country as a whole. The nation is then able to achieve relatively high levels of non-solidary integration by putting "on trial" communities or groups whose signs provide a powerful source of solidary feelings or shared moral obligation among their own members. It is this type of non-cohesive integration that is likely to be achieved through the courts and educational institutions of American society. Whether it will be the intentional or unintended consequence of social policy in other Western nations is clearly a problem for comparative analysis.

A society is therefore integrated to the extent that it has institutionalized settings and procedures for reducing the authority of corporate beliefs, values, or standards to purely personal convictions. By "corporate" I mean to refer to any social unit with a collective identity and purpose. Like the family that unit may be relatively small, informal, and with legal rights or liabilities that are not exhaustively defined by law. But a corporate actor may be as large as General Motors, as transient as a Committee to Elect the President, and have quite explicitly defined rights and obligations before the law. If these corporate entities enjoyed the rights to privacy accorded the individual, for instance, a society would quite clearly have serious difficulties in knowing what its corporate members advocate and do. Furthermore, the right of the

Catholic Church to exercise its religious freedom does not extend to the public classroom, although no law prevents the individual Catholic from engaging in private devotions in school. Conversely, the rights of individuals to keep their children out of public schools or to avoid serving in a country's armed forces are more frequently recognized by the state when they are safeguarded by the authority of a corporate actor such as the Amish. As James Coleman (1974) rightly reminds us, it is "corporate actors" that can most successfully influence or resist other corporate actors: not the isolated or atomic individual.

Individuals on trial for their beliefs in the court or in the classroom are most likely to be taken seriously when they represent a corporate actor of some sort, for example, an organized ethnic group, a religious community, or professional association. Corporate actors are like limited sovereignties within a larger society: like the Jewish nation, perhaps, within the Roman Empire. Dissident individuals are less threatening to societal integration, therefore, than a corporate unit with an identity and purpose of its own. It is always possible to allow one, isolated individual to die for public safety. The erosion of corporate signs and their meanings must be done more judiciously.

This is not to say that perfect integration is possible when all corporate actors' rights and duties can be reduced to questions of merely personal commitment. Individuals, as individuals, can be demanding and recalcitrant, militant and obstinate in their pursuit of happiness and liberty: acknowledging no rights beyond their own. Enough has been written in the sociological tradition concerning the disintegrative effects of individualism to make further elaboration of this possibility redundant here. I am also not ignoring the fact that on occasion individuals stand in need of protection from the very corporate actors that form the individual's guarantee against encroachments from the state. Unions and families, for instance, can so interfere with individual liberties that state interference is necessary on behalf of the threatened individual. I am saying that the authority of personal convictions is no match in a modern society for the corporate authority of the state, especially when those personal convictions are "merely" those of the individual concerned and not validated by the authority of the church or other corporate actors.

A number of examples may make the proposition clearer. In the United States the Selective Service allows individuals to avoid service in the armed forces if their own convictions are not "merely personal." Although the courts have stretched the statute to cover moral convictions that *are* personal (in order to avoid the possibility that the law can be construed as establishing organized religion), the law nevertheless stands as an exceedingly clear limit on the authority of personal conviction. In the courts the authority of a priest to speak for the church is often reduced to a merely personal construction of the church's teaching, just as the claim of a student to judge a classic work of art or literature can be reduced to idiosyncratic opinion by any authoritative academician. Religion is often recognized in the courts as *relevant* to individual liberties, but it is at the same time reduced to being a guarantor of a particular individual's sincerity or good character.

The extreme case of reduction before the law occurs when the state considers personal conviction to be so idiosyncratic as to be indicative of mental incompetence or disorder. To be authentic, convictions must be personal rather than merely conventional or official, but as merely personal they tend to lack authority before the law. Society can still be integrated although its population may consist of highly authentic individuals, for as citizens their rights and authority are conferred by the society as a whole and by its most important corporate actors.

The process of secularization proceeds by small but decisive linguistic steps. Words that in a liturgical context are guaranteed as signs of a corporate reality become mere symbols with a personal meaning. In a society with a firmly established religious culture, there are times and places where one can go to hear words that are adequate to the occasion and that will come true long after the moment is over. These utterances, associated with high liturgical developments, will still carry meaning and authority even before secular courts or in secular classrooms, but the force of these utterances may be drastically reduced and most of their original meaning may be lost in translation. Thus, outside liturgical contexts, individuals must follow secular rules for having their words understood, accepted, and considered respectfully.

We have already seen that a court's rules for legal testimony place severe restraints on the giving of religious testimony. The courts may define a speaker's convictions as "merely personal"; sincere, perhaps, but idiosyncratic. Even official representatives of a church may find that their testimony is regarded as a relevant and accurate symbol of their own beliefs but as lacking any corporate significance in the judicial context. Even a bishop's testimony may be ignored as a sign of the faith of an entire religious community and awarded a purely symbolic significance in court. Religious testimony is therefore reduced to a performance by which the individual gains credibility but lacks authority under the secular auspices of the court.

When a witness's statements cannot be classed as merely personal, because they represent the convictions of a corporate body like the church, the courts still may question the scope and relevance of the church's convictions by placing a narrow construction on the meaning of such words as "religion" and "ministry" or by taking their meaning as a metaphor for such non-religious facets of life as ethnic groups and loyalties. Academic institutions follow similar rules for constricting or reducing the meaning of religious terminology. Even when the church's statements are allowed to stand without challenges to their meaning, the force of religious testimony is still subject to legal challenge. In this event a speaker's testimony is classed as a mere "representation" of the church's beliefs rather than as an official pronouncement that directs the hearer's response. In speaking within a secular context, the religious witness finds that words of testimony often fall on barren ground or soon become tangled in a thicket of judicial or academic interpretations. It is therefore not surprising that some early Christians eschewed the secular courts entirely and preferred their own methods for "establishing the word" in situations of conflict. It is also not surprising that contemporary religious movements are reasserting the privileges of religious language in a secular society.

It is paradoxical that the religious sources of Western culture have laid the groundwork for the secular (non-cohesive) integration of Western societies. Western Christianity particularly, with its eschatological impulses, undermines the authority of all inherited meanings, both religious and secular. The Western ideal holds that the poor, the powerless, and those outside the boundaries of particular religious, ethnic, or political communities speak with as much authority to the ears of religious faith as do those whose authority to speak is certified by tradition, popular consent, or sheer power. The antinomian and equalitarian strains in Western culture derive from a tradition of religious prophecy and revelation that acknowledges no communal or class-based restraints on significant communication or authoritative speech. Religious tradition has certified the right of the ordinary person to be taken seriously.

But this tradition has been neutralized by the relative success of national governments in reducing the authority of religious speech or of ethnic language to purely expressive or representative functions. On the one hand, the state, through the courts and schools, treats many corporate convictions as merely personal, reduces open-ended or ambiguous meaning to literalisms, and turns signs of religious convictions, shared by whole communities of faith or speech, into mere symbols of relatively clear and restricted meaning. The state's unwillingness to argue its case in the courtroom on equal terms with the individual or an occupation's unwillingness to reduce its authority to the level of ordinary speech and speech-acts wit' out illocutionary force was dramatized in the trials of the Catonsville Nine and the Chicago 7 during the Vietnam War. Occupations continue to reserve for themselves the more authoritative speech-acts such as advice, direction, exhortation, and command, while leaving to individuals the right to represent or express their ideas and intentions. In this process it is individuals *qua* individuals who find themselves discredited before political and occupational authorities. This lack of reciprocity creates unfulfilled demands for personal authority and legitimacy or for the reduction of occupational and official speech to a level of linguistic equality with the speech of individuals. These demands may be met "privately" in various cults or sects until they are pressed — or challenged by the state — in the courtroom, at which point questions of the legitimacy of political authority are raised to a higher power.

Conclusion

While the secular world places individual and corporate actors on continual trial, so to speak, those trials are "finished" in the liturgy. The liturgy itself celebrates the vindication of the one who was tried in secular courts and found wanting. That is what the celebration is all about. The participants are also celebrating, however, the end of their secular "trials." First, in the metaphorical sense of "trial" as a process of testing, these secular trials are over and done with in each celebration. Confession, absolution, and the individual's participation in the new life of the religious community see to that. But in the more literal sense of the individual's trial before the divine judge, the ultimate trial is over and done with as the individual realizes the anticipation of the Last Judgment in the decisive moments of the community's faith: the rituals of death and resurrection. The secular trial makes it continually necessary for individuals and "collective" actors to identify and to justify themselves; in the liturgy that necessity is over and done with. In secular contexts it is necessary for meanings to be clarified and intentions to be spelled out so that even strangers may understand. In the liturgy those meanings are revealed and it is sufficient, at critical moments, to state one's intentions to be faithful in terms that are not open to challenge and misunderstanding. In secular contexts the authority of one's words may always be called into question, whereas in the liturgy the authority is given and invoked by those who use the proper Name.

The existence of liturgies alongside secular forms of the trial places the latter in some jeopardy. Secular scales of justice are challenged by the presence of another, authoritative scale. The liturgy stands as a prime example of what Holzner calls "a typical strategy of rebellion and revolution" (1978: 301). Not only does the liturgy confer a certain authority on believers, on conscientious objectors, on married couples and on parents, but that authority carries over into secular contexts that recognize the judgment of the religious community on such matters as whether two persons are married or whether a person is indeed conscientious in objecting to military service. But the threat posed by the liturgy to secular courts and contexts is heightened when liturgists go to court. In subsequent chapters I will refer to the testimony of the Berrigans and others of the Catonsville Nine who attempted to claim in court the privileges of authoritative speech that they enjoy within a liturgical context. The result, in part, was prophetic utterance: a testimony to religious convictions that became, in the words of one lawyer, "transcendent witness." Such witness tends to draw individuals out of their roles as actors within the court. The lawyer for the Catonsville Nine, who spoke of their "transcendent witness," also asked the court for permission to speak wholly as a person, and not as a lawyer for the defense (Berrigan 1970: 102). In the Supreme Court of New Jersey another lawyer, who had acted for the parents of Karen Ann Quinlan, also left his formal role under the impact of religious testimony in order to speak personally. Liturgical speech, as it becomes prophetic in secular contexts, tends to intensify the problematic character of secular identities and to demand that the individual actor speak as a person or that corporate actors, especially the state, clarify the sources of their own authority.

Sociologists have· been fascinated by the simultaneous and dialectical development in the West of personal and corporate authority. Critics have feared that the authority of bureaucracies and of the state will end the dialectic by crushing the authority, and even the identity, of individual actors; and they feared that individual actors will pursue their own authority to the point at which they experience no moral obligation to institutions or to the larger society. Others among the sociological community, however, have credited that state with preserving the dialectic between individual and corporate authority, since it is stateless persons who have no standing before the court and whose rights therefore do not exist. Others have similarly argued that the pursuit of individual goals has led to the formation of corporate actors and to the expansion of the state, whose legitimacy in the West depends, in fact, on its ability to serve the needs and protect the rights of individuals. The dynamic tension between corporate and personal authority in the West persists precisely because in secular contexts their authority is always problematic and "on trial." That authority is problematic because it is secular, and it is secular because the liturgy provides the one indisputably sacred context in which all trials are over. But the mere juxtaposition of sacred liturgy and secular contexts, such as the court, is only necessary for those contexts to remain secular; juxtaposition is not sufficient if corporate and individual claims to authority are to remain in dynamic tension. That tension depends on the effort of religious actors, both corporate and collective, to have their religious conscience honored in the courts. To preserve the dynamic tension between individual and corporate authority, individuals and corporate actors must be willing to go on trial for their religious beliefs.

Chapter 2

The Political Dimensions of the Liturgy

Every society demands that its citizens endure a trial or a testing: an event or a long process, either way, that ensures the fitness of the person to take a responsible place and to receive the trust and approval of friends and strangers. Most individuals, I assume, also have limits to their endurance of uncertainty and ask how long the wicked will prosper or their own sufferings persist. The demand for judgment and for justice is always present, sometimes latent, but sometimes approaching in times of crisis a demand for a last and enduring judgment. Fundamentalists in America are prophesying with rapture a final seizure or spasm in history, in which the Lord's forces will triumph over the evil-doers and the hard of heart. Fundamentalists in Iran are demanding a similar confrontation between their Lord and the pagan forces personified in the West and the tyranny of the Shah. Some in the West are tired of the long uncertainties of the Cold War and wish for a final test or consummation to end the long wait for judgment. The poor and subordinate in many countries weary of waiting for justice and administer tokens of their own justice in acts of terrorism. The righteous in America demand a return of capital punishment. The young weary of interminable years of evaluation and testing in an educational system which is often unjust and increasingly unrewarding. Kafka's metaphor for the present world, a trial without end, makes more sense as pressures increase for an end of testing or a final judgment. I assume that these pressures are always present, since the human capacity for endless trial has always been limited, but when super-powers or rival world religions or separate classes engage in prolonged testing, the desire for a consummate confrontation does mount.

The Christian religious tradition in the West supplies a somewhat contradictory response to these pressures. On the one hand, the tradition asserts that the final judgment has already begun in the events of Jesus Christ's life, death, and resurrection. Precisely because the Last Judgment is already in progress, however, the early church was cautioned against premature moral or religious judgments. Through exemplary stories about disciples and in direct instruction to new congregations, the early church was reminded that one must judge nothing before the time, that vengeance and judgment belong to the Lord, that radical forgiveness is the only realistic ethical posture under such conditions, and that one must pray continually that one *not* be led into the trial. The day of the Lord has already dawned, in which old scores, debts, transgressions, and instructions are neutralized once and for all. One must only wait for the setting of that sun that has already arisen. In the meantime, the light of that day is enough for one to find one's way. The day of final judgment is now at hand, but one must therefore judge nothing and no one: a fine contradication or dialectic.

The tension between these two positions is sometimes contained within a theological stance, as in the case of the Calvinist doctrine of election, but the tension is currently perpetuated between aspects of the Church and aspects of the secular world. Calvinists understood that the final word has already been spoken concerning the outcome of each individual's trial, but they also asserted the need to live as though one were being continually tested. To live consistently as though one were saved would attest to one's own salvation. Now, I am arguing, the same tension is acted out between the liturgical certainties offered by the church and the continuing testing or trial offered by institutions in the secular world. In the world, one is continually called upon to testify, to give evidence, and to have one's testimony examined and tested in the classroom, the doctor's office, the waiting room of a governmental agency, or in the court itself. In the liturgy one is also called upon to testify and give evidence of one's faith and identity, but for those who adequately confess their faith the trial is soon over and the outcome never in doubt. In the world, however, one is always called upon to support and up-date one's testimony, to have it compared with expert testimony on the same subject, and to wait for one's case to be reviewed. Review and appeal, whether in the educational system or in the courts, may go on for years, and the outcome is always in doubt, even if one has tenure. The secular statute of limitations can protect one against charges arising from fresh evidence but not fresh allegations of other offenses. The discovery of the unconscious, in fact, opens up a source of accusations or of offensive motives that turns a lifetime into a perpetual trial with fresh evidence continually arising from buried sources. No scientific or academic finding is immune from the challenge of new computations or evidence. No wonder that the biblical tradition names the devil as "the Accuser" and assigns to him jurisdiction over "the world" or the current aeon. It is only with the day of the Lord that all accusation ends, and the trial is over.

It is for that reason on the Lord's day that the people of God celebrate a mock trial, in which the law is read, confession and testimony obtained, and the verdict once again given as it was once before for all time. Otherwise all the days would belong to that secular sphere in which the trial never ends as new evidence gives rise to fresh charges or renewed appeals. It is also no wonder that in a secular world, the demand for a renewed and vital liturgy has increased rather than withered away. One can stand perpetual trial in every institutional sphere only for so long. It is ironic, however, that the demand for renewed and vital liturgies has led to the use of "trial liturgies," of services that are themselves being tested and tried before the opinion of the church. In that time of trial even the liturgy cannot appear to offer the same guarantees of a final judgment and acquittal to the people of God.

Most of the Christian churches have been in a period of liturgical reform for several years: a period initiated some decades earlier by the "liturgical movement" in the Catholic churches. Thomas Merton is probably right that this period of liturgical change is to be, and in fact already is, the greatest development in liturgy since the Patristic age and the most thorough reform in liturgy the church has ever known (1950; 1965: 2). But great development though it may be, it is also a time of serious disturbance within the churches undergoing strains of liturgical change.

Thomas Merton is only one of several writers who have traced the meaning of the term liturgy to the Greek *polis*, where *leit-ourgos* (liturgy) was the public act of citizenship that united the free and responsible individual with the Greek city-state. Merton notes, for instance, that in "providing for" the ceremonies of the dithyrambic dance and its later civic development, the Greek citizen simultaneously enacted the meaning of the community and its identity while affirming his own identity as a constituent member of the *polis*. To be a person, Merton notes, meant precisely to have a role in the public work of the community: a far different understanding from that which equates personhood with the private sphere of the self, family, and friendship. I will return to this contemporary reversal of ancient liturgical meaning in connection with specific innovations in the liturgy of the American Episcopal Church. But the point here is simply that to take part in any liturgy is to signify to oneself and others that one is constituting a community and onself as a member of that community. So to take part in the Christian liturgy is to take on one's role in a new kingdom: one that "shall have no end." It is the political act of all time and is therefore potentially seditious within the secular politics of a specific time and place. Caesar understood the political nature of the liturgy all too well.

It is meet and right, therefore, that liturgical change should arouse political suspicions and even passion. Certainly it behooves all Caesers to know what vows are being taken by their subjects and what freedoms are being claimed in the name of kingdoms other than their own. If, for instance, the final revision of the American Book of Common Prayer contains in its Catechism the instruction to the laity that they are indeed "ministers" of the church every bit as much as the ordained clergy, the church's members may be entitled, in principle, to the same constitutional protections as the clergy. Some laity may claim the right to keep silent about privileged communications, while others may demand the right to avoid military service: a right now granted only to the clergy and to those who successfully claim to be conscientious in their objection to military service. Liturgies give to ordinary people the right to make the world conform to their words: to be honored as indeed married, or to have their names and words remembered even at death. To be taken seriously, as free and responsible members of a commonwealth that has no historical boundaries, is the right of all who take part in the Christian liturgies.

The political aspects of liturgies have not been lost on those social scientists who have been preoccupied with the problem of "mobilizing" individual energies for the tasks of building a nation. These scientists may therefore agree with Daniel Bell that liturgies "drain" away the energies that belong more properly to political parties or civic institutions. On this view, the genuine public sphere is *outside* the church, which becomes the sphere of private self-absorption and self-celebration. But to the believer, it is the liturgy that is truly public, and to participate in the liturgy is to free oneself from the narcissistic, self-preoccupation of everyday life, from political pride and all forms of social prejudice. The true self emerges as the believer states "I believe" in unison with other souls who also proclaim their belief in a divine kingdom whose citizens they have been called to be.

The political nature of the liturgy arises in part, then, from the liturgy's claim to define the truly public sphere. That sphere is where individuals' true selves are manifest in symbolic actions that define and constitute their collective identity. The liturgy, by the sheer fact of existing alongside other forms of civic action, undermines the claim of secular politics either to manifest the individual's true self or to define what is collective about the common life of a society. A Eucharist that unites believers in Calcutta and Chicago in a common language diminishes the impact of a pledge of allegiance performed with more or less compliance in public schools around the country. But perhaps more seditious is the claim of the liturgy to be truly public in the sense of displaying the true self of the individual. Liturgies lead one to a self that is otherwise masked in such profane performances as conversations, commercials, or presidential press conferences. The managed spontaneity of these "public" performances arouses suspicion that the true self remains hidden despite publicity. On the other hand, Merton (1950; 1965: chapter 1) rightly argues that liturgies preserve the individual's innermost secret, known only to God, while at the same time the individual's true self is enacted in the public work of the *leit-ourgos*. At the same time, the liturgy suggests that there is something hidden even in the publicized activities of individuals whose selves do not come to light despite the glare of publicity.

Of course, any claim to define the public sphere is based on sometimes uncritical, but always ideological notions about the proper activities of free and responsible citizens. Sociologists are likely to criticize expressive or therapeutic activities as deceptive when these activities claim to enable individuals to realize their potential or to become their true selves (cf. Schur 1976). To engage in consciousness-raising techniques in small groups, so goes the argument, is really to lower one's consciousness of the impact of distant and impersonal social forces, whereas to take part in rational efforts toward changing a country's laws or an institution's rules is to become conscious of one's fundamentally social nature, endowment, and potential. I do not pretend to arbitrate the claims of liturgists and sociologists as to where the truly public sphere is to be found or where the truly responsible individual finds a voice, although I assume here that the liturgies of the churches make an uncompromising claim to embrace, even to monopolize, the public action of the truly free human person. The words spoken at the liturgy are ultimate, binding, and true: the Incarnate Word, to be theologically exact. Those who mingle their voices in the chants and creeds, litanies and hosannas of the liturgy can lay claim to be taken seriously in any other context because they have been addressed and have spoken in the divine liturgy.

Liturgies: The Politics of Sacrifice

The liturgy is the political act that calls all others into question. Certainly the radical nature of the Eucharistic liturgy is quite explicit, since that liturgy claims to inaugurate a kingdom that will eventually overthrow and transform the petty jurisdictions of "this world." But regardless of one's theological commitments, it is clear that liturgical language gives to the ordinary speaker a measure of control over those acts that constitute *any* human community and body politic: acts of witness to the individual's primary allegiance. Liturgies condense signs and symbols, so that statements about what is true become acts of allegiance to a human community that spans generations and crosses national boundaries. Other liturgical acts so concentrate signs into specific moments and places that the remainder of human activity becomes relatively empty of significance despite the claims of politicians or scientists that they can discern the signs of the times. Still other liturgical acts succeed in uniting what is spontaneous and inward in the individual to a collective creed and common hope, whereas few moments of political enthusiasm ever succeed in uniting the individual and the collectivity in such permanent and virtually indissoluble bonds. The liturgy also rehearses the givens of history while allowing space for new words of faith and hope to be spoken as individuals witness to their own visions within the context of the vision received once and for all by the faithful community. Where else does the private vision find itself taken up without being lost in traditional forms of belief? Other constitutions are eroded by amendments and bylaws or altogether suspended when political expedience or individual indifference require it.

In making these statements I am neither taking theologians at their word nor sacralizing language itself. It is not necessary to believe that through the liturgy a divine kingdom is actually encroaching on more mundane jurisdictions in order to affirm that believers undermine these secular jurisdictions by their liturgical acts. For instance, in praying for the Queen or for the President of the United States, the believer takes some ready-made meanings (Queen, President) and undermines or transforms them. The rulers become mere children: children of God who can err or stray like any other child and who therefore need support and guidance. But in praying for the Queen or the President believers also listen to themselves praying and thus discover what it was they intended without knowing that they were intending it: to establish, perhaps, a new human community in which all the children of God will be able to enjoy each other's presence and to confess their faults to one another without fear. The participants in the liturgy discover their intentions through the words and gestures of a service whose meaning was empty until they spoke its words, but as they spoke those words their own experience took on, as though for the first time, its true meaning (cf. Merleau-Ponty 1974: 86—94). This may indeed be the process through which the kingdom comes: leave that to theologians for the moment to decide. But it is indeed the process by which secular meanings are undermined and transformed as free individuals discover their freedom through others' words that they utter of their own choosing. The "one little word," that, according to Luther's hymn, will "fell" secular authorities may simply be "Amen" to another more everlasting kingdom.

In retrospect, however, Luther's faith in the nearly omnipotent force of religious speech seems like a residue of infantile narcissism in an otherwise adult speaker. To put it another way, the impact of liturgical language on the body politic is contingent on an array of social factors that, when considered together, comprise the facts of secularization in modern societies. It is one thing to participate in the liturgy as though one were engaging in another act of verbal expression among similarly like-minded individuals in a society that mixes religious themes with its justifications for political authority: quite another to take part in a Eucharist that recalls a lost, organic society in the midst of a militantly secular state. Certainly the possibilities of opposition between liturgical and political speech are higher in the latter than in the former: higher therefore in France than in the United States. Furthermore, as David Martin (1978b) reminds us, the conservative or liberal, even radical-left direction of liturgical speech will depend in large part on how peripheral and populist, as opposed to how central and elitist, have been the groups whose identities and styles have been expressed or discovered in their respective religious settings. High rates of participation in liturgies or the reduction of religion to a series of rites of passage will also affect the extent to which the hopes and fears, intentions and promises of everyday life are solemnized in liturgical forms or allowed to pass away with other secular artifacts like rumors, memoranda, and the daily newspaper. Finally, the interests and values of modern professions will determine whether individuals whose testimonies reflect their religious backgrounds are taken seriously or are required to transform their accounts of their experience into the more secular versions preferred by the therapists, lawyers, and the critical intelligentsia.

Eventually secularization and its effects impinge on liturgical texts. The words of liturgies wear thin, lose their capacity to make one feel alive in the spirit, and seem strangely inadequate at times even to the great occasions of life and death. Certainly no liturgy is eternal or immune to corruption as a manual of self-congratulation by privileged groups. Perhaps Thomas Merton first became convinced of the need for liturgical renewal when he heard a preacher favorably compare divine love (I Corinthians 13) to the virtues of the English gentleman (Merton 1965). American flags may accompany the cross in liturgical processions, despite the absence of appropriate rubrics for such displays of national pride. The self-conscious editing of archaisms and the improvement of the scholarship on which liturgical texts are based certainly cannot prevent such imperial corruptions, just as new ecclesiastical editions can only remind the worshipper that even these solemn words are potentially mere objects for critical scrutiny rather than the mysterious vehicles by which individuals come to their true selves through collective silence and speech. Ultimately Caesar has been right in applying a single test to the value and authority of liturgies: the test of sacrifice. That is, after all, the hard fact of the Eucharistic liturgy, that it announces, remembers, and calls for sacrifice. If it is hard for some in the churches to remember that fact, it has been equally hard for Caesar to forget it.

Liturgies: The Politics of "Representation"

The perception of signs is a political act in a radical sense of the term: making claims on the credibility and consent of others to accept the reality defined by the speaker. Whether the signs are "social indicators" of a trend toward a two-class system or psychological indicators of underlying trends toward fascism or rebellion does not alter the basic point: reference to underlying realities or to pervasive trends make implicit claims on the hearer's consent. The point is a mere truism among social scientists who recognize the essentially political character of scientific disputes and investigations. But there are important differences among these affirmations or attributions of reality, and it is these differences that are most illuminating in understanding the peculiar force and intention of religious language.

If we take liturgical language as our primary example, we will see most clearly the concentration of signs at particular times and places and the density of these signs within corporate, symbolic action. The liturgy of the Eucharist affords the most familiar and certainly the most dramatic example of such liturgical concentration and density. Words are indeed spoken, as they were spoken on the "night in which He was betrayed." Bread is broken, as He took bread on the same night and broke it. The tone of the celebrant's voice is itself a sign of the solemnity of these acts, and the cadences of the liturgy re-enact the dramatic actions of the divine in history. The liturgy is eventful, as the events are re-created and renewed in the actions of remembrance, breaking, consecration, and the administration of the sacrament itself. Music, silence, standing, kneeling, words, shouts of praise, acclamations, and mumbled devotions concentrate at these extraordinary moments in which every symbol becomes a sign of shared belief and common commitment, and every belief itself takes on a symbol in word or deed.

The most useful term by which to describe the force of liturgical language would be "representation," had not the word been secularized almost beyond recognition of its original meaning. The sacrament is the means, of course, by which Jesus of Nazareth chose to represent himself: His body and His blood represented under the signs of bread and wine. But the sacrament re-presents the person of Jesus in a more active and literal sense. The early church spoke of the liturgy as "showing forth" Jesus, until His coming again is completed on the last day. This "showing forth" is a representation that makes Jesus "present again" for the time being, during the time that must elapse until He is all in all. I would want to add that in this concentrated and dense form of language, the ordinary individual gathered in liturgical action with others of common heart and mind, is capable of reconstituting all of reality in a form that transcends elite definitions of reality or imperial claims on the layman's consent and credulity.

By way of contrast, consider the meaning of the term "representation" in secular courts. According to the ritual of the courtroom, the lay person is permitted to represent that a statement stands for an adequate description of that person's memory, intentions, standard practice, or viewpoint. But the meaning of representation is drastically reduced in that secular context. Instead of being able to "present again" words and deeds that are of crucial significance in defining the person's present condition, the lay person in court is allowed simply to "represent" that a certain statement conforms adequately to reality in the sense that others, given the same opportunity to observe or understand, would say the same thing. But the lay witnesses' representations are mere affirmations without authority and await confirmation through cross-examination, through the examination of other witnesses, and finally through judicial pronouncement on matters of fact before the court. As Foucault (1974) reminds us in his discussion of representation, language in the modern world has become an object of study rather than the sphere of the spontaneous expression of the knowing individual. How few individuals in court are allowed to represent themselves: let alone to speak freely of the truth as they know it.

The secularization of language turns liturgical events into mere symbols or at best into symbols that signify underlying more or less common and intense social commitments. Of course, the liturgy of the Prayer Book indeed deserves to be taken seriously in this more secular sense as "representing" irreplaceable and unique aspects of a people and their history. Social scientists take the English liturgy seriously because they also take seriously the human achievement of a historical community: of common memories and a common hope in and through suffering and failure. In a similar vein the American sociologist, Robert Bellah, insists that the symbols of the American civil religion are not to be despised because they have been ill-used by tedious or vicious politicians, since the same symbols stand for what is uniquely real about the human community within the American body politic. But even when religious language is thus credited with "standing for" the solidary and enduring ties of a nation and its people, language is being treated as merely representative of something outside and beyond itself and as serving a function of maintaining and pointing to that external reality. Religious language, however, properly concentrated in the dense structure of the liturgy, re-presents the reality itself within the words and phrases of liturgical action. Liturgy thus provides the *substance* of representation, whereas, from the point of view of the observer, religious language, liturgical or otherwise, at best serves to represent enduring social realities. The difference is between language that constitutes reality by being uttered and language that simply stands for reality. Secularization drives the opening wedge between language and reality.

In the secular courts of "this world," the individual faces the "fallen" character of language. In contexts such as the classroom, for instance, the individual student confronts the distance that may exist between what others mean by a certain word and what that individual actually intends in using the word. Good grades are won in part by individual strategies for closing the apparent gap between meaning and intention, as sociologists who have struggled with the term religion before saying anything at all know particularly well. In other "courts," such as the therapist's office, the individual confronts the distance between idiosyncratic or metaphorical meanings and meanings that stand the test of consensus and "reality." In each case the individual who speaks confronts the dialectic between what David Martin (1978b) aptly calls the collectivist constraints on meaning and a pure interiority.

Liturgical Change and the Political Vulnerability of the Churches

Certainly common hopes and fears and an openness to the mutual expression of the deepest human emotions are as important to the liturgy as they are to the family, community, or larger human gathering: and perhaps even more important to the liturgy than to these other institutions, since the liturgy identifies the supernatural unity of believers through the practical and tangible relationships of those who worship together (cf. Merton 1950; 1965: 237). Natural human emotions are the precondition and sign of liturgical action, as in the ancient kiss of peace that occupies in some revised liturgies a renewed place of importance as a symbolic act constitutive of the life of the churches. The refusal to *exchange* the "peace" would destroy the fabric of the religious community. In the same way, the refusal of the worshippers to respond to the priestly invocation, "The Lord be with you," with the response "And with your (thy) Spirit" would end the liturgy at that point. Revelation, in the liturgical sense, occurs between God and the human community only to the extent that it occurs between persons.

The orderly exchange of responses may gain its vitality from the spontaneous and mutual exchange of personal emotions and intentions, but the liturgical setting guarantees the ultimate reality of the relationships constituted in these symbolic exchanges. Liturgies thus challenge other human exchanges that lay claim to authority and credibility. The liturgy stands alongside, for instance, the orderly flow of presidential pronouncements in the apparently spontaneous give-and-take of press conferences as a measure of ultimate reality and corporate authority. And the contrast can be politically unfortunate for Presidents whose grasp of the liturgical is, at best, precarious.

Once, intrigued by the text of one of Nixon's press confer- ences, I eliminated the questions of the reporter. Uninterrupted by words from the reporters, Nixon's statements made more sense than when they were read as though they connected with something that someone else had said. His words had no necessary beginning and no necessary end. Least of all did they promise to lead anywhere except to more presidential talk at a later press conference. His words offered little hope that his later statements would be more adequate, heartfelt, or memorable than were his current statements. The Nixonian years were a famine of language: a period in which Americans came to realize that when the connection between language and reality is broken, people and institutions hunger for a nourishing word.

Contrast the flow of Nixon's words with a liturgy. Whereas Nixon's press conferences could begin and end anywhere, not so the Eucharistic liturgy. The liturgy begins with a greeting and ends with a dismissal. Liturgies begin with the blessing of God by man and ends with the blessing of man by God. They begin with an invitation and end with a command to go in peace. The dialogue between speakers that was superfluous to Nixon's flow of words is essential to the liturgy. If a congregation refuses to respond, for instance, to the exhortation to "Lift up your hearts" by saying "We lift them up to the Lord," the liturgy ends. Liturgies require responses. Without the "Amen" the action of the liturgy cannot proceed: an early linguistic example of rule only with the consent of the governed. The Nixon administration, however, could proceed in its press conferences without appropriate response and displayed little regard for obtaining the consent of the governed. On more than one occasion he reminded the electorate that he would promise little, and his utterances were as unpromising as they were inconclusive. They fit Michel Foucault's description of language in modern societies:

For now we no longer have that primary, that absolutely initial, word upon which the infinite moment of discourse was founded and by which it was limited; henceforth, language was to grow with no point of departure, no end, and no promise. (1970; 1973: 44)

Churches therefore tamper with liturgies at the peril of leaving unsatisfied the human hunger for an imperishable, utterly true and life-giving language. Granted the theologians' objection that the object of the liturgy is to be obedient and to sacralize life rather than language. Nonetheless, to revise a liturgy is to create, in effect, a new one and at the same time to remind the faithful that the connection between language and reality depends upon the scholarly and critical discretion of those with esoteric and historical knowledge: not upon a divine command and upon the faithful response of the believer alone. But words that enjoy a contingent connection with reality tend to become secular in the sense of passing away. They join the world that is dying rather than create a world that will not end.

The radical implications of liturgical acts thus may be forfeited under the impact of successive liturgical "revisions." Of course, the linkages between reality and language always require the maintenance of commentary and criticism provided by scholarly elites, but a living liturgy dispenses with these specialists' services. Commentary on the liturgical texts is always permitted, and authoritative commentary from the pulpit or by the priest interpreting the sacred mysteries embedded in the liturgical text is often required. But these services are required the more the liturgical text no longer participates in and recalls what it also represents. Here I will assume that liturgical revision is a sign that liturgical acts have partially lost their radical attachments to reality itself. A liturgy undergoing revision, like a lobster growing a new shell, is vulnerable to its enemies and sells rather cheaply in the market. Liturgical revisions turn liturgies into dispensable objects, but a liturgy, by its very nature, claims that its words will not pass away; they are not part of this present age, this passing aeon.

Although liturgical acts are not secular, liturgical change secularizes liturgies in the same way that criticism erodes the authority of all texts. Criticism, Foucault notes, asks how language functions:

what representations it designates, what elements it cuts out and removes, how it analyzes and composes, what play of substitutions enable it to accomplish its role of representation. (1970; 1973: 80)

The lay worshipper thus becomes a lay critic of the liturgical text during periods of liturgical revision. Where today shall we put the Gloria, do you suppose? Is the purpose of the Gloria best served during the first part of the service as an act of public praise or immediately prior to consecration as a secret act of exultation among the faithful? Similar reflections govern the self-conscious analysis of whether to incorporate elements of the Penitential Order when it is not quite necessary. "Is this a suitable day, all things considered, for a confession and absolution, or does the season and the special intention of this particular observance warrant their omission?" The lay person becomes aware of the *function* of liturgical language in being reminded that omissions and inclusions, changes and reversals in its sequences, and the play of circumstances and events may rearrange the parts of the liturgy just as they affect the ordering of a poem or a play. But to reorder the parts of the liturgy is to affect the whole in a far more radical sense than applies to secular texts where the meaning of the whole is itself problematical.

Once the wholeness of the liturgy is a matter for critical reflection rather than a taken-for-granted order, the reality expressed and established in the liturgy also comes into question. That reality, however, is nothing less than the divine polity into which one enters and in which one for a moment dwells during the liturgy. It is not a polity that one enters or inhabits unadvisedly or lightly.

To engage in liturgical acts establishes one as a citizen with other loyalties that take precedence over those required by the politics of "this aeon." But if the liturgy becomes an object for critical reflection, functional analysis, and the exercise of certain options, the constitution of the divine polity itself is then subject to amendment by the people. Under the impact of successive amendments, furthermore, even a republic can become a totalitarian regime or a series of parts unable to unite for purposes more enduring than the temporary allocation of rewards and opportunities.

Conclusion

Like other modes of speech, liturgies are not immune to historical forces. The secularization of liturgies may masquerade as liturgical renewal, just as most historical change is disguised by its proponents in the name of continuities with the past. But as soon as scholars, antiquarians, revisionists, or prophets among the clergy and laity sense a gap between what the words of the liturgy "really mean" and what the faithful mean by them, official pressures for reform or popular pressures for renewal through the vernacular join forces to revise the received text of the liturgy.

Some aspects of a revision may seek to permit genuine interiority and inwardness to flourish in (prescribed and permitted) moments of silence between passages of collective expression: the revised American Book of Common Prayer is full of such official interstices for private devotion. The revision may also seek to synthesize the givenness of prescribed passages with opportunities for spontaneity in the form of readings or unrehearsed devotions offered by the laity from their own resources; again, the revised American Book of Common Prayer is a case in point. But it is then the *text* of the liturgy rather than the liturgy itself that seeks to overcome the fallen character of language by resolving the antinomies of givenness and spontaneity, or of collectiveness and interiority. The text, however, provides a space for the antinomies without resolving them. Indeed, no text can do for a people what they or God cannot do for themselves.

Once, however, a people have their own liturgy they become a people, and neither death nor the state nor other peoples can do more to them than simply diminish their numbers. So long as the liturgy provides for "the means of grace and hope of glory," that people will survive as a people whether they wander in a wilderness or gather in convents and monasteries to await better times. But a liturgy no one is willing to die for, least of all those who have authored it, will lack authority to unite the spontaneous and personal with the collective and the given aspects of social life. Regardless of how carefully the authors have interpolated moments of interior silence and spontaneous prayer with passages of collective language, the text is synthetic and will remain so until it is kindled in the hearts of a people or in the flames of personal sacrifice.

The liturgy, however momentarily, resolves the dialectic between the interior meaning and sense of the individual speaker and the collective meanings inherited by a people who are chosen by God and who choose Him for themselves "by grace through faith." All language, as I have suggested, is caught up in the dialectic between what is given and what is spontaneous: between the rite itself, the right order of doing things, and the original order to "do this in remembrance of me," on the one hand, and, on the other, the free, spontaneous, fully intended and wholly understood act of prayer and praise from each individual in the speaking congregation.

Outside the liturgy, individuals can properly be confronted with challenges to their speech from those who, like therapists, find fault with inadequate signs of inwardness and awareness or from those who, like teachers and lawyers, carry the requirements of collective meanings into their encounters with students and clients. But within the context of the liturgy itself, these antinomies are resolved by each person in concert with the people of God who realize their true selves in responding liturgically to the divine word.

Liturgical language may never wholly satisfy man's hunger for words that are full of meaning and fully adequate to the occasion. Occasions carry their own particular meanings, and individuals always edit and interpret even the words of the liturgy. But the gap between words and meanings is narrower in the liturgy than elsewhere. I agree with Merleau-Ponty that language and meaning constitute each other and seek each other out. His formulation is especially helpful here if we apply it to liturgical or political language:

> What we *mean* is not before us, outside all speech, as sheer signification. It is the excess of what we live over what has already been said. (1974: 80)

Applied to political rhetoric and to ideology, his insight suggests that in these cases the excess of life over speech is great. The meaning of political rhetoric can only be established by a historical record of deeds done or deeds to come. But in the case of liturgical language there is little more to be said than what has already been said and done. There is in the liturgy no excess of life over speech. Meaning has been constituted in words, and words have been fulfilled in deeds until, at the end, "It is finished." Liturgies alone can say that the word is done: Go in peace.

Efforts at liturgical change, however, are driven by a more objective view of language, as though language is separate from its meaning. Liturgists examine the succession of meanings acquired by words over time as they are spoken first in one context and then in another. Language becomes for them the object of thought rather than the "happy" or "spontaneous" animated body that is inseparable from the meaning the speaker conveys (Merleau-Ponty 1974: 80, 83). It therefore becomes a language comparable to any other: comparable even to ideologists and political rhetorics. The danger exists that liturgy will become similarly objectified in the mind of the worshipper: an object for study and manipulation like any other. In this event, the worshipper loses what is the last remaining possibility for speaking spontaneously yet in collective rhythms and for speaking from the heart in words that are understood by the entire community. As I noted at the outset, the patchwork solution of liturgical scholars, that pieces together moments of spontaneity or private reflection with the given order of the text, will not put together what has already been torn asunder.

Chapter 3

Religious Testimony on Trial:
The Secularization of Witnessing

At the heart of many cultures (perhaps of all) are themes of a major test or trial: an odyssey or a battle between two cosmic armies, a covenant with the gods or with the devil, and the promise of a fruitful and protected land to a faithful people tested in the wilderness. In Western culture, the theme of the trial is coded in terms of a Last Judgment that lends significance to earthly trials in everyday life or in courts of law. In the Old Testament the plaintiff is frequently Yahweh, who wishes to plead his cause against his people. In the New Testament the trial theme is enacted within an eschatological scenario; thus the trial of Jesus before Pilate and the Sanhedrin initiates the Last Judgment, in which the world is indeed convicted, but final sentencing awaits the return of the one who has been judged by the world yet vindicated by the resurrection. The irony of the New Testament lies in the reversal of the trial, which to "the world" appears to be a judgment on one who pretends to a divine throne, but which is revealed to have been a judgment on the world itself.

These themes lie at the "heart" of Western culture in ways that are often obscured by their location in peripheral groups and movements. While religious sects in America, for instance, still herald the coming of the end in which the evil-doers of this world, already found guilty by the prophetic community, will receive their proper sentence, the trial theme is carried in more subtle ways in the language and rules of secular institutions. It is commonplace to note that Marxism and liberalism assume a secular eschatology based on the eventual triumph of a proletariat or of freedom and reason in human affairs. But the theme of the trial exercises a far more pervasive and indirect influence on social life than might be suggested by references to religious sects or modern politics.

Even the language of everyday life evokes the theme of a trial. Take, for example, the current uses of the term "witness." In ordinary language witnesses are simply people who observe a crime, an accident, or perhaps an eclipse. Ordinary language also includes the notion that witnesses report what they say or what, as "expert witnesses," they know on a given subject. But there is also a second meaning of the term that makes witnessing a religious duty and a witness one who fulfills a religious obligation. Sometimes a person's language, role, and the social context make it clear that one is witnessing in the first, ordinary sense of the term, as in the case of a doctor called as an expert witness to speak in technical terms to a secular courtroom on the medical definition of death. But at other moments, language, role, and context may obscure the boundary between the ordinary and the religious or "symbolic" meaning of the term, as in the case of a father testifying in a secular courtroom to the religious convictions that support his role as a Catholic layman and as guardian of his comatose daughter. I am referring, of course, to the case of Karen Ann Quinlan, but there are undoubtedly many cases in which religious language and roles are not clearly separated from the secular speech and from the role of a witness within a secular courtroom. When the Catonsville Nine stood trial for disrupting the activities of a local Selective Service Board, for instance, the language and role of the witnesses were prophetic: so much so that the witnesses acted out their intention to put the court itself and the state on trial with God, once again, as the plaintiff. The irony of the New Testament theme of the trial occurs whenever secular contexts fail to impose stringent constraints on the role and language of religious witnesses.

When the context does not succeed in constraining the meaning of testimony, so that the distinction between secular and religious roles and language becomes problematical, trials

take on ultimate significance to those who take part in or
observe them. But even where the boundary between the
secular and the religious is more clearly drawn, secular trials
take on a seriousness that derives from the implicit meaning
of witnessing, of testimony and confession, and of judicial
decision itself in a society whose religious culture places aL ꞓ ꞓˆ
history within the context of a Last Judgment. Wherever on.,
wishes to be taken especially seriously, one witnesses, con-
fesses, or gives testimony. Otherwise one's report or statement
may be taken seriously without personal reference to the one
who tells the tale. No judgment is given, and one's statements
become empty: "mere words," to be placed on file.

The theme of a trial gives implicit meaning to many activities
that are remote from courtrooms or that do not involve witnessing, confession, testifying, or judgment. Max Weber was
fascinated by the extent to which work and capital investment
in the West were serious activities rather than the spheres of
arbitrary self-interest or undisciplined risk-taking. In the
Protestant tradition he found sources that made all of life a
testing of one's ultimate standing before a divine tribunal and
noted the search of the early Calvinists for signs or testimony
to their ultimate status. In the status-group of the bourgeoisie,
that seriousness lent a certain discipline, rigor, and continuity
to decisions concerning production, marketing, and investment. In studying Protestant sects he also noted an emphasis
on consistency between faith and action that became in secular
contexts a standard requiring consistency between words and
deeds. That standard assured that certain individuals would
receive moral credit in the community and perhaps even
financial credit from banking institutions. Just as Protestant
souls could no longer gain immortality by the last-minute
purchase of ecclesiastical favors by their relatives, but only
by a lifetime of creditable testimony, so individuals could
achieve continuous and effective economic organization only
by a lifetime of disciplined investment and productivity.
What began as an eschatological testing at the end of time
became, after fifteen-hundred Christian centuries, a lifetime
of testing of one's vocation. Neither acquiring merit from

works nor spending merit from a divine treasury, the Christian's freedom consists of remaining on trial while knowing that indeed the verdict is already in and only the last sentence remains. Perhaps, given a faithful lifetime on probation, the sentence will be suspended for those who have already acknowledged their complicity in the crucifixion.

A lifetime on probation can fairly characterize social life in secular institutions. In the schools, colleges, and universities of Western societies the majority of youth are subjected to a process of continuous testing and evaluation. Positions in these institutions are initially probationary, and even tenured faculty at every level are increasingly subject to repeated evaluation. But probationary processes and appointments characterize other institutions beyond the educational. "Management by objective," for instance, guarantees that covenants between supervisors and employees will be carried out faithfully if the relationship is to continue, and policy itself is made subject to periodic evaluations that test its merits as well as the effectiveness of procedures that implement it. Indeed periodic elections ensure that policies and politicians are on probationary terms, subject to a review by the electorate that resembles the deliberations and verdict of a jury. Political campaigns themselves resemble a primitive test of stamina and valor combined with a quasi-judicial review of political testimony. In the scientific community hypotheses enjoy a probationary status and require repeated testing: a clear indication that scientific propositions, like the elect, will be known empirically "by their fruits" after a trial period in which they are subjected to repeated testing by the scientific community. People entering the professions require repeated tests before they are certified as reliable, just as programs are only provisionally accredited by professional organizations that provide periodic review and certification. In the scientific community and in many secular organizations, language lacks any specific religious terminology, and individuals are inducted into authoritative roles without passing any religious tests. Nonetheless, scientists or literary critics are occasionally compared to priests and prophets by those who wish to call attention to how seriously critics and scientists lay claims to authority and authenticity. But in politics it is not unusual to find politicians using religious language as they claim to be born again or as they invoke divine blessing on their endeavors. Even induction into political office is usually celebrated with religious symbols, oaths, and ceremonies. Indeed, one American President frequently used a phrase from Isaiah, "Come, let us reason together," to express his fundamental attitude toward the role of the President. It is not coincidental that this phrase comes from that part of Isaiah in which the writer describes a lawsuit by God against his people: a lawsuit carried out in this instance, perhaps, by the politician-turned-President against a stiff-necked people who resisted his commands and refused to offer the proper sacrifices. When the verdict of the people was unmistakable, moreover, the President in question, in a public address that had the marks of contrition, announced that his trials were over and that he would not seek renomination to another term.

In its prophetic language, then, religion places the world on trial, but in the course of secularization the trial is institutionalized in all areas of social life until even religion itself is tried and, on occasion, found wanting before secular tribunals. The question of whether it is God or Caesar who is on trial is at the heart of the biblical tradition and in the critical events of the New Testament. The question of who is on trial continues in the dynamic relationship between religious and secular authorities: sometimes resolved in favor of the former, and sometimes in favor of the latter, but never resolved indefinitely or for all parties. Slowly the dynamic takes root in secular social life through a continuous process of trying, proving, and testing individuals, ideas, and policies. The biblical tradition that ultimately expresses itself in secular standards of utility, as an emphasis on continuous testing and validation in the religious life, is carried over into work and politics, into science and education. But in the nineteenth century the same utilitarianism provided the standards that put religion itself on trial. It is this reversal that Goldstein (1975) finds in the personal biography of Tocqueville, who first lost his childhood faith under the impact of secular rationalism, only to find in that rationalism a precarious set of standards for validating religion as expressing and meeting the deepest human aspirations. Tocqueville "confessed" (ibid.: 10) that, in terms of traditional Catholicism, he was an "unbeliever," but he claimed to believe in an "ultimate judgment of good and evil," (ibid.: 6), in the immortality of the soul, and the justice of God. Thus religion was both "a trial" for Tocqueville (ibid.: 11), on trial in the court of secular effects, and ultimately vindicated by those same effects:

The fact that the teachings of the Gospel were able to inspire a pure and ethical life was an ultimate test for Tocqueville. (ibid.: 6)

It is clear that the theme of a continuing trial for the world and for faith itself was as deeply rooted in European Catholicism as in Protestantism, however much Catholicism's terms concentrated on the soul or immortality and borrowed heavily from utilitarianism.

The cultural theme of a trial has therefore lent a certain seriousness to social life in Western societies. To everyday life, that theme lends the awareness that the individual is on trial, perhaps being tested by God, or undergoing trials that, as the spiritual has it, will "soon be over." To the life cycle the theme lends the significance of a lifetime of testimony, in which the individual gives and seeks signs of his or her eventual status before a divine tribunal. To social institutions the cultural theme lends the right and obligation to be certified as creditable or authoritative witnesses to truth embedded in molecules, legal texts, medical records, or other significant repositories of information. To the person the theme of the trial generates a demand to be taken seriously as an authentic and credible witness to what one knows and has seen with one's own eyes. Personal authority, like the authority of the biblical witness, ultimately depends on personal experience and is exercised through personal witness. Not to be taken seriously as a witness, therefore, is to fail before human tribunals and perhaps before divine judgment as well. Religion in the West has therefore made everyday life and social relations serious, because they entail the justification of individuals, of social institutions, and of the larger society itself. That is why, of course, religious dissent often makes the claim that everyday life does not matter or that, in fact, the trial is over. Such is the claim, as I see it, of many of the Eastern religious themes imported in Western societies primarily by the young who have tired of being on trial in educational or other institutions and despair of a lifetime of secular and moral testing.

There is another perspective from which to view the theme of the trial, however, that I will also explore in this discussion. That perspective is less interpretive, more analytical, than the one stated in the preceding paragraph. I will argue that the trial is a social institution that certifies the relationship of words to reality. As such, the trial is undoubtedly a primitive institution or arrangement. As a human product, words are often deceptive or empty. Wishes may be mistaken for promises, false witness may be given, and even promises may be forgotten or ignored. Individuals may speak of that which they have heard rather than seen, or they may give directions without proper authority. Their own deeds may belie the speakers' words, and two witnesses may not be able to concur on their testimony. The trial, long before it became a model for the justification of God's words and for judgment on human language, was and is a social arrangement for closing the gap between language and reality.

The relationship between the trial and language, however, is triangular. At the apex, so to speak, is religion itself. On the one hand, even secular courtrooms require religious oaths before individuals may give testimony or be inducted into judicial offices. On the other hand, individuals in secular courtrooms lay religious claims to a form of justice that may go beyond the letter to the spirit of the law. The institution of the trial cannot guarantee the relation of language to reality without the higher guarantees accorded by religion, but religion in turn guarantees and can transcend the claims of the court to be a legitimate tribunal for justice in human affairs.

Like most triangular social relationships, therefore, the relations between language, religion, and the social institution of the trial are inherently unstable. The court may set limits on religious testimony, define religion as irrelevant to the issues at hand, or reinforce the plaintiff's or defendant's claims to justice on religious grounds. On the other hand, in the name of religion, individuals may place the court and the secular authority of the state itself on trial, or by the power of religious testimony convince the court that a gap in the law exists: that a gap exists between the circumstances of their situation and the language of the law. Under these conditions new laws must be written, new words spoken, and unprecedented decisions be made by virtue of an appeal to certain values held sacred by a people if not actually encoded in legal texts. How religion functions to reinforce the role of witnesses and the authority of the court depends on a wide range of factors that I can only begin to explore in this discussion.

In the process of secularization, the intimate connection between religion and language is dissolved as language becomes established in a variety of secular contexts. As speakers cannot always rely on religion therefore as a guarantee that they are speaking *seriously*, the authority of the speaker inheres in the act of speaking itself far more than on external sources of authority. But in exchange for this autonomy, speakers face constraints from other sources: for example, from rules for discourse in the classroom and the court. In these contexts speakers lose a certain *force*, and their words may be of no avail. The implications of this general thesis, of course, would require far greater scope for development than is possible in this short introduction. But it should be possible here to sketch the basic outlines of the process of secularization in order to suggest a picture of language that is separated from guarantees for its seriousness and effectiveness by losing its liturgical context. Language in this process becomes problematical therefore and subject to skepticism concerning "mere words" or "the prisonhouse of language." As a widow is reported to have commented on the recent visit of Pope John Paul II to New York City: "What we need is less rhetoric, more action," (*New York Times*, 3 October 1979). It is a comment, I am suggesting, far more likely to be made about religious speech when it occurs in the secular contexts of Yankee Stadium or the United Nations than in St Patrick's Cathedral, where the distinction between rhetoric and action is overcome by the liturgy itself.

Religion guarantees, first of all, the *seriousness* of the speaker. It is prohibited to utter oaths or to take certain names upon one's lips without meaning what one says; the penalties for unserious speech in religious language are severe and lasting. In a liturgical context, years of preparation determine that the ordained will speak without irony or insincerity the mind of the whole church. Idiosyncratic and unintentional speech is literally ruled out by the liturgy even at the moments when they are most possible, as in the homily or sermon. Of course, outside liturgical contexts, religion still serves to warrant the seriousness of the speaker, as in the religious oaths taken by witnesses in secular courts, where the penalties for unseriousness are also severe but not quite so lasting, perhaps, as in a strictly liturgical setting. Prophets who use religion to guarantee the seriousness of their intentions are also likely to be taken seriously by their followers, but others who follow their activities for the media or for the state are known to entertain doubts as to whether the prophet's speech is wholly serious rather than merely symbolic (expressive) or even strategic (manipulative).

Questions on the seriousness of religious speech are now at the center of public policy in several Western nations that have become host countries to Eastern religious movements. The questions are often quite specific, in fact, as courts seek to determine whether the speeches of the Rev. Mr Moon cloak political intentions with religious language. In the courtroom itself, moreover, the testimony of individuals to their religious convictions is closely scrutinized for signs of a merely strategic purpose, as, for instance, conscientious objectors have discovered in pressing their cases against service in the armed forces. But even the protestations of an American President that he can be taken seriously because he is "born-again" have not brought the full guarantee of religion to presidential speech. Outside a liturgical context, the guarantees of religion do not ensure the seriousness of speech or the willingness of hearers to credit the speaker as being wholly serious. In the complete absence of any religious language, however, speakers are left to their own devices to make claims to seriousness of speech. In ordinary language it is therefore entirely appropriate for the listener to ask, "Are you serious?" and to entertain doubts even concerning a speaker's affirmative response.

Religious language also makes speech-acts more clearly *identifiable* than they would otherwise be outside liturgical contexts or in wholly secular terms. Take, for instance, the act of promising. As I noted in the Introduction it is often problematical whether a specific utterance is indeed a promise. Children learn to trust or to doubt their parents' words on the basis of implicit understandings as to whether, in fact, a parent made a promise rather than expressed a pious hope (to take the child to the zoo, for instance), and secular philosophers construct a range of conditions that promises must meet if they are to be full-fledged promises: conditions seldom found in their entirety outside the philosopher's text. But in religious language, it is not in doubt whether the promises of God are promises rather than statements of good intention. In the liturgy, moreover, promises are set aside as such by special markings in the text and by special gestures, such as giving rings and taking hands under ecclesiastical direction. In prophetic speech, of course, promises are understood as such only by the faithful for whom they are intended, as the non-faithful are more likely to be the recipients of warnings and threats. But even the faithful are known to require that promises be interpreted, for example, as to when the prophet will return or his words fulfilled. Outside liturgical contexts and the somewhat contingent guarantees of religious speech, however, promises are notably ambiguous: they are easily mistaken for warnings, predictions, or statements of intention.

The process of secularization makes any act of speech susceptible to misinterpretation, but promises are among the most
vulnerable of such acts to misinterpretation in the absence of
religious markings or outside a liturgical context.

In the secular language of presidential utterances, Americans
have become accustomed to find that certain statements have
become "inoperative," in the sense that they no longer can
be taken as constituting a set of directions for action, but
religious language guarantees the *operative* character of speech,
as I will shortly indicate in a brief discussion on biblical rules
of discourse. Divine speech is quintessentially operative, as
the divine word creates its own effects: the word "light"
brings light, and the promise to be with His people becomes
self-fulfilling as the promise is heard and remembered in later
generations. In the liturgy, of course, the operative character
of language remains, as when words of consecration turn
bread and wine into sacraments of the divine presence. But
even in the liturgy the operative force of language becomes
contingent on the dialogue of the speakers. The consecration
is not complete without the congregational "Amen." The
naming of a child in baptism, as operative an act of speech as
one may find in a liturgical context, is contingent on the child
being presented and received with that name by the faithful.
In prophetic speech, moreover, the religious guarantee that
the words of the prophet will indeed be operative, in the
sense of coming true, are contingent on the faith of those
who hear the prophet, as the New Testament formula ("Your
faith has made you whole") makes clear on repeated occasions.
But outside liturgical contexts and in the absence of prophetic
speech, language depends entirely on negotiated social arrangements for its operative character. Commands are given, sen-
tences handed down, declarations of war made, and verdicts
announced under social arrangements that are politically
designed to guarantee the operative quality of the speech
concerned. The less carefully arranged the circumstances,
however, the more problematical is the operative quality of
the language. Especially in the absence of careful, and legitimate arrangements to guarantee the operative quality of

language by force, speech that declares and pronounces is likely to be empty, to be "given the lie" by unforeseen circumstances or resistance, and to reinforce skepticism concerning the illocutionary force of secular language. Few secular statements are unimpeachable.

Religion has also guaranteed the *authority* of the speaker: a relationship between religion and language so common as to appear commonplace when put in so many words. Take, for instance, the traditional Trinitarian formula still used in many liturgies: "In the name of the Father, and of the Son, and of the Holy Ghost." Not only does the use of the Trinitarian name illustrate the operative function of religious speech: the name thus invoking the divine presence. But the formula signifies the authority by which the cleric pronounces couples husband and wife, or gives a child a name, or concludes a part of the liturgy. The use of the name carries great authority, and at the use of certain names, "every knee shall bow." The right therefore to use the name is itself a source of authority conferred only on those who are set apart for an authoritative role and entrusted with the liturgical elements and functions of the religious community. The use of operative speech, the right to declare and pronounce, and the permission to preach are also forms of speech that require and convey the authority of the speaker within a liturgical context.

Outside the context of the liturgy, however, religion reinforces but cannot guarantee the authority of the speaker. The authority of the prophet, of course, is reinforced by religious claims: claims, for instance, to follow in a certain prophetic tradition, to be an exponent of a religious worldview, or to represent the mind and doctrine of an entire religious collectivity. But these claims are more precarious in the courtroom than in the pulpit. A liturgical context guarantees that no contrary claims to be an authoritative spokesman for the tradition will be raised, and at strategic points in the liturgy the faithless or the merely interested are expected to depart. But in the courtroom other witnesses may be present who claim equal religious authority for a contrary interpretation of the tradition, and on cross-examination a prophetic witness may appear to have spoken only personal convictions rather than the mind of the religious collectivity as a whole. Under these conditions, claims to authority on religious grounds are vacated, and the prophet must rest a claim to be taken seriously entirely on the grounds of the prophet's credibility or authenticity; that is, the prophet may yet claim to have had certain experiences that warrant a serious hearing, or the prophet may demand to be taken seriously in view of a certain consistency between his or her prophetic words and deeds. In either event, the claims to authority may be considered moot, since in a secular context it is the judicial authority itself that prevails even over such traditional questions as the definition of religion and the location of its boundary with the secular.

The guarantees of religion to the *credibility* of the speaker are venerable, although their value in secular contexts is increasingly limited by the guarantees afforded by professions to the credibility of "expert witnesses." The word of revelation is the quintessentially credible word: a word, as the Old Testament has it, that is "solid." God's word is credible to the point of being able to create the faith it requires; it is the word, therefore, of grace. In a liturgical context efforts are made to ground the credibility of the liturgical text in the founding words of the tradition: "On the night in which he was betrayed he took bread . . . and said, Do this in remembrance of me." But the credibility of the liturgy ultimately rests on more than a historical liaison with the founding utterances of the prophet or savior. The liturgy *re-presents*, in the sense of presenting again or making present, *the reality* of the initial utterance; thus the doctrine of the real presence, regardless of its metaphysical elaboration, captures liturgy's claim to re-present not only the speech but the speaker at the founding event. Of course, the representative function of the liturgy also guarantees the authority of the liturgical event, just as in secular contexts a claim to represent an authoritative figure lays claim to that figure's authority. But the liturgy is primarily a "showing forth" (until the second coming, perhaps), a demonstration that is a serious, perhaps the most serious, communicative action that conforms to ideal standards (cf. Luckmann 1979: 20–1). Outside a liturgical context, and especially in courts, witnesses are allowed to "represent" that certain events took place, but the witnesses' claim to credibility is itself being tested in the judicial examination and cross-examination. To "represent" on the witness stand is merely to allege, even though one represents under a religious oath that one speaks the truth.

The claims of the prophet to credibility stand between the liturgy and the speech of the witness in a secular courtroom. The prophet's claim to credible speech rests on the "I say unto you": on the relation between prophet and hearer. Of course, prophets claim to have seen and heard realities that escape ordinary attention, and prophets also claim that their words are guaranteed by things that others soon will hear and see. There is a strain toward empiricism in prophecy, as in the admonition of Jesus to his questioners to "look around" them and observe what it is that they see: the lame walking, deaf hearing, etc. But the primary source of prophetic credibility is in the relation of the prophet to the hearer, in the "follow me," and in the force of prophetic utterance itself. Even in a secular courtroom, prophets rely for credibility on the relationship conveyed by speaking itself, as in the Berrigans' testimony in the trial of the Catonsville Nine. There Philip Berrigan reiterated the formula thus: "To lawyers we say . . ."; "To federal judges we say . . ." (Berrigan 1970: 31). It is the *we say* that is the guarantee of prophetic credibility, since the prophet speaks only of what the prophet truly knows. But in a secular courtroom the *we say* of the prophet is out of order, in the sense that it violates or ignores judicial rules for crediting testimony. In the court, as in the secular classroom, the credibility of a statement depends on the statement itself and its relation to what can be observed. Even the poet's credibility rests on a statement concerning the "concrete particular," an observation as specific and detailed as one observation out of the many hundreds, perhaps, that are accumulated in scientific laboratories and sociological surveys of public opinion. Thus the sociologist (far more than the poet), lays claims to credibility that does not depend on the relation between speaker and hearer. Scientific statements indeed stand or fall on the basis of tests that can be applied without reference to the speaker or author and are entirely subject to the question-and-answer, the give-and-take of ordinary language.

The separation of the speaker from the speaker's own statements turns conversations into texts that are understandable without any personal relationship between speaker and hearer. As Bernstein (1974) notes in his discussion of the elaborated code, it is the function of that code (style, usage, variant, cf. Gouldner 1976: 58f) to enable strangers to understand the speaker's statements by making the speaker's intentions and meanings entirely open from the outset rather than available only to disciples, friends, students, or intimates. Even in face-to-face encounters, academics often speak as though they were addressing a distant audience or creating a text (cf. Davies 1975: 137ff). On some occasions, of course, academics do converse for precisely that purpose, and because they intend to be quoted they specify their intentions, the force of their statements, and their particular meanings by such phrases as "I would like to suggest," or "By 'religion' I meant to refer to . . ." very much as a witness in a courtroom attempts to create a record for later judicial review. Academics and other professional witnesses thus speak as though they were on trial and weigh their words carefully, since their words will often be scrutinized by those who were not present at the time and who will remain forever strangers to the speaker. The word "stranger" here is chosen, I might add, because I wish to suggest that there is indeed something alienating in the process of separating the speaker from the meaning and in allowing words to be considered apart from a relationship between the speaker and hearer.

In a society in which it is the norm to interpret statements without a personal relationship between speaker and hearer, it is not surprising for churches to pursue the vernacular, while courtrooms and classrooms too exert strong pressures against the use of vague and open-ended meanings. The judge in the trial of the Catonsville Nine protested against Daniel Berrigan's use of metaphor, and in both academic and judicial contexts the purpose of ordinary language is to make possible the determination of as nearly a literal meaning as possible. The questions of "What, precisely, do you mean?" can only be answered in ways that reduce the ambiguity, open-endedness, and opacity of language. Under these institutionalized constraints, for instance, it was well-nigh impossible for Joseph Quinlan to convince the court that his daughter Karen was virtually dead, since expert witnesses were available who could remove the religious and moral openness of that term and substitute instead the criteria of electronic measurements of brain waves over a twenty-four hour period and of the unassisted effort of the body to inhale. The court did not have to know the expert medical witnesses personally to understand and test their statements about the meaning of the term "dead," but Joseph Quinlan's use of the term was sufficiently ambiguous and open that only an extended personal relationship with him and perhaps with his daughter would have made his statement plain. Secularization turns the rules for credibility into requirements for literal usage.

The spread of literal usage no doubt is related to the one-dimensionality of language lamented by Marcuse. Even the rising tide of biblical literalism empties the prophetic word of its opacity and open-endedness. Since the believer is related primarily to a text rather than to a person, the words of that text are susceptible of being given one, and only one, meaning. It is this flatness of communication that other observers have noted as a loss of the "backside" or other-sidedness of social life, such that individuals are perceived in their social roles as policemen, perhaps, rather than in their more hidden and unpredictable dimensions (cf. Luckmann 1979: 10). Clearly Max Weber understood this loss of transcendence in social life, especially in institutionalized interaction between individuals, to be at the root of the "disenchanted" universe in which only "this-worldly" meanings could be communicated and understood. More recently Bellah (1964), without specifically relying on a hermeneutical approach, also refers to the collapse of dualism in a world with clear and specific meanings. It is a transition that literary critics have understood or at least described more thoroughly than sociologists. One thinks of Northrop Frye's (1976) observation that contemporary radicalism is what one would expect in a world that, to its youthful observers, lacks any continuity, any embedded purposes or intentions, either in nature or history; and it is a radicalism that complains about the inability of the students themselves to understand the personal and subjective reality embedded in medieval texts or in the texts of a foreign culture (Frye 1976: 43–4). It is a world in which images represent only the surface or face of a reality rather than its "backside" (Luckmann), in which bread, so to speak, cannot re-present its original reality as the body of Christ or claim an "inward and spiritual grace." Of course, in more folk-oriented cultures myths persisted, like the creation story, in which statues themselves have souls because they are animated with divine or demonic purposes. The world was enchanted because its symbols, whether they were pictures or statues, embodied souls which could speak to humans and in turn respond (Ziolkowski 1977: 18ff). As Ziolkowski himself notes, it is the "process of secularization" that "disenchants" these literary or mythical images, so that they are no longer resonant with thoughts and feelings from beyond themselves.

The literary critic thus documents what sociologists in the Weberian tradition essentially have argued, that secularization brings a fundamental change in the relation of individuals to symbols. The symbols no longer are "constituent" (cf. Ziolkowski 1977: 14) or constitutive (cf. Ricoeur 1977; Parsons and Platt 1973), because they no longer evoke or embody what the symbols represent. Applied to the symbols of national identity, and especially to the religious symbols or themes that define the nation's identity and purpose, this process leads to the disenchantment of nations and the withdrawal of moral and emotional commitments from national goals and institutions. When applied to the analysis of literary or other texts in the classroom or to the scrutiny of testimony in the court, the separation of words from the speaker's own meaning enables these words to be interpreted and tested on grounds other than those directly implied or chosen by the speaker. Thus literary critics can improve on the metaphors of John Donne, and lawyers can ignore, bracket, or reinterpret the testimony of witnesses, as personal testimony becomes a text that is literally separated from the passions and purposes of the original speaker. Call it disenchantment; call it a loss of immanence or of a sacramental view of symbols; or call it the loss of constituent symbols. It is a world in which literary critics not only note the loss of continuity between present and past generations but exacerbate that loss by subjecting texts to radical rearrangements and criticisms in the absence of their author. Students in the classroom, and witnesses in court, often therefore prefer silence to speaking, when they cannot call for the response or interpretation that they most desire. Even the English Book of Common Prayer, whose text has for three centuries linked the particular spirit of its author, Thomas Cranmer, to the hopes and fears of the English people, is being rearranged by a committee of scholars. The paradox is simply that literary critics, liturgical scholars, and academics go on to deplore the loss of continuity in a world that they have helped to separate from its own most personal past.

It is indeed paradoxical, in an age in which the value of the individual or the person is apparently so deeply founded in social policy and in secular values, that individuals should be required to abandon religious beliefs and experience as a source of their authority or personal credibility in secular contexts. It is not as if religion did not appear to provide the themes of modern literature or enter the experience of modern individuals, but the situation is rather that, in order to be taken seriously, the individual does well not to take religion or the sacred itself too seriously in secular contexts. But secular contexts are where the serious work of the society is carried on — the work of setting the minimum wage or of determining what to include in courses on literature. To claim authority for one's beliefs or convictions on religious grounds in such contexts is to risk dismissal as not being serious or to risk not being taken seriously. As Frye notes, of course, religion is still available as a source of themes in contemporary literature and folklore, but it is in such unserious literature as the Poseidon adventure, designed primarily to entertain in the leisure-time of a modern society, that the Moses myth endures, rather than in serious literary allegories on the Holocaust (Frye 1976: 20). Bryan Wilson (1976:42) argues essentially the same point concerning modern religious movements: that they make use of ancient themes, but that they are not focussed on the central institutions of modern society or entertained by individuals playing important roles in those institutions. Without the benefit of religious beliefs and institutions to guarantee that the individual is speaking credibly and with authority, individuals are left, without religious guarantees, to claim that they are at least authentic and so worthy of being taken seriously.

Clearly the standards or norms for authority, authenticity, and credibility, that determine when a speaker is to be taken seriously, are not entirely secular in origin regardless of their widespread control over discourse in such contemporary secular contexts as the classroom and the court. Weber argued that the norm of consistency between word and deed, that appeared in entrepreneurial and bureaucratic organizations in the West, originated in Protestantism and was carried specifically by sectarian groups in which "individuals were to act in terms of conscientious adherence to principles of normative consistency" (Robertson 1979: 20). Robertson notes that, in Weber's view, Protestant sects took individuals seriously on the basis of trust because they believed that individuals are both free from the status quo of "this world" and responsible for the consequences of their actions in everyday life (ibid.: 16). To put it another way, we might note two kinds of consistency that are at work in the familiar Weberian thesis on the Protestant ethic and the spirit of capitalism. The first is a consistency or congruence between sectarian norms for individual freedom and responsibility, on the one hand, and, on the other, the relatively flexible and impersonal world of the entrepreneur prior to the development of an "iron cage" of bureaucratic regulations. This point has been well enough understood, despite the ensuing controversy, and needs no further elaboration here. The second type is a consistency that is required of the Protestant between faith and action, so that *action* is justified by reference to an authoritative faith and *actors* are justified by their claims to consistency. Robertson (1979) points to the secular development, in professional and bureaucratic contexts, of corresponding standards for certifying individuals as trustworthy and authoritative. Indeed, as Robertson points out, other writers are deriving a "culture of professionalism," in which individuals are certified as responsible for carrying out a professional mission, from the same sectarian emphasis on freeing individuals from direct ecclesiastical control and on entrusting to them a mission in this world that is authenticated by consistency between the individual's faith and work. It is this line of analysis, moreover, that has governed sociological interest in religion since Troeltsch's first claim that every major religion carries within itself a "general fundamental sociological theory" concerning the relationship of the individual to society: a theory "which in some way or another will exert an influence upon all social relationships" (Troeltsch 1931; 1960: 30).

While it remains for scholars to chart the paths by which the Protestant, and especially the sectarian, ethic was taken up by secular professions and organizational groups, it is clear that Protestantism has inspired the rules by which individuals may be taken seriously in secular contexts such as the classroom and the court. The relationship of secular to religious speech is therefore complex and problematical. In the same courtroom in which oaths on the Bible must be taken before individuals will be considered as authentic and credible witnesses to their experience, the same individuals will find that their testimony to their religious faith is restricted by strict standards of reliability and relevance: standards set by secular professions that derive their authority from the state. Individual witnesses may be regarded as authentic and therefore as "sincere," moreover, without being taken seriously as authoritative witnesses to their church's teaching or as entirely credible witnesses to their own past experiences. The chances are relatively high, in other words, that an individual's "score" on a judicial "scale" of authenticity will vary independently from that person's score on authority or credibility. Only religious prophets like the Berrigan brothers demand to be taken seriously on all three dimensions of religious language. In any event, the witnesses' scores and their relative weights are assigned by a panel of peers or judges whose own standards for taking individuals seriously may be difficult, at best, to determine. Consistency is still a norm in secular contexts, but consistency among secular norms remains to be determined.

The claim to *authenticity*, as I have noticed, derives from a Protestant emphasis on consistency between faith and action that was carried specifically in Protestant sects in Europe and America. Authenticity still carries with it the connotation of consistency, which in secular contexts has been a consistency between word and deed. As Benjamin Franklin noted, in a passage that caught Max Weber's (1958: 48f) attention as expressing the secular ethos once derived from the Protestant ethic, the artisan whose words are as good as his deeds is taken seriously and receives financial credit precisely because of his this-worldly consistency. But religious expression, particularly in charismatic and the more enthusiastic of contemporary non-Western religious groups, provides a third type of authenticity: not between faith and action or word and deed, but between inner experience and outward expression. As Cox (1977: 18) noted of a young woman chanting in Arabic while dancing in the Sufi tradition, the dancer did not know that she was praising Allah. She was simply achieving a unity between inner states and outward gestures through chanting and the dance. In that process religious symbols are not "serious," in Habermas's sense of signaling the serious engagement of the speaker or a claim upon others to be taken seriously. It is rather merely symbolic-expressive and provides a mode of authenticity that guarantees only that outward gestures are reflective of inner states. It was a similar drive to achieve authenticity that many observers noted in the silent vigils of the 1960s before cemeteries and selective service boards, where religious beliefs, even when they were voiced, conveyed less a claim to authority than a message that the individual was authentically expressing inner states in these outward actions. It has therefore been relatively easy for critics to belittle these gestures as ineffective, dramatic, narcissistic, immature, or self-serving rather than to understand them as the one claim to be taken seriously on religious grounds that is left when claims to authority and credibility are no longer guaranteed in secular contexts by religious tradition and experience.

In this discussion I have mentioned the transcripts, edited by Daniel Berrigan, of the trial of the Catonsville Nine to illustrate these uses of speech. The defendants in that trial claimed credibility as reliable witnesses. When they found their credibility being attacked in court, they protested, as did Daniel Berrigan when he stated: "I must protest the effort to discredit me on the stand. I am speaking of what I saw" (Berrigan 1970: 90). When the defendants were challenged concerning their authority, they claimed validity in terms of traditional Christian standards, to wit: "This is a legitimate form of social protest. It is well documented in Christianity" (ibid.: 43). When the defendants were challenged about their authenticity, they simply claimed that they were trying to achieve consistency between their religious intentions and their social actions: "I was trying to say that the style of one's action must coincide with the style of his life," a religious style, in the case of these defendants (ibid.: 75). These transcripts are extraordinarily useful in illustrating the serious use of language, rather than symbolic and playful or merely practical usage, because the defendants' testimony reflected their own desire to be taken seriously as witnesses, not only to their experience and to their own actions, but also to their faith.

The Catonsville defendants asked to be justified and understood on a basis that, in Habermas's terms (1979: 63–4), is "speech-act immanent." *Immanent* within a statement about certain facts is the speaker's obligation to cite certain experiences. The defendants therefore sought to provide knowledge which, if understood, would justify their claim to credibility since both speaker and hearer would share the defendant's understanding of the costs of the Vietnam War. Also immanent within a claim to be authoritative is what Habermas (1979: 64) calls the "obligation to provide justification" by referring to a specific "normative context," like the traditional Christianity cited by several of the defendants among the Catonsville Nine. Immanent, finally, in the speaker's claim to be authentic is what Habermas (1979: 64) calls the obligation to prove "trustworthy" by showing, as the Catonsville defendants attempted to show, that their deeds were wholly consistent with their moral intentions. Now, it is possible for both speakers and hearers to agree or to disagree on whether certain facts or certain actions support a speaker's claim to be credible and authentic. After all, experts disagree on whether certain facts are reliable or sufficient for a diagnosis or judgment, and consistency is likewise a matter for thoughtful reflection and judicious argument: a matter for deliberation by juries and justices. But as Habermas points out, a claim that one's action can be justified by a certain norm is even more vulnerable, since norms themselves are not self-justifying. What is the standing in court, for instance, of a traditional Christian standard that justifies civil disobedience? Where agreement on the basis for justification cannot be assumed, justification is problematical and other rules of discourse for reaching agreement prevail. In the case of the Catonsville Nine, the court's rules, entirely practical ones for determining whether a law had been breached (and if so, how, when, and by whom), took precedence over the rules that would justify the speakers who were testifying in their own defense.

When there is tension and conflict between two sets of rules for discourse, the conditions are ripe for what Habermas and many other sociologists would call a crisis in legitimacy. In such a crisis, other forms of language-use seem more promising than the use of language to achieve understanding and agreement. Symbolic or playful forms of language seemed to flourish during the 1960s in the United States as I have already suggested, as life was "celebrated" and non-verbal symbolic action was used for the sake of demonstrating rather than for reaching shared understanding in many forms of public action. Similarly, purely strategic forms of language use, where the emphasis was on getting results with or without shared understanding, became the object of public criticism during the anti-war and civil rights movements, as the public became increasingly sophisticated concerning the "management of news" and the manipulative aspects of political rhetoric both by officials and by dissidents. But whereas symbolic or strategic language-uses may be susceptible to complaints that the one is ineffective and the other too conducive to distrust, "legitimacy crises" *per se* attend the breakdown of the use of language for the purpose of establishing relationships based on shared understanding. It is this capacity of language that Habermas (1979: 65) refers to as "illocutionary force": "The illocutionary force of a speech act consists in its capacity to move a hearer to act under the premise that the engagement signalled by the speaker is seriously meant." A more acute version of the crisis occurs when hearers do not take seriously a speaker whom, they might agree, is speaking seriously.

Other writers (of whom Habermas is perhaps too critical at this point), would consider illocutionary force to mean something more than the capacity to be considered as speaking seriously; viz. the capacity to make the world *conform* to the spoken or written word (cf. Austin 1962). When a priest pronounces a couple married or a judge passes sentence, such a transformation occurs. In either sense of the phrase, however, it is my thesis that legitimacy crises are marked by the loss of illocutionary force: by widespread questions concerning whom to take seriously, by severe doubts that one's own speech will be taken seriously, and by confusion, above all, on the grounds by which anyone can speak — and be taken — seriously. The crisis is precisely one of "legitimacy" because of the uncertainty as to what rules or norms justify certain statements. What standards justify a speaker's claim to legitimate civil disobedience? What standards indeed justify an official claim that the only applicable standards derive from a narrow construction of the relevant law governing disturbances of the peace or the protection of property? In a legitimacy crisis, decisions on such matters can be actually handed down and even enforced, but in the absence of a mutually acceptable relationship and understanding. A slogan of the peace movement captured this possible loss of illocutionary force quite nicely: "Suppose they declare a war and no one comes?" In a severe legitimacy crisis, offical declarations become mere words. So also do prophetic statements that lack force until they are "justified" by obedience or future events.

In referring to Habermas here for a theoretical background to this study, I do not intend to take theoretical sides or to be drawn too deeply at this point into a discussion of theoretical questions. Having mentioned an area of disagreement about the meaning of illocutionary force, however, I wish to elaborate on one point concerning the efficacy of speech. It is a point fundamental to the analysis that follows. Of course, I regard speech as efficacious when it operates within institutional contexts, as when a judge pronounces or a doctor declares. Speech is also efficacious when it is inseparable from certain consequences, as when speech carries conviction, produces a change of heart, enlists loyalties, makes enemies, stimulates action, or transforms one's definition of one's situation. Perhaps Habermas has in mind a psychoanalytic model, in which speech is suggestive and authoritative without too explicit a dependence on a normative institutional context. Such speech is therefore capable of overcoming resistance without limiting the hearer's freedom and capable of establishing new and shared understandings on the basis of a relatively full disclosure of otherwise restricted information. Although I do not have in mind such an ideal-typical model, I will draw heavily on secondary analyses of language within the biblical tradition to suggest that the potential for a legitimacy crisis is rooted in two divergent rules for discourse carried in Western civilization from biblical and Hellenistic sources.

As Habermas and others have pointed out, most statements are not only "uttered" (and therefore have the capacity, under the right conditions, of evoking a response and establishing a relationship); they also mean something. That meaning may be more or less embedded in, or distinguishable from, the utterance. The meaning may also be more or less dependent on being uttered: no particular matter, since the fact remains that, in principle and under certain conditions, that meaning may be separated from the utterance itself and subjected to quite unintended forms of scrutiny, testing, cross-examination, and interpretation. Precisely such a process, I will point out, occurs in courtrooms. Under these conditions, it is the *non-operative* aspects of language that become particularly salient.

As utterances come to be separated from their meanings, their meanings become particularly vulnerable to the process of "secularization." The secular world is the world of meanings subject to change, of meanings that pass away or do not come true, of meanings that are subject in the end to death itself. The biblical tradition, however, recognizes the word of faith as that which produces faith, which inspires the commitment that it also demands, that separates individuals from their past and creates for them new situations even as it is heard and accepted. That word is "operative" and therefore comes true. In the process of secularization, however, such utterances lose their immediate connection with their meaning and are subject, as in the myth of the Garden of Eden, to reinterpretation. It is indeed the secular serpent who asks "Did God say . . .?" As meanings become separable from their utterance and can therefore be taken outside of the relationship in which they are spoken in order to be subject to reinterpretation, a secular "fall" begins: a fall into problems of justification and legitimacy. The process continues when words can be separated not only from meanings but also from an object to which they refer. Thus separated, the divine name no longer makes for a divine presence, and parables can be interpreted metaphorically, turned into allegories, or even reduced to a literal meaning. This separation, I suggest, is made *possible* by the separation of religious from other institutions, and it is *legitimized* by rules of discourse that derive from Hellenistic rather than biblical sources.

Western civilization carries both Hebrew and Greek rules for discourse, just as it carries biblical and Hellenistic notions about life, death, reality, nature, and history. Of course, the two sets of rules for discourse are not wholly opposite to each other, and within each there are important differences. But oversimplification is permissible here for the sake of making clear two ideal-typical rules for discourse: ideal-typical in the classic sociological sense of abstract descriptions of social life that always fail, more or less, to fit particular, concrete examples. Now, if Boman (1960: 56) is an adequate guide, it appears that the Greeks were more concerned with correct and incorrect speech, whereas we would expect to find a biblical distinction between speech that is effective or fails to come true. Greek culture thus distinguishes between truth and error in language, whereas Boman finds in the Old Testament a pervasive contrast between language that is effective and language that *lies* — not because it is in error — but because it comes to nothing in the end: "If the Israelites do not distinguish sharply between word and deed, they still know of very promising words which did not become deeds; the failure in such instances lies not in the fact that the man produced only words and no deeds, but in the fact that he brought forth a counterfeit word, an empty word, or a lying word which did not possess the inner strength and truth for accomplishment or accomplished something 'evil' " (ibid.: 65–6). It is very biblical to judge a fig tree by its fruit and not by scientific or aesthetic criteria. The question is not whether an utterance is supported by the data but whether it produces the data which it implies. An empty word is for the Hebrew what a false one is for the Greek (cf. ibid.: 66).

One set of rules calls for faith in the speaker, whereas the other calls for a fidelity between words and such other criteria as a text or signs in nature itself. Hellenistic rules for discourse therefore approve words which distinguish correctly between appearance and reality (Boman 1960: 56), whereas biblical

discourse approves words on the basis of whether they themselves determine, and not merely express or expose, the distinction between what is real and what deceives. For there
are indeed words that deceive precisely because they are not
in themselves deeds. Boman (1960: 66) thus approves Goethe's
notion that "in the beginning was the deed," precisely because
that initial deed was an utterance, an act of speech. To declare
war is to go to war. To pronounce a couple husband and wife
is indeed to marry them. To pronounce a person dead is to
cut all ties with the deceased. And, for some, to proclaim the
faith is to place those who hear in an ultimate situation, a
moment of final judgment, in which according to their
response their eternal fate is determined one way or another.

It could be misleading to characterize Hebraic discourse as
operative if our only examples were to derive from secular or
religious rituals. Of course, it is often in rituals, both secular
and religious, that such powerful and effective words were
spoken. But, of course, ritualistic discourse does not exhaust
the type of speech that follows the Hebraic model. Prophetic
discourse, whether or not it is ritualistic, follows the Hebraic
pattern, as contrasted with more metaphoric, allegorical, and
especially with literal modes of speech.

The Protestant, and originally biblical, use of language as a
vehicle by which individuals achieve serious communication
and understanding has been successfully institutionalized in a
number of secular contexts. These contexts, in turn, are
controlled by secular professions who value, as highly as the
church ever valued it, a language that enables individuals to
be taken seriously as credible, authoritative, and authentic
speakers. It is a language that is operative, in the sense that it
established the relationships that it requires for the sake of
genuine understanding. But in these contexts, religious language itself is deprived of authority and lacks its operative or
illocutionary force. Furthermore, the standards by which
individuals are credited with speaking authoritatively or
credibly reflect Hellenistic rather than biblical notions of
validity and reliability. Individual's meanings are therefore
assessed in the absence of a mutual relation between speakers

and hearers, and individuals are required to divest themselves of operative or forceful speech that might otherwise create a relationship which would sustain and reflect their personal meanings. Meanings, in being differentiated from relationships between speakers and hearers, are subject to clarification and reinterpretation that may result in contraction of the speaker's meanings far more often than their expansion. In these secular contexts, where meaning and validity are determined by institutional standards and procedures independently of personal relationships and of the speaker's particular motives or intentions, testimony to religious understandings and convictions is bracketed as personal in the sense of idiosyncratic, subjective, and unreliable. It is a process that Barfield has captured well in his analysis of the changing meaning of the word "subjective."

As the history of philosophy reflects the latest stage of this age-long process, so the semantic history of the words "subject" and "subjective" reflects the history of philosophy. Thus, for "subjective" we find in the *Oxford English Dictionary*, supported by quotations, the lexical meaning, in the seventeenth century: *pertaining to the essence or reality of a thing; real, essential.* A further lexical meaning, but dating back now only to the first half of the eighteenth century, is: *having its source in the mind.* By the second half of the same century we have: *pertaining or peculiar to an individual subject or his mental operations...personal, individual.*

So far, we have the connotation of reality plus a steadily increasing emphasis on the activity of the individual. It is reversed for the second half of the nineteenth century to go to the length of actually reversing the meaning in one respect, so that the adjective whose lexical meaning was *real, essential,* becomes an adjective whose lexical meaning is: *existing in the mind only, without anything real to correspond with it; illusory, fanciful.* (Barfield 1967: 114)

Conclusion

While exploring the unstable triangle relating religion to language and to reality in such secular contexts as the classroom and the court, we have found that the process of secularization leads to a simple paradox. On the one hand, by taking all formal trials with a nearly ultimate seriousness, as well as by institutionalizing stringent standards for credible and authoritative speech in the professions and requiring authenticity of persons over the course of a lifetime, the cultural theme of the trial casts what Geertz (1973: 120ff) might call a "derivative, lunar light" over the secular landscape of modern Western societies. On the other hand, however, the requirements for judicial testimony or for authoritative and credible speech in the professions are more or less free from the support and control of religious contexts. Language, in other words, is virtually on its own, although speech itself remains serious business whether or not it occurs within the context of a trial. What appears, then, to be a purely secular form of testing and verification in public affairs, in scientific inquiry, or in the trial itself owes its seriousness to the implicit seriousness attached to witnessing and testimony and, indeed, to all speaking as an activity of ultimate significance. But the sacred dimension is suppressed even when speech is taken seriously and surfaces in secular contexts only briefly when speaking is taken most seriously, for example, in times of trial or in trials themselves, where oaths of truthfulness are required before anyone is permitted to speak, to take office, or divine the future. Human speech, then, is "on its own," as it were, even when the sacred dimensions of serious speech are understood, implied, or even forgotten rather than uttered in oaths and formulae. The ultimate, religious sources of authority and credibility are therefore of uncertain relevance to most secular speaking: of questionable relevance even to speaking under oath on subjects that the court determines to be secular rather than "religious" in significance. The key terms here are "uncertain" and "questionable," because they denote the vagueness of the boundary between the sacred and the secular wherever testimony is given and especially where speaking is most serious, viz. in the formal context of a trial. Sociologically speaking, the secularization of the trial theme and of the judiciary itself may cause an anomic confusion of standards for taking speakers seriously.

Not all situations for speaking seriously are equally anomic. In the preceding discussion, I have compared liturgical contexts and religious prophecy with speaking in formal secular contexts such as the court and in more informal secular settings in the classroom and in everyday life. This comparison ranges along a dimension of contextual constraints on language: the more highly constrained contexts requiring strict observance to rules for speaking by incumbents of particular roles. In a liturgy, for instance, only a priest may consecrate bread and wine or absolve sins, just as in a court only a judge may pronounce sentence. In a liturgy, however, all responses are constrained in advance by a text and allocated to particular roles, whereas in a trial the rules for speaking are occasionally suspended and the text is created by the speakers in the form of briefs and a transcript. The comparison also ranges along another dimension, however, in which religious language is more or less separated from the give-and-take, the question-and-answer of ordinary language. Few sermons, for instance, are interrupted for dialogue and cross-examination of the speaker, and all sermons are examples of religious testimony. In courts, however, even testimony to religious convictions is subject to interruption and cross-examination, and that testimony is less direct than the homiletic; it merely represents the speaker's perception of his or her religious convictions at a given place and time. The two dimensions are depicted in table 3.1 with illustrative kinds of speaking in particular settings given for each of the entries of the table.

It is the anomic situation that has most attracted the attention of sociologists in the Durkheimian tradition, who have focussed on situations in which it is difficult to know how seriously to take politicians and professors, let alone priests and prophets. In a society in which religion no longer guarantees the relation of language to reality, social authority rests on such uncertain foundations as legal texts and, at times, tape recordings. Under anomic conditions credibility is equally as uncertain as authority, since words are often rendered inoperative by circumstances, and representations of reality are more like allegations than liturgical re-presentations. But

Table 3.1 Degree to which constraints on religious testimony
are institutionalized

Degree of separation from everyday life in the giving of religious testimony	*Highly formal*	*Forms open to occasional exception*	*Least formal*
Highly separate	1 Liturgical speech	2 Testimony in the courtroom	3 Testimony in the classroom
Highly integrated	4 Prophecy	5 Witnessing in face-to-face conversation	6 Ordinary conversation, "gossiping the Gospel"

from another sociological viewpoint, the separation of language from reality without the guarantees of religion leads to disenchantment and to alienation. A Weberian perspective would find that as the meaning of a speaker's testimony is separated from a relationship with the particular speaker, words themselves are emptied of the subjective emotions and personal commitments that make them capable of conveying a person's seriousness or inspiring serious commitments in others. It was Weber, after all, who argued that students should not seek in a professor's lectures any guides to personal commitment and ultimate meaning. Taken to an extreme, moreover, the process by which speakers' meanings are separated from any particular speaker is an alienating one. Just as a worker's product is taken from a craftsman and sold on the open market regardless of the consumer's awareness of the worker, so words become embodied in texts, like this one, that are sold on the market and create a value that is determined by the impersonal response of the consumer or reviewer. The speaker-writer no longer has the right to secure a response from the reader, nor can the reader demand to know how serious is the speaker. No wonder that authoritarian politicians claim that their words are guarantees of action and will issue in deeds, if only the electorate will lend their hands to the task. Secularization creates a hunger for words that require a relationship and issue in solid deeds, that a nation's and a people's trial may one day be over. It is in the absence of religious guarantees to secular speech, however, that the trial never ends.

Chapter 4

Eventful Speech, Prophecy, and Secularization

Secularization as the Loss of Eventful Speech

The secular world is, by one theological definition, the world in which "nothing is happening" of far-reaching and lasting significance. The religious world, however, is the world in which the Real is coming to pass; it is eventful. The distinction between the two worlds is not merely analytical or philosophical, but the result of an act of faith. Whether one is speaking of Christianity or Islam, religious views "correct and complete" what is missing in the matter-of-factness of everyday life and common sense (Geertz 1973: 94–5). In everyday life, words are not eventful, they are "mere words," whereas religious speech either makes things happen or fulfills them. Rosenstock-Huessy (1970: 120–1) captures the distinction this way:

When we chat about God and the world, our mind is on a vacation. And this chatter, gossip, talk, is the shell or the chaff of the real and full power of speech when things speak through us. It is a gross misunderstanding to judge speech by its play-variety, small talk. That is mere reflection on real speech. Through us, the world quite literally comes to know itself . . . The ubiquitous and omnipresent character of life on earth depends on man, since through his traditions, his story-telling, his observations, *the passing events in the remotest corner of the globe* are kept as an eternal present before all the generations and the nations of the earth. (emphasis added)

Serious or powerful speech, then, must capture the eventful aspects of human history and society so that what happens, say, in Vietnam or what once happened in Africa can be told in such a way as to define the situation of Americans in the present. But even the news lacks the truly eventful character of religious speech, since the religious proclamation itself defines the situation of an individual or group in society and history.

Words that are used to conceal, while appearing to communicate, heighten whatever latent distrust lies between friends or between governments and the public. Words that are abstract and lifeless liturgical or theological formulae tend to disenchant congregations and to lead the young and old in different ways to search for more expressive forms of religious belief and practice. Language itself becomes a "prison-house" which prevents the individual from fully encountering the reality of which language speaks. Language "does our thinking for us" and traps us in a prison of ready-made thoughts about men, women, children, God, and the world. Sorel is said to have uttered a fascist's oath on his death-bed, when he cried, "We have destroyed the validity of all words. Nothing remains but violence . . ." (Rosenstock-Huessy 1970: 163). For violence, after all, substitutes the language of hard deeds for the meaningless talk of bureaucrats and politicians. Where speech makes nothing happen, only deeds can talk. Without action, as Marx used to insist, words were mere abstractions that prevented individuals and entire classes from coming directly to grips with their actual situations.

Fascism, madness, apathy, meaninglessness, distrust of governments and of personal acquaintances, the abandonment of traditional religious forms, and the pursuit of new or bizarre religious experience: all these have been traced by various writers to a pathological state of language and speech. But cynicism about the actual conditions and powers of language in modern societies is, I would argue, a reflection of the utopian hopes that certain modern intellectuals entertain for language itself. Of course, language may indeed be the "primary institution" in all societies (Berger 1972: 72f). Language creates human communities, preserves memories, provides records, and so is the indispensable source of leverage

on the present and of hope for the future. It is utopian, however, to credit *language* with defining social purpose, preserving
social boundaries, linking individual personalities with social
institutions and with the ongoing identity and purposes of
the larger society, while still expressing what is unique to the
individual in symbols that are shared by an entire people. On
this view, language does what religion used to do. It enables
an individual to take on the thoughts and purposes of other
individuals: to stand in their place and at the same time to
transcend any single social location, so that in discourse a
transcendence is achieved which is more than the sum of the
meanings uttered by single individuals. Speech through discourse does indeed create a language that transcends, as
religion once transcended, the limits of a single speaker or of
a particular social context. But as religion has become more
private and increasingly subjective and esoteric, some intellectuals have turned to language as the very secret of how societies
form, endure, and regenerate themselves.

In addition to these critical or utopian views on language,
there is a third view which, for lack of a better word, I will
call the romantic. It is ably expressed by Rosenstock-Huessy
(1970: 162) in this passage that celebrates the role of language
in making experiences eventful and significant. "It is the
essence of language to be momentary, fluid, fleeting . . .
albeit a mathematical proposition, a law, or a book." Therefore any attempt to take language out of its immediate,
intimate context is responsible for the barren, abstract,
formulaic character of language. The romantic view insists
that any effort to speak so as to create a record, to be intelligible to those who are not present but who will hear at
another place and another time, vitiates language and prevents
the spoken word from being eventful. Only words that are
truly spoken in a given context can transcend that context.
Only words that are intended to fulfill the possibilities of the
here and the now can have lasting influences.

Each of these three viewpoints addresses the question of
what makes speech and language eventful. By eventful, of
course, I mean several things. Eventful language clearly makes

something happen. Once certain words are spoken, something is changed: a marriage is formed, a death sentence passed, a sinner forgiven, a friendship established. Eventful language is "full" of an event in the sense that the word, spoken or written, somehow captures and expresses the significance of what is happening and so fulfills the meaning of the occasion. A situation comes thus to be defined through speech either as hopeless or as the proverbially dark moment before the dawn. The sufferings of the working class come to be defined as a punishment for sin or as the inevitable effects of expropriation. When language ceases to make things happen or no longer significantly defines situations, language does indeed become verbiage: a barrier to authentic communication and to a realistic grasp of actual conditions.

This notion of eventful speech impinges on the traditional questions of Western theology. The possibility of eventful speech may belong to God alone; in which case human efforts to speak eventfully are a form of pride that will not enjoy much historical success. Otherwise, in ascribing to God the sole power to speak eventfully, humankind has alienated from itself the powers that belong to all humans and are capable of historical expression. I will not attempt to explore, let alone to resolve, the theological issues at this point. The theological reference here is important simply because it requires that we trace the potential for language to be "eventful" to a residue of primary religious speech. It is therefore not surprising to find references to eventful speaking couched in traditional religious metaphors, as when Rosenstock-Huessy says: "Only in rare moments do we use language for the purpose of recognizing each other in the spirit and in truth, and in unconditional surrender" (1970: 159). As one writer notes, true and effective speech can occur only under relatively ideal conditions of "truth, freedom, and justice" (Scott 1978: 9). Otherwise some speakers would reveal more of themselves than others; some would obey more than others; and the consensual base for arriving at a common and unconstrained definition of the situation would be flawed by partial and distorted communication. There is a wholeness to the human community implied in this ideal of "communicative competence" that suits a religious ideal to which few religious communities can realistically aspire. It is a vision of radical self-exposure and mutual reticence, safeguarded by shared understandings and by the equalitarian distribution of opportunities to give direction.

Religious Languages as "Eventful"

In an earlier chapter I took up the liturgical movement and liturgy itself in order to explore the distance separating ordinary, secular language from the eventful speech of religious ritual. In the next chapter I will suggest that ordinary talk is very "ordinary" in several ways. It separates the speaker from the speaker's own meaning, so that matters can be discussed more or less impersonally and outside of a given relationship, as in a seminar. "Seminar talk" uses words with some attention to what they mean and how they refer to specific events, objects, or even to other words; and it is literal-minded rather than metaphoric or prophetic in usage. Seminar talk is usually less intense, and the speaker seeks to be credible rather than authoritative: a far cry from the authoritative statements of command and prohibition, from the pronouncements of a beginning and an end to things in the liturgy. Speakers speak for only themselves in everyday life, however credible they appear or however authentic they may claim to be. But in the liturgy speakers speak from the authority of a tradition, of a myth or other theory and use signs that convey the corporate commitments of the religious community. Language in the liturgy is quasi-ideal and seems autonomous, even though it is segmented from everyday life and concentrated at specific times and places. But secular talk goes on and on and seems dependent on the interaction of speaker and hearer. In fact, ordinary discourse is caught up in the process of give and take, of negotiating praise and blame, following and leading: so much so that it is seldom able to achieve "symbolic closure" or the last word. Ordinary talk seldom gives one the sense that all has been said and done.

There are in seminar talk ways of ending without finishing, as the speaker calls for further research or continues to revise the record of what has already been said: but not so with liturgies.

In this chapter I will use the term "eventful" to point to the distance between seminar talk (as an example of ordinary discourse) and liturgical speech: the former being talk in which nothing happens, the latter being speech in which the sacred happens. The notion of an eventful language or of a language-event has a history that I cannot explore here without too long a digression, but I will refer briefly to one helpful discussion of the notion that will suggest its origin and development among literary critics and students of New Testament language. Here, in exploring the space between liturgical language and everyday speech, it is important not to exaggerate the distance while keeping it in mind that, as individuals abandon liturgical speech for ordinary and uneventful talk, they obey a different set of rules of discourse and so, in certain contexts, forfeit their claims to speaking with credibility, with authenticity, and especially with authority.

The space between liturgical and ordinary speech is partially filled by prophetic speech. Rather than refer back to the model sketched in the preceding chapter, I will adapt that model to illustrate the relationship of prophetic to liturgical, poetic, and ordinary speech here in figure 4.1. Whenever individuals testify to their religious convictions in secular contexts, they close the distance between liturgical and secular speech. The effect of breaking or suspending the rules of discourse in the courtroom, for instance, is often profound. In examining the responses of certain lawyers to the testimony of Joseph Quinlan concerning his religious faith (as we will do in chapter 7), it will become clear that a breakthrough of prophetic speech into a secular court has the effect of at least momentarily separating individuals from their roles: long enough for speakers to be identified with their speech, and for the speakers' meaning to be attached again to the act of speaking itself. To the participant, secular discourse in the classroom or in the court takes on the power of prophetic speech or the solemnity and force of ritual when the rules of secular discourse are broken. But the effect is disruptive, just as when an individual breaks into poetry during an otherwise ordinary conversation. It is at such times that the boundary between the secular and the sacred becomes obscure indeed.

FIGURE 4.1

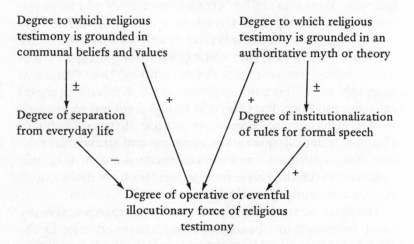

Degree to which religious testimony is grounded in communal beliefs and values

Degree to which religious testimony is grounded in an authoritative myth or theory

±

+

+

±

Degree of separation from everyday life

Degree of institutionalization of rules for formal speech

−

+

Degree of operative or eventful illocutionary force of religious testimony

In the life of churches, however, liturgies do not always and for all participants carry the force of ritual. The corporate beliefs and values that find expression in the life of a church or congregation may become too abstract for liturgical expression. Many Catholic churches, for instance, have relied heavily on ethnic or linguistic sources of common commitment, but as these communal sources disappear, become absorbed in large, urban contexts, or become forgotten with disuse, the liturgy itself becomes more of a text than a celebration. Similarly with the change or disappearance of the beliefs and values of the ecclesiastical tradition; any change in Catholic piety concerning the saints or in the Protestant faith concerning the Incarnation may erode the mythic base of liturgical expressions. As a liturgy becomes deprived of traditional or communal sources of authority and commitment, the liturgy itself may seem more like a text than a ritual. Under these conditions, movements for liturgical "renewal" are likely to develop, and indeed the Catholic and Anglican churches have institutionalized a number of changes in the text of their liturgies. But, as I attempted to argue in the second chapter, the boundary between the sacred and the secular, between God and Caesar, or between religious speech and secular language cannot adequately be defined by changes in a liturgical text, unless the changes express and support an ancient faith and corporate values. Otherwise, to participants in liturgies, a new text leads to renewed disappointment that one can say all the proper words with nothing "happening."

Liturgies share with parables and prophetic speech generally the operative dimension of language: of speech that changes the situation of the speaker and hearer. I will avoid the use of the term "operative" here and substitute the word "eventful." The latter term enables us to draw directly on the discussions of "language-events" in the hermeneutical study of the New Testament, at the same time as we tap more commonplace understandings of the notion of an "event." The point here is that under certain conditions, as when the rules of discourse are suspended or broken, secular languages can become eventful, just as under other conditions even liturgies can become the uneventful recitation of sacred texts. Here our attempt is to focus on how prophetic speech closes the distance between ritual and courtroom, between liturgical speech and ordinary discourse, and between proclamation and seminar talk.

Literary critics engaged in the hermeneutical study of the New Testament sometimes argue that the parables, for instance, gain their eventful ("operative") force because they are metaphoric. But we must ask why the thesis of "the parable as metaphor" obscures the distinction between ordinary discourse and the operative or eventful aspects of religious language. The key is in the unique relation of the speaker to the words themselves.

Perrin's (1976) recent summary enables us to treat the argument rather briefly. The parables gain their effectiveness through metaphor, he writes, because of certain linguistic characteristics peculiar to metaphors. Perrin argues that metaphor has the power "to produce an impact on the imagination, to be the bearer of reality, to induce vision" (1976: 135). It gains that power through its realism, through the strained interaction of related meanings joined by the verb ". . . is," and through its lack of symbolic closure, or, as Perrin puts it, its "open-endedness." As a result, metaphoric language involves the hearer in making judgments, in applying the metaphor (in a parable or other saying) to new contexts, and thus in extending and elaborating the meaning suggested by the original metaphor. So far so good: the analysis places metaphor somewhere between literal truths, where meaning and language are separable from one another, and myths embodied in rituals, where meanings are continually elaborated within the contexts established by the ritual itself. Metaphor is an appropriate vehicle for language that upsets conventional speech and understandings while stimulating the hearer to elaborate and apply its meaning in new contexts. Why, then, does this emphasis on the metaphoric properties of language fail to account for the eventfulness of *prophetic* speech?

The answer lies in the importance of the speaker's own commitments. According to Perrin (1976: 131), certain New Testament interpreters insist that the power of Jesus's metaphors lies in Jesus's own orientation, intensity, and faith. Jesus, on this view, makes good use of metaphor, but the metaphor derives its transforming power from the speaker's (Jesus's) own commitments to a people and to a myth of the Kingdom of God, without which the metaphor may be suggestive or interesting but hardly transforming in its potential effect on those who indeed have ears to hear. Taken out of the context of Jesus's preaching, the sayings and parables become interesting exemplary stories or extended metaphors rather than prophetic and liberating speech. On this view, furthermore, the parables can thus only be heard and understood in a modern context through the church's own preaching. The alternative view in New Testament hermeneutics rests on a new appreciation of metaphor itself and argues that prophecy does not therefore depend on a peculiar and dynamic relation between a speaker's *act* of speech (e.g. the "I say unto you . . .") and that speaker's meaning ("The Kingdom of God is like . . .").

Occasionally speakers break the rules of courtroom testimony. Some of these rules insist on attributing and restricting the force of a speaker's utterance only to the credibility or meaning of a speaker's statement: *not* to the force of the utterance itself as a command or proclamation. In making this separation, the secular rules of judicial discourse are very much akin to the secular rules of literary criticism that, as I have noted, attribute the power of certain sayings to their (metaphoric) meaning apart from the process of preaching or prophetic utterance. On the view of the new hermeneutic, the boundaries between the sacred and the secular are eroded successfully through the "power of metaphor." On the view I have adopted here, metaphor is not of itself sufficient to make speech eventful, and although notably employed by Daniel Berrigan, it may not be essential to prophecy. Instead, it is the dynamic interaction between a speaker's utterance and a speaker's meaning that allows the sacred to break open the secular rules of discourse and to raise questions about the boundary between the sacred and the secular.

Generalizations about the "power of metaphor" are thus misleading if they place in the background the force of prophetic utterance that arises from the particular commitments of the prophet. I would argue that judges do not demand restrictions on the poetic language of all witnesses: only of those witnesses who claim to speak with the combined authority of a sacred tradition and of a religious community, and especially of those who have taken liberties with ritual by enacting it outside of religious contexts. Under these conditions, precedents for which are relatively easy to find in New Testament accounts of Jesus's preaching, metaphor indeed is powerful, but its power also depends on the forceful utterance of a speaker and on that speaker's unique commitments. I will illustrate these points in our final discussion of the trial of the Catonsville Nine. Here my point is simply

that it is not disembodied metaphor that obscures the boundaries between the sacred and the secular, but speakers who
take liberties with the rules of discourse in particular contexts
by insisting that they themselves be taken as seriously as their
words. Under these conditions speech is again eventful: things
"begin to happen."

The eventfulness of the early Christian preaching, I suggest,
is partly the result of that preaching's synthesis of several
speech-acts in a single announcement: Jesus is Lord. For
instance, it is not merely the *telling* of the Christian story
that enables Jews and Christians to redefine their situation
in relationship to each other. It is the *announcement* or
declaration itself that redefines the situation of ancient
hostility as one of reconciliation and harmony. Indeed telling
is announcing: that is why preaching changes the situation
even while the proclamation itself is being made. The evangelical imperative is thus central to the New Testament; to
obey is to preach, since preaching carries out and carries
forward the central event of the new age. The distinction
between the words and the works of faith is, as Luther later
pointed out in an attack on the Epistle of James, eccentric
to the Gospel. The Gospel is the evangelical pronouncement,
and the pronouncement is part and parcel of the event. In
this way the declaration that "Jesus is Lord" claims to transform the world.

The speech-act of declaration and announcement, however,
is synthesized in the Christian preaching with four other acts
of speech. To say that "Jesus is Lord" is also to utter a direction to the hearer to believe the proclamation. Otherwise one
has not truly "heard" what has been proclaimed. Just as true
preaching creates faith, true hearing believes the proclamation.
In addition to declaration and the command to believe, moreover, are other speech-acts that are equally implicit in the
message. The speaker, in proclaiming that "Jesus is Lord," is
stating what the speaker believes to be a true "representation"
of the world as it is. According to the preaching, Jesus is, in
fact, Lord. But those who ignore this announcement do so at
their own peril; hence the speech-act of representation con-

tains an implicit direction: a final warning. In addition to this
(less forceful) act of representation in the preaching is an
additional speech-act of expression, since the proclamation
claims authenticity as an expression of the speaker's own
beliefs. It is the one statement that cannot be made insincerely
except at the speaker's own peril. Finally, the preaching contains the act of communicating the speaker's intention to act
according to the proclamation, even if the speaker's own death
should ensue. When the acts of intention, representation, and
expression are fully joined, preaching gains authenticity and
credibility. When such speaking claims also to transform the
world, through declaration, warning, and command, we have
before us a model of religious language as event-ful.

There are innumerable biblical references to this distinguishing characteristic of religious language. The Old Testament
attributes to God the capacity to speak eventfully: light being
brought out of darkness as God speaks; people being brought
together out of assorted tribes by standing under the Mosaic
word. On occasions certain individuals are endowed with the
capacity to approximate or to report this powerful speech,
but the approximations are just that; mere proximity rather
than divine utterance itself. The prophets report what God
has said or predict what God will say. Their words, however,
are not fulfilled in the utterance itself but only in the people's
own faith and obedience. The relationship between prophetic
word and event is intended to be intimate rather than identical.
Words bring about a response which completes the act of
speaking. Only when the word is heard and believed is it truly
spoken. When God speaks, the Word itself is inseparable from
being and event. When man speaks, however, the utterance is
complete only when the relationship to being or event is
made apparent. Prophecy waits for faith and obedience,
because the prophetic word calls out the appropriate response.
Even in the context of the liturgy, the consecration of
certain elements is not complete until the priest repeats
certain words of institution, speaks for the assembled community, and hears that community add its own words of
assent and commitment. The relationship of word to event,

integral in divine speech, is attenuated, although still intimate, in the speech of the prophet and in the speech-acts of the liturgy performed by the priest.

In secular speech the relation of word to event is still further attenuated. In pronouncing an individual dead, a secular physician announces an event which has occurred, but the pronouncement does not constitute the death quite so intimately as the priest's pronouncement constitutes the marriage-event. Still further along a spectrum of continuity between word and event lies the authorship of games. In writing the rules of a game, some have argued, the game itself is constituted, regardless of whether or not anyone plays the game. But here we are on ambiguous linguistic ground, since the authorship of the rules of a game does not itself either announce that a game has been played or itself constitute the playing of a game. The framework merely has been established whereby certain events will be interpreted as events within a game if players assemble and consent to following the rules. The words of the rules are a necessary but not sufficient condition for the game to be played. Scientific prediction is still further removed along the continuum, since the speech of the scientist is considered true speech if and only if the event described or predicted is subsequently observed under the specified conditions. And, at a still farther point along the continuum are words for which there are not events either before, during, or after their utterance. These are autistic utterances which do not require to be heard or read to be completed or valid. Nothing happens when they are spoken because nothing is intended to happen. The secular world, from this perspective, is the autistic result of mankind speaking only to and for itself.

The Irreconcilable Conflict between Religious and Secular Discourse

Throughout these pages we will be considering the dilemmas faced by those engaged in prophetic religious utterance within secular contexts. The dilemmas are caused by inconsistencies, even by conflicts, between the rules for secular and for religious discourse. Conflicts arise because the rules for secular discourse set stringent limitations on prophetic utterances. This effect is nowhere more visible than in the impact of literal usage on prophetic speech.

A few examples may help to demonstrate the conflict between literal and prophetic rules for discourse. The particular rules at stake govern the speech-act of referring, or making reference, by means of some words either to objects or to other words. Now, as Searle reminds us quite succinctly, ". . . we have the institution of proper names to talk in words about things which are not themselves words and which need not be present when they are being talked about" (1969: 75). The proper name of a tree or a dog, for instance, enables one to refer to an elm or a collie without pointing to a visible object: simple enough. Literal usage thus makes sense under these conditions, and there is little danger that a name will be misconstrued for the thing itself. Thus naming leads to a sort of nominalism, in which words are quite distant from either their meaning or the object to which they refer.

As the Old Testament is likely to suggest, however, religious names obey different rules for discourse. First, it is clear that God is not a thing; and it is possible that God is word rather than flesh. There is also a possibility that God needs to be present when talked about; otherwise he becomes objectified rather than worshipped: an idolatrous consequence that the Old Testament is at some pains to avoid. Thus religious language at the outset clearly follows rules for discourse in which the distinction between words and objects, or between the presence and absence of what is referred to in words is a moot one. Circumlocutions are necessary, and one must substitute for the proper name of God a word that means the Name itself. Otherwise, with improper reference in secular or even in sacred contexts, the presence of that ultimate word may be invoked, with consequences that no creature can withstand. Thus, when Jesus invoked the symbol of the Kingdom of God, the words themselves introduced the kingdom that prophets had for ages waited to see. By exploiting the powers of prophetic utterances, the prophet from Nazareth disrupted secular rules for discourse and the relationships that those rules helped to express and to maintain in everyday life. Neither the local priests nor the secular governors approved the change in the rules for discourse, and it is not accidental that in the secular trial of Jesus the phrase "King of the Jews" was clearly reduced at first to metaphor and finally to a mocking literal usage in the form of a sign placed, according to the Passion narratives, above Jesus's head on the cross, where it referred quite simply and ironically to the dying body below.

Secular rules for discourse provide powerful strategies therefore for keeping certain words, phrases, or statements from enjoying their liturgical force. Searle gives an example of one such strategy: a rendition by an ornithologist of the sound made by a particular bird. To the speaker and hearer, it is clear enough the ornithologist's rendition is just that: a rendition rather than the real thing, just as a performance of a particular symphony is a rendition of the "original" as first composed and performed in a far distant context. But on the face of it: ". . . an ornithologist might say, 'The sound made by the California Jay is . . .' And what completes the sentence is a sound, *not a proper name of a sound*" (1969: 76) (emphasis added). Secular rules for discourse make it clear that one is not really hearing the jay's own sound when the ornithologist performs, just as Searle expects his reader to understand, through the use of quotation marks, that one is not really hearing the words of the ornithologist saying "The sound made by the California Jay is . . ." But to a "primitive" mind, the distinction between the original and the performance is not so clear. To the primitive, both the jay and the ornithologist are as present in these later renditions as they were when they themselves first spoke, so long as the renditions are faithful. Only to a modern speaker, who is fascinated by a religious world-view that disregards secular distinctions, is the separation of the word from the original utterance also not entirely clear.

Let me add a word on this latter point. Owen Barfield,

for instance, finds it difficult to distinguish an expression (it does not matter for a moment whether it is a name or description) from the thing itself. In a careful discussion of scientific theory, Barfield (1977: 130ff) argues that it is difficult, indeed impossible, to separate a description of say, quantum theory from the theory itself. Suppose, for instance, that I were to take a digression here in order to lay out the essentials of quantum theory: a task I am neither competent nor intending to undertake. Would you, then, not have before you the theory itself in outline, if not in all of its particulars? Does one require the original text to encounter the theory, or will another rendition do? It is the same problem as the distinction between the ornithologist's rendition of a bird's sound and the sound of the jay itself. A primitive, or one devoted to a metaphysics that confounds Western distinctions between subject and object or between symbol and thing symbolized, would answer in a way that calls for an understanding of religious language as event-ful.

When in religious discourse certain words are repeated, they have their original force. The giving of the Mosaic commandments is as forceful centuries later as when first uttered: no less immediate, no less binding, no less disruptive of other transactions than the original Sinai proclamation. In certain religious communities to repeat the words of Jesus at a certain supper is also to evoke the same consequences: bread becoming the vehicle for his identity, blood the tenor of his life (to use a metaphor Barfield finds suitable to this argument; cf. Barfield 1977: 33ff). The rules for secular discourse are therefore contrived to keep these powerful events from reoccurring, whereas religious discourse insists that quotation marks are no barrier against the original force of divine utterances, even when the context shifts from Sinai or Jerusalem to Chicago and New York.

Summary

As a paradigm of religious speech I have been discussing a particular "speech event," the early Christian kerygma or announcement that "Jesus is Lord." A kerygmatic speech event is one in which the widest possible range of "speech-acts" is present in a *single* utterance, for example, expression, representation, intention, direction, and declaration. It is also impossible in kerygmatic speech to distinguish the meaning of what is said from the act of utterance itself. Speaker and meaning are inextricably related to one another, just as the types of speech-act are undifferentiated. That is why I have chosen kerygma as the "paradigmatic" case of religious speech.

Secular speech, on the other hand, uses utterances which do not cover the complete range of speech-acts. In fact, most secular utterances are limited to one or two speech-acts at a time. Although the paradigm of secular speech is more diffi-cult to locate, I will use for illustration in the next chapter a few excerpts of seminar talk among academics and researchers concerned with language. In the course of speaking in such a seminar, some participants engaged in several speech-acts, but they occurred *sequentially.* The longest and most authoritative utterance covered a larger portion of the range from expression to declaration, although no *single* utterance incorporated all possible speech-acts at one and the same time. Furthermore, the participants rigorously called attention to the meaning of what they were saying, as distinguished from a statement about their own utterance, for example, as to whether they themselves were "suggesting" (or engaging in a more forceful act of speech). Finally, some speakers engaged in speech-acts of relatively little force, such as "suggesting," whereas a few were more insistent, and only two engaged in commands or prohibitions. This continuum appears along the horizontal rows in table 4.1.

As we have noted in connection with the act of naming, religious language assumes an intimate relationship between word and event. Of course, the most formalized language assimilates all discrete events to linguistic symbols in such a way as to make ambiguous the specific, historical and unrepeatable character of each event (Bloch 1975: 15). But while some religious language is conducive to this ambiguity, other kinds of religious speech-acts, such as prophecy, naming, pronounce-

Table 4.1 Differentiation of types of speech-act from each other

Religious utterances	Kerygmatic proclamations	Prophecy	Liturgical formulae	Testimony in court or classroom
Secular utterances	Ideological, condensed statements, e.g., in manifestations	Poetry	Formulaic pronouncements, petitions, representations, etc.	"Seminar talk"

ments, and oaths, achieve a forceful and immediate relationship with specific times and places. The event is the spoken word, and vice versa. The formalized varieties of religious speech-acts, which resemble the priestly and the liturgical, are most eventful if they occur in the context of a particular speech-community. (By speech-community I mean a social unit which is attuned to hear the meaning of speech-acts and to respond appropriately.) A sacrament, for instance, is the result of an event that occurs when the proper words are spoken appropriately within a speech-community that hears, believes, discerns, and responds with the appropriate verbal and non-verbal actions. When a priest states, "I pronounce you husband and wife," an event is occurring, even as the words are uttered, which indeed constitutes the couple in question as "married." Here there is no doubt about the cause-and-effect relationship between the word and the event: the two being the verbal and non-verbal aspects of the same event.

The prophetic, as opposed to the priestly, type of speech-act, of course, may disrupt one speech-community while calling for the formation of another. When Jesus read the celebrated passage from Isaiah which announced and defined his own ministry as one of liberating the captives and healing the blind, he closed the reading with this statement: "Today these words are accomplished in your hearing." Prophetic religious language creates, in the act of speaking, a community of those who hear, understand, and believe. The impact *may* be revolutionary, if it is not concentrated entirely in the segmented liturgical contexts in which it is most often repeated and most fully elaborated. Prophetic language that occurs within the context of a *secular* ritual may be the single most disruptive type of speech-act, although its eventfulness depends on circumstances beyond the prophet's control.

Of course, the distinction between religious and secular rituals is not entirely clear even in the absence of disturbing prophetic utterances. Some sociologists emphasize the religious nature of secular rituals, since the latter also impose a world-view and foster a sense of justice being done, claim authority, and are concentrated at special times or places and segmented apart from everyday life (cf. Lukes 1977). Secular rituals, whether they are judicial, scientific, or political, resemble religious rituals in that they "foreclose debate on all manner of questions which, given an alternative construction, might well be live political questions" (Goodin 1978: 287). It is their "symbolic closure" as I will call it, that partially accounts for the resemblance between secular and religious rituals. But despite this resemblance, some writers are concerned to separate the secular rituals of the sports arena, the scientific community, or of the state from those religious rituals that appeal to magical interests and evoke the aid of the supernatural (ibid.: 281–2). The separation is especially important if one is concerned to gauge the extent of secularization. Without a clear distinction between religious and other rituals, social life takes on a quasi-sacred character as pervasive as ritual itself.

In fact, it is exceedingly difficult to separate religious from secular rituals on such formal occasions as a Coronation or an Inaugural Ceremony, in which traditional liturgies or prayers are intertwined with clearly political acts and intentions. Although I will treat the burning of draft files outside a local Selective Service Board in Maryland as a secular ritual, it was performed with religious intent under the auspices of two priests of the Catholic Church. Even within the context of the court, many of whose activities are both secular and ritualistic, testimony to religious convictions by devout and committed believers may break the rules of discourse and transform the setting into one more clearly religious and even prophetic. Under these conditions it will make more sense to distinguish between the religious and secular aspects of the judicial ritual.

The same distinction is applicable even to the sacred liturgies of established churches. On the solemn occasions of liturgical celebration, the liturgy may seem uneventful and casual not only to observers but even to participants in the order of worship. When, for instance, the liturgy depends on a text that no longer unites individual believers in a community of shared values and commitments, the action of the liturgy loses its corporate character. When, furthermore, the text codifies a myth or belief-system that is traditional but no longer believed in by most worshippers, the language of the liturgy may also become inoperative or uneventful. It is not unusual to pronounce a couple married "In the name of the Father, the Son, and the Holy Ghost" when neither party takes seriously the doctrine of the Trinity; thus the authority and eventfulness of the pronouncement is undermined. To be authoritative, liturgical actions need the support of binding commitments both to a community and to a creed. Otherwise the liturgy is "mere words," however reminiscent of a people's past or of a church's ancient faith. Under these conditions, however, liturgical texts are not only ripe for revision. Their ceremonies seem contrived because they do not mark out enduring relationships of authority and loyalty. Their words do not transform hearts, minds, or relationships because the words no longer represent and make active again an authoritative belief-system. Liturgies thus are experienced as being uneventful and private, although they are intended to be eventful and to disclose what is truly public about each devout participant. One might be tempted to say that liturgies become "secularized" if it were not for the ordinary-language distinction that preserves the identity of certain rituals as "religious" even when they lack authority and make nothing happen.

In this chapter I have argued that "prophetic" religious language is eventful, by which I mean to say that it brings about, re-creates, as well as expresses the reality that it refers to. Jesus's parables about the Kingdom of God initiate that divine activity, prepare hearers to recognize and respond to divine activity, and are misunderstood if they appear simply to refer to and describe divine activity in the secular world of everyday life. The secular world is the focus and context of these parables, but in speaking these parables Jesus disrupts the ordinary course of everyday events in that secular context.

To take the preaching or parables in context, then, means not only to understand what rules of discourse cover their original utterance by Jesus, but to allow them to disrupt the secular contexts of the modern world. Otherwise the parables are reduced to descriptions, similes, metaphors, allegories, or morality-narratives. That process of removing them from their secular context begins even in the New Testament, as the parables are uttered no longer in the Palestinian streets but in religious groups gathered under the church's new principles of organization to instruct disciples. The first fate of the eventful character of religious language, then, is that it loses its secular context and focus while being encapsulated within the terms of religious discourse, as those terms are understood, say, within the church. We will return to this aspect of secularization in chapter 8.

The ritual context allows a residue of eventfulness to remain in religious discourse, but only within the limited context of the church, at stated times, in certain places, and on certain occasions. Liturgy establishes the word of religious discourse in such a way that it holds only an *indirect* but not unimportant potential for disrupting everyday life. The encapsulation of religious discourse preserves the symbolic demonstration of what eventful or prophetic public action means, and so the liturgy embodies the possibility of a public realm that is not coterminous with any secular political system.

Liturgy does not itself disrupt the secular polity, but exists as a setting within which the possibility of that disruption can be remembered and hoped for once again.

Quite paradoxically, the process of reducing — secularizing — religious language occurs at the outset by efforts to "establish" the word: by making its meaning and interpretation perfect and inviolable. Religious discourse, in its original secular context, is never beyond doubt. That is why liturgies separate those who respond from those who do not. Liturgies allow only those to participate who will respond appropriately without carping at the Word of God. No serpents are allowed in the liturgical garden. The price of establishing this word, of course, is to make it less eventful in everyday life. That is why prophetic religious speech seeks to break out of the liturgical context: to be less concentrated and segmented. On the other hand, the price of this liberation is the loss of certain immunities against misinterpretation. The liturgy, however, gains authority at the price of being fixed in a text and encapsulated in special contexts: a price too high for prophecy. In seminar talk, there are no immunities against misinterpretation as participants scramble to create a record or text that embodies not only their convictions but their doubts. No wonder such talk is experienced as interesting but uneventful. Each individual speaks as though on trial and gives testimony subject to cross-examination and revision. Unlike a trial, however, there is no final adjudication, no resolution of discrepancies, and no last word. In ordinary secular discourse, as in seminar talk, the "trial" never ends.

Chapter 5

Seminar Talk: Uneventful Speech

Secularization clearly affects the relationship between religion and language. On the one hand, language has been the primary medium for religion in most societies, primitive and modern. From symbolic acts and gestures, from sacred words that create worlds and whole communities, to the most elaborated and edited religious messages, language has been the primary vehicle of religious influence and control. When institutions like the court or the university therefore develop their own rules of discourse, for asking questions and giving answers, for stating the facts and drawing conclusions, those separate rules are likely to make religious language seem inappropriate, irrelevant, or disruptive. A defendant who gives prophetic commands to the legal professional within the courtroom has clearly violated the court's rules of discourse. On the other hand, the development of what I have called "non-operative" and "non-liturgical" rules of discourse in secular contexts creates a hunger for speech that has effects and can justify in turn the one who speaks. Empty words that carry no authority and come to nothing only undermine the authority of politicians and professors. No doubt that the secularization of speech stimulated and shaped the liturgical movement, the revival of biblical literalism, and even the widespread phenomenon of glossolalia or "speaking in tongues."

Here I will try to make clear what I mean by secularized language and to draw illustrations from transcripts of a sample of what I will call "seminar talk": a type of discourse often found in (but by no means restricted to) the conversation of academics. It is ordinary talk: as non-liturgical a type of speech as one is likely to find in everyday life. In it the individual speaks with very little authority, personal tones are muted, editing and elaboration leave little to the imagination, and no lasting effects flow immediately from the speech itself.

Changes in language and in the rules for discourse are likely to affect the ways in which individuals try to justify them-selves: to claim credibility, to speak with authority, or to present themselves as authentic and therefore as trustworthy spokesmen whose words are wholly consistent with their deeds. In the course of secularization, the use of religious language for these purposes becomes problematical as individ-uals testify to their convictions in such secular contexts as the classroom and the court. It matters, of course, whether these convictions are stated with the authority of a corporate body and of a tradition, or whether they are (merely) the personal convictions of a believer. Indeed to establish and apply this distinction is one of the primary tasks of legal defense and prosecution. In the case of Karen Ann Quinlan, for instance, her parents claimed that their convictions were authorized by the church, whereas the prosecution argued that their convictions were personal and idiosyncratic, how-ever harmonious they might be with the teachings of the Catholic Church. When individuals seek to gain credit in one context, like the court, for authority that is borrowed from another context, like the church, their testimony is likely to suffer from translation. Prophetic speech loses its force when it follows secular rules of discourse for asking questions, reaching conclusions, and for negotiating degrees of freedom and authority.

Individuals are most likely to fare well in court, I would argue, who base their testimony on an authoritative text or tradition; hence the importance of liturgies and of liturgical change. Individuals speak with less authority who defend the quasi-sacred commitments and obligations of the family or of other intimate relationships. Individuals are least likely, I will argue, to fare well who base their authority in the bureaucratic organization of the church rather than on more intimate or traditional religious associations. But these are speculative propositions that will guide our discussion of particular legal cases in later chapters.

It is not necessary here to exaggerate the differences between liturgy and seminar talk. In fact, the distinctions are relatively small compared to the total range of language that could separate "ordinary" from special or specialized ways of speaking. The term "ordinary" is placed in quotation marks here simply to indicate that it requires explanation. Some writers are convinced that ordinary language exists as a way of asking questions and getting answers, as a way of negotiating roles so that some individuals have more or less influence and responsibility than others, or simply as a way of arriving at mutual understanding (cf. Ward 1979; Habermas 1979). Other writers are not at all sure that ordinary language exists (cf. Wootton 1975: 27). In any event, ordinary language has its own mysteries, since to speak it and to be understood require the use of understandings that are often implicit, vague, and occasionally erroneous (Wootton 1975).

Many of the skills and understandings that are used implicitly in "ordinary" conversation are made explicit and are dramatized in ritual, since ritual itself serves to mark out the roles and rules for discourse that undergird social life and conversation. Liturgy, like ordinary language, also asks questions and gets answers: Q. "Who made you?" A. "God . . ." The people respond to the priest's intonations and exhortations in poetic rhythms that mark and renew an existing social order. In the prosaic discourse that I call "seminar talk," however, speakers ask questions and are only sometimes answered. They make plans and reach decisions that create, at best, only a temporary ordering of who does what to whom in roles. Seminar talk helps to construct a visible but negotiable and temporary social order among more or less equal speakers. The degree of equality among speakers is problematical, and the understandings reached may therefore be flawed and lacking in authority. The last word is seldom spoken in seminar talk, which is characterized by what I will call low levels of "symbolic" closure and by personal or idiosyncratic statements of opinion and conviction.

The degree of literalism and metaphor varies among speakers who self-consciously work at freeing language in general, and particularly their own speech, from contextual or personal constraints.

Poetry lies somewhere between liturgy and ordinary speech. As with the liturgy, poetry is read only at certain times and on special occasions. People who quote the liturgy or poetry to strangers on the street or while paying bills and making appointments are likely to be ignored, kept at a distance, or occasionally held for examination. For a distinction between poetry and ordinary discourse I will quote Ward here, who says it very well.

Any imaginative figures, assonances, or formally exact linguistic frameworks such as couplets or pentameters cannot be allowed to overwhelm the trend of discourse itself, whose business is always to get or to be an answer; to negotiate a social, economic or other relationship through interaction. Consequently the economy and intensity characteristic of poetry must always be diluted, in discourse, by the need to adapt language to interactive ends; to put in the extra words that justify the discursively less expected material. In practice, parties to discourse will, implicitly at least, apologize for any poetic modulations or effects, keep them insulated from each other to avoid an intensity that would be intolerable, or maintain a detached and throw-away tone in them and switch off quickly. (Ward 1979: 92)

But liturgy is still farther from ordinary discourse than poetry. Although liturgy makes poetry serve what Ward calls "interactive ends," it makes poetry become the discourse of social life without losing too much of its poetic intensity and rhythm. Daniel Berrigan demonstrated that usage in court when he read a poem to express in condensed fashion the meaning of his actions outside the draft board, in which he and others offered official files as a burnt sacrifice. Both poetry and religious language are eventful in the sense that they claim to unite the hearer to the speaker, to place a new interpretation on familiar events, but liturgies have the power to create the response that they require, where poetry cannot construct its own order for interaction. Poetry therefore stands somewhere *between* liturgy and seminar talk. It is its proximity to ordinary language that gives prophecy its capacity to disrupt everyday life, but the same proximity makes it vulnerable to ordinary give-and-take, especially when it is dispersed rather than concentrated and segmented in special readings. There is no mistaking the intensity and disruptive potential of Daniel Berrigan's poetry in the context of the court. The fact that it was given a hearing in that secular milieu indicates that the poet, for the moment at least, broke the rules of secular discourse. The judge therefore reinforced the court's rules in his charge to the jury, very much as an academic would remind a seminar that papers will be evaluated on their ability to ask and to answer the proper questions rather than for their dramatic potential.

In the next section of this chapter I will apply these rather general remarks to a transcript of seminar talk taken from a volume reporting on the papers and discussion of participants in a seminar on language, learning, and transmission (Davies 1975). The seminar considered in particular the problems of teachers who are charged with helping the young to write. Despite its "applied" focus, the seminar generated a range of comment on language and is of general socio-linguistic interest. My purpose here, however, is to listen to how these participants talk rather than to attend to what they say about language, and I am particularly interested in illustrating uneventful language. Although it may seem unfair to single out seminar talk among socio-linguists for examples of uneventful speech, the transcript which we will explore here is particularly useful for this purpose since the academics and researchers are notably articulate about the types of speech-acts in which they are engaging and their reasons for doing so. We can take them at their word without imposing another, somewhat artificial, scheme on their own accounts.

The purpose of this excursion into the transcript of a seminar is not to caricature seminar talk as uneventful but to establish the basis for a comparison with religious speech as the paradigm of eventful communication. In the previous chapter I agrued that the earliest Christian preaching is an example of eventful religious speech. In that preaching it is virtually impossible to separate the meaning of the speaker from the act of speaking itself. The two are intertwined in the logic of the message and in the experience of the hearer. In this way the preaching creates the shared understandings that it actually requires to be effective. That is the claim, at least, of the early ecclesiastical records of the preaching events. Seminar talk, however, makes no such assumptions about the connection between speaking and being understood.

The comparison of seminar talk with religious preaching would be biased if I were to argue that all religious speech is by definition eventful, whereas also by definition all secular speech is as uneventful as seminar talk. On the contrary, in the process of secularization religious speech loses much of its eventfulness and secular speech becomes relatively more eventful. To some extent the process of secularization begins within the churches, as liturgical words become less expressive or representative of individual speakers' real wishes and ideas, as the clergy monopolize opportunities for speaking with authority, and as shared understandings yield to private or idiosyncratic opinions. The process continues, however, in settings such as the courts, in which the many speech-acts that are fused into the event of preaching are separated from one another. There individuals are permitted to utter only the less authoritative speech-acts, to the limited extent that these acts of speech are considered relevant or reliable within the judicial framework. Finally, as I will argue in connection with liturgical change, the secularization of language "feeds back" into the churches' own language to reduce the eventfulness of the liturgy itself and to separate utterances from their actual meaning.

In the first set of excerpts from the transcript of the final session of the seminar, I have selected the statements of several speakers who illustrate the secular code of academic talk. It is always somewhat speculative, of course, to infer the existence of such a code for speaking from any transcript. But such codes exist in the mind of the observer, whether or not they exist also in the minds of those actually engaged in speaking to one another.

From my somewhat distant vantage point, I observe a code that requires speakers to display considerable mastery over the act of speaking. That mastery is displayed in part by the speaker's ability to identify the act of speech in which he or she is engaging: whether it is a suggestion, a representation of an idea, or merely the expression of a state of mind. The code requires relatively high levels of verbal planning, and indeed few speakers appear to be fumbling in these passages for words. Mild emotions may be expressed in the form of an indirect report that the speaker entertains a preference ("I like 'exploration' "). And speakers who might otherwise be heard as directing the group reduce directives either to statements of intention ("I should like to suggest") or to representations of fact ("I *feel* that *we need to widen* . . ."). Intentions or ideas are stated in ways that leave little to the imagination and indicate relatively full disclosure on the part of the speaker. There is no mystery here, just as there is little to suggest either a will to dominate or the presence of feelings and commitments that might interfere with rational discourse.

The relatively high degree of planning, editing, and elaboration reflect a code which may exist in the mind of at least one of the participants, Basil Bernstein, who has written at length about the existence of an "elaborated" variant, code, or style that governs discourse among the more highly educated members of English society.

Notice in these speech-acts the explicit, planned, and judicious expression of ideas, feelings, and wishes by members of the seminar:*

HALLIDAY: I want to comment . . .
GATHERER: I like "exploration." Up to now I have used the term "action research" but in the future I propose to call it "exploration" . . .
DAVIES: I wonder whether . . .
SLOMAN: We have had experience . . .

* From Davies 1975: 135–40 (excerpt 1).

WIDDOWSON: Following up the notion . . . it seems to me . . .

HALLIDAY: I agree that written discourse has been neglected, but I do not see any need for choice here . . .

JOAN TOUGH: There are necessarily different kinds of research . . . I myself think that . . .

JESSIE REID: The suggestion has been made . . . May I say that I very much disagree with this.

SPEITEL: I should like to see . . .

SINCLAIR: I should like to probe . . .

MERRITT: Can I comment . . . What I tried to say was . . . and

DAVIES: I should like to make a point . . . But if my guess is right . . .

HALLIDAY: I agree with this. The reason is, I suggest . . . I still think it would be useful.

T. BROWN: I want to take up Bruner's point about writing . . . But the fact is, I suggest . . . Moreover, I should like to suggest.

BERNSTEIN: I feel that we need to widen the terms of our discussion . . . We need to ask the basic question of how the distribution of power and the principles of control affect this TA matrix. I would want to look at . . .

BRUNER: Doesn't that — if not politicise — at least sociologise the topic?

Often the speakers identify the speech-acts in which they are engaged. For instance, Davies *wonders*, Gatherer *proposes*, Halliday *agrees* or *corrects*. There is also a pattern of giving names to the speech-acts that the speakers *wish* to make. Sinclair would like to *probe*, Merritt and Halliday want to *comment*, Brown wants to *take up a point* and to *suggest*, while Davies announces that he would like to *make a point*. A few speakers couch directions to the seminar as a simple report of perceptions, or feelings, as did Bernstein in the brief excerpt above, while others articulate their current thoughts without labeling the speech-acts in which they are engaged. There is virtually no single, direct statement of a personal vision that compels response. Relatively few of the speech-acts express strong feelings, while most of them fit within the constraints of disciplined reflection. The expression of wishes is muted, and feelings or ideas are rather blandly reported. Indeed relatively few speakers respond directly to what others have said, except to agree or to make corrections. There is a conscious verbal mastery here over the act of speaking itself. The speakers provide their own commentary on the nature of the speech-acts that they are performing. Their commentary identifies them as knowledgeable and responsible speakers who know what they are saying. In fact, their mastery is conveyed in the very separation that the speakers make between their meaning and their utterances.

These acts of speech are very different from those of the poet who performs for a larger audience than he or she will ever know. Poirier notes that for one poet at least (Robert Frost), ". . . not being listened to and not being answered in sound is equivalent to the horror of loss of creative power" (Poirier 1971: 100). The poet risks being ignored in ordinary give-and-take but longs for the certainty of liturgical response. Although persons engaged in seminar talk may wish to shape reflection and direct inquiry, their acts of speech are apparently more dispassionate than those of the poet or the prophet. Consequently, there is little in the seminar speaker's words to suggest an overweening or narcissistic drive to be taken at one's word, to be heeded and taken seriously. Indeed their analytical task does not readily evoke strong, expressive statements. As one participant put it in an earlier session of the same seminar, "the analytic is an important part of life . . . because it gets the 'me' out of things, enforces a self-denying ordinance" (Davies 1975: 133). Indeed, the price of being taken seriously in the secular world of the seminar is to speak without apparent effort to be taken too seriously: a sacrifice, as it were, of the spirit of the self to the collective academic purpose.

Not all speakers were so self-abnegating, of course. In a penultimate session of the group, one speaker is recorded as saying; "I would like to challenge your approach . . ." (Davies 1975: 132). Later another participant spoke emphatically, in the hortatory mood, as follows: "Teachers must forget the idea that . . .": an unusually forceful utterance for an exploratory seminar. Still another participant in the final session stated "May I say that I very much disagree with this . . .": a forceful disagreement, although prefaced by a rhetorical request for permission from others to disagree. Some speakers appear to specialize in taking the more self-denying role of the analytic and inquiring speaker, whereas others point the seminar to neglected or newly discovered obligations and opportunities. The seminar as a whole therefore, rather than specific speakers, develops a wide range of acts of speech, from the purely representative and expressive statements that we first noted to those statements that require a response and entail changes in the direction of attention and energy.

Beneath the tranquil operation of the elaborated code, even the distant observer can sense a struggle for control of the discourse. The struggle for control takes many forms, but perhaps the most important struggle took place in the indirect expression of directions by Bernstein and Bruner noted above. Bernstein seeks to focus the attention of the seminar on the *political* factors that affect the relationship between those who transmit and acquire language, while Bruner senses that Bernstein wishes to sociologise the topic: a change in the framework of discussion that would apparently not satisfy Bruner's own interests. (I say "apparently" since, in a previous monologue, Bruner calls for studying the code of speakers in a "much more sociolinguistic context.") In view of Bruner's earlier directive, it is therefore all the more surprising that Bruner later goes on to say, "Power and control, yes, but that leaves out a great deal, all the intrapersonal uses of language." Here the struggle for control appears to place Bruner in opposition to Bernstein, as each speaker seeks to widen the terms of discussion and to set the direction of future inquiry. But this effort to control also leads Bruner to shift from an emphasis on socio-linguistics to an apparent concern with what happens *within* the individual: a change in focus which makes sense in terms of maneuvers for control of the discourse.

Even these directives, implicit in the statements by Bruner and Bernstein, are *only* implicit: couched as they are within statements of intention or expressions of feeling. But in his long monologue Bruner engages in two quite explicit directives:

Do not, that is, stop your study of Adam and Eve when they have mastered the acquisition. *Go on* as they now learn to acquire transmission. (Davies 1976: 138)

Earlier Bruner, in the same monologue, had stated somewhat less forcefully:

So what needs to be done, I suggest, is to look at kinds of situation of use in which there are the maximum opportunities for learning the structures that are to be converted for use. (Davies 1975: 138)

Although less forceful, this earlier sentence is clearly a speech-act that directs the hearer to certain activities: a suggestion, however, rather than the explicit, later command "Do not . . . stop" or "Go on." On my reading of the transcript of the final session of the seminar, Bruner more than any other participant engages in explicit directive speech-acts to the seminar.

Of course, many participants sought to direct the group, but in each case the direction was buried in a statement of intention, feeling, or in a representation of the speaker's idea. Gatherer stated that "we have to specify quite clearly . . ." but he prefaced this speech-act with another, "so I think," thus reducing the act of direction to an act of representing his own thought. Halliday also sought to direct the seminar's discussion, but he couched his directives in the form of statements of wishful intention:

I would like to see this Seminar having two kinds of results . . . I hope we may be able this afternoon to identify suitable areas for such exploration. (Davies 1975: 135)

When authority is not evenly distributed among speakers, some participants in dialogue will more frequently mute their directions by casting them in the form of wishes, intentions, ideas, or feelings.

Authority in the seminar, then, revolves around two primary speakers, Bruner and Bernstein. Bernstein's opening remarks as chairman of the seminar summarize what he considers to be the important points of the discussion. Next to Bruner's later monologue, his is the longest reported speech by a single participant in that session of the seminar. In length alone, the remarks appear to fit an authoritative role in the seminar, as befits the chair, but it also contains an unalloyed directive. Bernstein, like other participants, often speaks in less forceful forms about the directions that he wishes to see inquiry take, but here he states:

We have to bring the two together and then ask ourselves: what is the role of language in the transmission—acquisition matrix. (Davies 1975: 134—5)

We have to — a clear statement of an imperative that, if followed, would lead the seminar's participants to attend to a crucial linkage between the ways that language is transmitted and the ways in which it is acquired. Unlike Gatherer's "we have to," it is not prefaced with "so I think." The directive force is clear. It is clearly not an accident that Bernstein and Bruner later disagree on the crucial issue of framework and topic, when they disagree whether power and control should be central elements in the seminar's field of inquiry.

We have explored the relevance of speech-acts to understanding the uneventfulness of secular seminar talk: first, by examining the code that separates the speaker's meaning from the act of speaking itself; second, by exploring the maldistribution of authoritative speech-acts in the seminar. Speech-acts clearly indicate the relevance of personal biases to the group, just as they reveal who is free to speak with authority. Of course, not all the speakers' contributions have been transcribed and published: the record itself therefore may be misleading. But if seminar talk is uneventful, it appears that part of the uneventfulness may be due to a process and to a code that together take relatively few witnesses seriously on their own account, at their own word, or in their own right.

I stress this here because similar observations will occur to us in other contexts. Transcripts of personal testimony to religious beliefs in secular courts exhibit the same process and code that I have inferred from the above record of seminar talk. That is, witnesses to religious beliefs find that very few individuals enjoy the right to direct the inquiry of secular courts and to raise topics for discussion. Similarly, when speaking of religious beliefs and intentions to the court, witnesses find that their words are frequently interpreted as representative of personal convictions and therefore as lacking in authority before the court. Personal convictions are usually regarded as "merely" personal and even therefore idiosyncratic. Expert witnesses are taken more seriously as exemplars of a code that subordinates personal commitments to the rational and disinterested statement of putative facts. Only officers of the court may engage in talk that is intended to be eventful. Official words spoken there are intended to be adequate to the occasion, especially among officers who give a verdict or opinion. Such words, furthermore, issue in action or clearly define a situation in authoritative terms.

To be eventful, speech will at some point in a discussion define the situation that prevails among the speakers. That definition may be a judicial opinion or verdict: it may be an agreement concerning where responsibility lies for failure, or it may be a statement by friends as to what they have in common. In the transcript of seminar talk we have been examining, many participants attempted to define the situation, in the limited sense of trying to locate the central topic and the relevance of such concerns as power and control. The seminar appears not to have eventuated in an agreed-upon definition of the participants' central concerns or future goals. I have already indicated that, instead of achieving a consensus, participants chose to speak for the record by correcting misunderstandings and misquotations, by affirming what others had said, and by reporting their own central ideas for future reference. Instead of eventful discourse, the seminar eventuates in an approved text. Like participants in a trial, the participants in this seminar tried to create a record as "a basis" for future appeals and justifications. Unlike a trial, however, the seminar does not lead to a single conclusion.

To bring discussions (or history) to a point is to speak

seriously. Merleau-Ponty (1974: 314) argues that "action would not bring some sort of finality to the whole enterprise of the past, if it did not give the drama its last act." In the published transcript of the seminar there is one speaker, and only one, who toward the close engaged in the serious act of attempting a *final* definition of the situation. (Of course, there may have been other attempts to do so, but these are not reported.) Bruner's lengthy monologue attempts to bring some finality to the previous discussion (cf. Bruner's monologue, Appendix III). Bruner alone has a vision that compels him to testify as well as to agree, to resolve rather than to explore, and to give both a prohibition and a direct command that emerges from his vision of "what is really needed here." He has discerned the meaning of the seminar participants' struggles and sees a way out of them. And he witnesses to that vision at greater length than any other participant at that point in the discussion. Bruner's lengthy speech is therefore not simply an act of authoritative speaking but an attempt at serious speech that will give finality to the seminar by correcting and completing what has been done or said and by pointing the way to new tasks and duties. Bruner's speech, if effective, would bring "the trial" to an end.*

There are other speakers who try to achieve closure in the seminar following Bruner's testimony, but they speak with a view to achieving an accurate text or version of the past, rather than toward a consensus on what is to be done. The closing comments of several speakers indicate a desire to correct the record of what they have said or to make a record on the basis of which they may raise objections in the future to what others have said. For instance, Halliday wishes "to correct a misquotation" of his earlier remarks by Bruner,

---

* Such testimony is not authoritative, however, unless it is authorized by those who hear it, and in this case three participants disagree either explicitly or indirectly with Bruner: a point evidently not lost on Bruner himself, who then comments negatively on Bernstein's statement that "we need to ask the basic question of how the distribution of power and the principles of control affect this TA matrix" (Davies 1975: 140).

while in closing Bernstein wishes "to widen the terms of our discussion": an act that creates a record for future reference when decisions are being made as to the direction of further research. Bernstein's statement for the record follows Brown's indirect disagreement with Bruner, whose testimony might otherwise have a determining effect on the course of future inquiry. Of course, the participants appear to assume that what individuals say will affect decisions made in other contexts on what is "really needed," "basic," or "fundamental" in the field. No wonder some of these individuals wish to make statements for the record, to heighten points of disagreement, and to correct misquotations.

The concern for correcting the text indicates that the last judgment, the last word on the subject, has not successfully been spoken: whether by Bruner in his later monologue or even by Bernstein at the outset of the final session. A similar process occurs in trial courts when attorneys make closing statements in order "to make a record," as legal jargon would have it, as a basis for review by a higher tribunal, since in their opinion the trial court is not likely to render an adequate definition of the situation. In the same fashion, students occasionally make statements in class or in writing that serve as a record on the basis of which to influence or appeal from a teacher's judgments: especially when they sense that there has been too much asymmetry in the distribution of authority in the class and too little opportunity for a serious judgment. Speaking to create an adequate text or record, however, is not always an aspect of uneventful talk or speech, since some forms of religious witnessing intend to create a record on the basis of which the divine, final judgment can be made about the person who has received the witness. Witnesses to the faith of many religious sects tend to believe that those who fail to receive that witness as authoritative can be convicted of faithlessness on the basis of the oral record created by the speech-act of the witness. But religious testimony of this sort, unlike seminar talk, satisfies the major conditions for eventful speech. I will shortly argue, furthermore, that the same motive (to establish an adequate record) underlies liturgical revisions and that these revisions may be entirely successful in creating an adequate or final word.

Conclusion

The distance from liturgical speech to seminar talk is one measure of secularization. In the final chapter, we will trace part of the process by which religious language loses its power to interrupt everyday life and to transform the taken-for-granted meanings of the world until individuals are alert again and responsive to the possible breaking-in of the divine kingdom. Corporate-mythic meanings degenerate in this process to a mere biblical literalism. The parable of the Good Samaritan thus becomes either a parable about a good Samaritan or a metaphor for neighborliness, rather than a narrative that symbolically evokes the Kingdom of God in its very telling. The fall of prophetic religious utterance makes it possible for the hearer to separate speaking from its meaning: to ask, in effect, "Did God *really* say that?" The secularization of religious speech makes it possible to inquire whether the speaker is using words as metaphor, as allegory, or quite literally. Language thus becomes clearer, more complete, and more likely to have a single referent in the real world (like the Good Samaritan), but in the same process language thus loses its power to create an immediate and transforming connection between speaker and hearer. Once there is a serpent in the linguistic garden who takes it upon himself (or herself, of course) to clarify the intention and meaning of God's words, language has begun to fall from grace. The ability to separate a speaker's act of speaking (utterance) from that speaker's meaning is conferred by rules of discourse in secular contexts. Liturgies confer no such critical right or ability to separate the two.

Once it is possible to separate what a speaker means from a speaker's actual utterance, it is possible for other speakers to claim for themselves a larger measure of authority and to identify themselves in ways that are not always possible in the immediate and spontaneous give-and-take of personal communication. Within the sphere of everyday life, of small communities, familiar colleagues, or members of one's family, it is seldom necessary to elaborate on the meaning of one's words, since the context supplies the meaning and a reservoir of common assumptions. But beyond such everyday contexts the meaning of words and a speaker's intentions are not easily taken for granted. To justify themselves, to identify their intentions, and to claim authority individuals must elaborate, make their meanings plain, and carefully point to what their words actually refer. As the Eden myth puts it, outside the Garden justification is always problematical, and, as I will argue here, attempts at justification are likely to have negative, although wholly unintended, consequences.

As individuals use religious terms to justify themselves in secular contexts, those terms lose their prophetic power and become mere metaphors or allegories, terms separate entirely from their meaning and from the objects to which they refer. This process reduces religious prophecy to a set of meanings that are incidental to the prophetic words themselves. It is therefore not surprising that the earliest instructions to Christian believers included injunctions against taking quarrels before secular courts and against casting verbal pearls before swine. The dilemma is clear. Religious communities may seek to spread their prophetic word and so to make it eventful in the courts and classrooms of the larger society, or, they may keep that word limited to a religious context where it becomes fixed in text or ritual, but largely uneventful outside the religious community. If religious communites seek to establish the word outside of the community of faith, it becomes available to others who seek, for a variety of motives, to justify themselves before secular authorities. Whether or not individuals in this process have their credentials accepted, the religious word is likely to become mere metaphor or allegory, to be reduced even further to a literal and therefore uncompelling usage, or to become associated with motives that religious communities find embarrassing or actually abhorrent.

A religious hope that finds expression in Western theological doctrine is for a word that does not lose its power when uttered in secular contexts and does not lose its authority when mixed with wholly human and personal motives. The doctrine of the Incarnation, in fact, asserts that such a word is spoken in the person and work of Jesus. That word endures although it is not fixed in text or ritual: hence the function of the Holy Spirit in Christian mythology. That prophetic word, uttered in a secular context, seeks to transform the secular powers without being reduced to metaphor or literal usage. But from a secular, sociological viewpoint, religious speech, especially prophetic utterance, loses meaning and force when uttered out of context or associated with individuals' claims to authority.

Seminar talk, as I have illustrated it here, represents ordinary language in secular contexts. A speaker's meaning is radically separated from the act of speaking itself, and that act is usually of the less forceful variety. Few speakers declare or announce in evangelical or prophetic utterances. The meanings themselves are literal, and speakers seldom use metaphors that open the gates to religious meanings. Speakers attempt to create a text or record, as in a court, since the final judgment lies outside the context of the seminar. The talk is uneventful on the face of it.

Chapter 6

In the Matter of Karen Ann Quinlan: The Secularization of Religious Testimony

The process of secularization imposes severe limitations on religious witness. Only certain religious topics can be raised on appropriate occasions, but even then religion, like politics, can be discussed only with appropriately low intensity. Otherwise intimate relationships and smooth routines will be disrupted. In secular contexts, even individuals with strong religious convictions find that they are expected to engage in a version of "seminar talk": to advance personal opinions or to make suggestions rather than to proclaim and declare. When religious witness does occur, moreover, constraints are imposed on the witness's ability to exhort and direct, let alone to declare, pronounce, and to judge. These more authoritative speech-acts are reserved in secular contexts to those licensed to speak with authority. The religious witness is therefore left with brief, highly constrained reports of personal beliefs or with appropriate expressions of attitude and feeling.

Not all secular contexts, of course, are equally constraining. The courtroom is simply one very fruitful source of observations on the way secular authorities constrain the religious witness. In the courtroom even expressive acts of speech are limited, and the witness is seldom allowed to speak about commitments to future courses of action. Thus, a secular society tends to place individuals in a dilemma by placing them "on trial" in many contexts while limiting the occasions on which they can turn to religious beliefs as a source of personal credibility and authority.

It is this dilemma that helps to account for the paradoxical revival of religion in societies with highly developed and autonomous secular institutions and authorities. I suggest that many secular contexts, like the courtroom, impose severe limitations on speech-acts that direct and declare, reserving these acts of speech to those properly authorized and trained to pronounce, judge, evaluate, order, direct, implore, beg, or even persuasively to suggest. Some religious groups, in other words, flourish precisely because they provide the unauthorized and untrained, the laity, with opportunities to declare, pronounce, and direct. Utterances in the spirit, of course, cannot be easily constrained, despite the tendencies of priests to question the authority of laymen inspired by the Spirit to pronounce and direct. Inspired utterances clearly provide opportunities for speech-acts that are often prohibited to those with little education, training, power, or authority in secular contexts. Religious groups with Pentecostal fervor and authority in their acts of speech may indeed flourish precisely because of the successful secularization of educational, economic, or political institutions in modern societies.

Of course, not all movements for "free speech" occur under the auspices of religion. In the free speech movements of the 1960s, some constituencies, already fluent and able to take their own opinions seriously, demanded opportunities for the type of speech that seeks to conform the world to the word through declarations and directives. The protest songs of the 1960s also provided models for speech-acts that deplore and celebrate, praise and lament, as well as for acts of speech that commit the speaker to certain ideals or courses of action. The point here is simply that secularization creates a demand for the kinds of speech-acts reserved only to elites in modern societies.

Rituals provide individuals an opportunity to speak and to be taken seriously if they speak within prescribed limits. Some rituals place very stringent constraints by limiting individuals to certain words or phrases of acclamation and assent, such as "Hosanna" or "Yes, sir." Rituals of the courtroom allow witnesses to be taken seriously if they observe judicial constraints on evidence and testimony. Only witnesses that can speak with authority about a given body of knowledge will therefore be considered "expert" or authoritative. Others will be considered as representing only their own, personal interpretations and opinions of medical or ecclesiastical knowledge and teaching. *In the Matter of Karen Ann Quinlan*, a case we will consider in this chapter, the religious witness of a layman, Joseph Quinlan, and of his priest was reduced to mere statements of their own opinion, regardless of how authentic and sincere the witnesses may have been in claiming to speak of an entire tradition. Public rituals may make short shrift of personal religious witness and reduce official, corporate teaching to expressions of the personal understanding of the spokesman in question.

A speech-act theory of secularization must therefore focus first of all on power: power defined as the ability to engage in such forceful acts as declarations and directions. That power could be measured in terms of the number and range of directions that a particular role entitles its incumbent to make: for example, to order, invite, suggest, demand, inquire, or to question the incumbents of other roles. Power could also be measured by examining the number and range of declarations that a particular role entitles its incumbent to give to others: for example, to nominate, appoint, decide, constitute, initiate, or terminate, to name only a few of the declarations mentioned by Searle (1976: 13–15). A theory of secularization utilizing these concepts would then be able to assess the relative power of religious institutions and their spokespersons in various non-ecclesiastical contexts. For instance, courts claim for themselves the right to determine the location of the line separating the sacred from the secular: a line on which depends the scope of the church's authority and rights *vis-à-vis* other institutions, notably the state. The Constitution thus gives, with one hand, the right to the churches to be free of governmental transgressions across the line between church and state, while giving to the courts the right to draw the line between the sacred and the secular wherever they see fit. As the courts draw a more limited line describing the church's periphery, the process of secularization is advanced.

A sociological analysis of secularization that focusses on the distribution of such authoritative speech-acts notes other constraints on the force and integrity of religious speech. Some constraints, of course, reflect particular distributions of power, but other constraints arise from the distribution of certain functions, like education or the care of the sick, to organizations and institutions, like schools and the medical profession. Of course, that distribution is itself partly the result of conflict between various groups for larger shares of those speech-acts that involve the direct exercise of power. But I shall take it as a fact of modern societies that certain institutions lose some functions while engaging more intensively in others. Churches, for instance, are credited with specializing in emotional support, the release of tension, and the re-enactment of traditional and conventional values and beliefs, although they appear to have lost some of their ability to influence work, education, and politics. Even Joseph Quinlan's own priest, Father Trapasso, claimed at the end of the trial only that he had given emotional support to his parishioner rather than authoritative teaching on the church's definition of life and death.

The separation of institutions that specialize in religious speech-acts places severe limitations and constraints on the range and intensity of religious witnessing in other contexts. Religious witnessing becomes inappropriate in formal situations within a modern corporation or political organization, for instance, although religious witnessing is not unusual in informal settings or by businessmen and politicians outside their immediate occupational contexts. Jimmy Carter witnessed to his religious beliefs, and so does Senator Hatfield, but their testimonies have usually been given off the floor of Congress and outside the context of formal congressional hearings. Conversely, religious witness in the church seems to occur primarily in situations specified for such purposes, while informal situations are found appropriate for talk on secular subjects. Religious witness either occurs off the secular stage or primarily on cue within religious institutions. Neither setting is therefore conducive to an event that makes powerful demands on the hearer or on the host institution. Church members can discount religious witnessing as "mere talk," however solemnly delivered, while secular organizations can compartmentalize the effects of religious witness to half-time, coffee hours, or prayer breakfasts.

The Quinlan case, however, reminds us that on occasion this formal separation of institutional contexts for religious witness may begin to dissolve. By relaxing the rules for giving testimony and evidence in the courtroom so as to permit a more narrative construction by Joseph Quinlan, the court itself opened the door to a partial breakdown of those institutional barriers to the speech-acts characteristic of the home and of church. Joseph Quinlan was allowed to tell his story, to represent his beliefs in a narrative fashion that permitted greater force and intensity than the statement of abstract religio-ethical propositions. He therefore expressed attitudes and feelings ranging from hope to anguish and elaborated on his own intentions for himself, his family, and particularly for his daughter, Karen Ann. But in the last analysis even this enriched religious witness lacked the full power of religious witness to transform motives, situations, and actions according to its own directives and judgments.

The first brief submitted by Joseph Quinlan on behalf of his daughter, Karen Ann, claimed that she was beyond hope of recovery according to the religious beliefs and judgments of her family. Joseph Quinlan petitioned the court to permit a dramatic reversal of Karen Ann's situation from enforced artificial respiration to less heroic or extraordinary measures, in order to allow nature or the Lord's will to take its course. But Quinlan amended his brief in order to satisfy the legal— medical definition of death: a definition later elaborated by "expert witnesses" in testimony before the trial court. In amending his brief, Quinlan forfeited his religious claims to the right to declare that Karen Ann was beyond earthly hope and should be allowed her hopes of heaven. Joseph Quinlan was still allowed a directive speech-act, viz. to "pray" that the court would authorize his guardianship and the possible removal of extraordinary measures of life-support from his daughter. But no stronger directive than such a prayer was permitted. No latitude remained for Joseph Quinlan to demand, let alone patiently to insist, but only to inquire, to seek, and to ask for a decisive response from judges and attorneys who might, he prayed, discern or unwittingly articulate the proper thing to do: the will of the Lord.

The process of secularization thus radically restricts the range of topics and occasions on which religious witness can give declarations, authoritative judgments, final decisions, and verdicts. In the Quinlan case the courts made two such restrictions with compelling force. They reminded Joseph Quinlan that declarations as to what constitutes "life" or "death" are clearly authoritative only when given by members of the medical profession. The courts also reminded Joseph Quinlan that what he defines as a religious issue is not a religious issue unless the court so defines it. Without the power to make either declaration with authority, Joseph Quinlan's religious witness was reduced, in the light of further testimony by the church, to mere opinion permitted the Catholic laity and to a sincere expression of personal faith. Authentic representation and sincere expression constitute two highly limited speech-acts within the total spectrum that potentially constitutes religious witness.

The Quinlan case is not the first time that Christian churches have found the force of religious witness radically restrained when given according to the rules and within the constraints imposed by secular judicial authorities. But for the early church the last judgment had already been initiated. Thus, only one "advocate" was essential for those whose capacity to witness to their own faith was otherwise limited in secular contexts, viz. the "advocate with the Father," the Spirit. Secular trials could not determine an individual's ultimate vindication. Indeed, to rely on secular advocates deprives a religious witness of an opportunity to testify with the authority conferred by the Spirit. Some Christian sects still observe the early prohibition against seeking the support of secular advocates and will therefore not go to court, at least against other Christians. It is not unusual, furthermore, for Christians to refuse to testify, on religious grounds, in a courtroom that constrains religious witness to a rehearsal of memories and beliefs. The churches on the whole, however, appear to have accepted the authority of the courts to constrain religious witness, with incalculable effects, of course, on the power and scope of their testimony.

Speech-act Theory and Secularization

In this discussion of religious witnessing, I am relying rather heavily on the concept of speech-acts as developed by Austin (1962) and adapted by Searle (1979). Testimony in secular contexts is unconstrained, I would suggest, if it opens up the full range of the powers of speech-acts. I have suggested, furthermore, that prophetic speech is relatively unconstrained, as in the case of individuals who rely on the "advocacy of the Spirit" in secular courts. We need, however, an analytical scheme to denote the range of possible speech-acts. I follow Searle, then, in arguing that speech-acts may *declare* something to be true, *express* a speaker's feeling or attitude, express an *intention* of the speaker or an *order* or request to the hearer, or simply *represent* a state or set of facts as being true. The words used to perform these speech-acts may be able to perform only one of them or more than one, depending on the structure of the sentence and on the social position of speaker and hearer. But if Searle is right, we have here an exhaustive list of "illocutionary points": the representative (of "the truth of the expressed proposition"), directive (attempts "by the speaker to get the hearer to do something"), commissive (that "commit the speaker . . . to some future course of action"), expressive (of a "psychological state"), and declarative (that makes the world conform to the word when the speech-act is successful). Clearly other typologies are possible and useful for different purposes, but this brief list suggests the range of speech-acts that are conceivable under the right conditions (Searle 1969).

Unconstrained speech, then, would enable the speaker to declare that someone is married or that a certain player is out, to use two of Searle's examples. It is immediately clear that only individuals such as civil servants, clergymen, or umpires are qualified, by virtue of their position in a particular institution or organization, to make these declarative acts of speech. Thus wholly unconstrained speech is possible only in a society where anyone can conceivably occupy any position. Such a society is not entirely fanciful, although historical examples escape me for the moment. Think only of those periods in the early church, however, when various individuals could be — and did become — clergymen for short periods of time, as in the early church and in the Gnostic controversies of the fourth century, and the possibility of such unconstrained speech will seem less remote. Of course, for students to pronounce that they have failed or passed a course would be possible only when certain cherished constraints on their speech have been removed. It might be well to pass quickly on to other institutional spheres like the church, where laymen do, in fact, pronounce themselves or other laymen to be saved without always observing the constraints imposed by clergy. I am driving at one quite obvious point: that even a cursory inspection of social situations suggests that the most potent verbal acts, by which the world is made to conform to certain words, tend to be the privileged preserve of those who are qualified by licensing or social position to utter them, but that even these privileges are subject to democratizing pressures. The audience in a court pronounces its own verdicts, the fans countermand the verdicts of the umpire, the laymen pronounce one another saved, regardless of the acts of declarative speech by particular officials, who turn a deaf ear to these lay or unofficial voices only at their long-term peril.

Imagine for a moment a speech that is constrained so that only one "illocutionary point" can be uttered: the representative. These constraints permit an individual to state, report, or describe something and to represent these statements as being true to the stated, reported, etc. facts. But that same individual is not permitted to declare — and so bring about — a state of affairs, let alone to get someone to do something by speaking certain words. Statements of intent, on the part of the speaker, are equally proscribed, as are statements of feeling or attitude. Just the clearest, most accurate and concise, representation of a limited range of facts is permitted. Cases of such speech abound in the academic world, in scholarly journals, as well as in student papers. Scholarly articles, for instance, represent a certain segment of the world and ask nothing of the reader except to credit the author with sincerity and to judge for himself the truth-value of what is said. But such articles never declare, seldom beg, pray, entreat, advise, or invite the reader to do anything (except, perhaps, to continue reading), and seldom lament or celebrate the state of affairs reported, explained, or argued in the article. These more expressive or authoritative acts of speech might be appropriate for discussion, but they betray non-scholarly interests and highly subjective attitudes and standpoints that might interfere with the claims of the author to credibility.

The courtroom is a situation that constrains speech-acts in several ways, the most important of which is to allow only specialists in certain speech-acts to use them. Thus attorneys are permitted to state their intentions prior to a course of questioning, whereas witnesses are required simply to represent their beliefs about a particular set of facts or observations. Attorneys may urge juries and judges to reach certain decisions, while judges alone may direct attorneys and witnesses to engage in certain speech-acts. Judges, perhaps more than attorneys, also appear to be permitted to express such feelings as impatience or fatigue. When the ritual of the courtroom proceeds without disruption, each participant engages only in the speech-acts appropriate to the role. The very specialization of roles is itself a constraint on speech, so long as the requirements of the role are honored.

These formal requirements of the courtroom are occasionally dispensed with. The attorney for Mr Quinlan successfully asked the court to relax its rules for the giving of testimony in order to permit a freer narrative by his client. In this relative freedom, Joseph Quinlan went on not merely to *represent* his beliefs, but to state his intentions in coming to court, to direct, however politely, the court toward a line of action that included discerning the Lord's will, and even to express certain attitudes and feelings of his own. The power of these combined speech-acts is evident elsewhere in the proceedings, where various participants, including the judges, agreed that the authenticity and sincerity of Joseph Quinlan as a devout Catholic and concerned parent were beyond question. Other more indirect evidence can be found in the comments of at least one commentator on the trial, the court-appointed guardian for Miss Quinlan, Attorney Daniel Coburn, who, shortly after the New Jersey Supreme Court gave its final ruling in the case, told a panel at Columbia Law School that the Quinlan trial was "religious" throughout in its concerns and awesome seriousness (see Appendix II). I will not document these assertions in any detail here in order to allow space for the following excerpts from the transcript of expert witness on religious belief by Joseph Quinlan's priest. They document quite tellingly the tension between religious witness and those speech-acts that are normally permitted within the usual constraints of the judicial process. In these excerpts from the testimony of Father Thomas J. Trapasso before the Superior Court of New Jersey, *In the Matter of Karen Ann Quinlan*, Father Trapasso is progressively constrained to speak in a way that reduces authoritative religious witness to a matter of mere opinion within a permissible range of options. The court is especially careful to ascertain that the Pope's words are not a "declaration," a term which the court uses in the same narrow sense as does Searle, but only a mere "clarification" of directives earlier issued or widely understood by Catholic morality and piety. In these excerpts the illocutionary force of Catholic dogma is reduced from strong to weak directives, from declarations to clarifications, and from directives to statements of mere opinion or personal belief. These are the symbolic steps by which the process of secularization advances within the judicial system.

Where necessary, for emphasis, I have italicized the key words and phrases of the testimony and examination.

THE COURT: Gentlemen, good morning.
             All right, Mr Armstrong, will you begin?
MR ARMSTRONG: Thank you, Your Honor.
             Your Honor, I would like to call Father Trapasso, if I may?

THOMAS J. TRAPASSO,
called as a witness [*sic*] on behalf of the plaintiff, being duly sworn, testifies as follows.

DIRECT EXAMINATION
BY MR ARMSTRONG:
Q: Would you state your name in full, please?
A: I'm Reverend Thomas J. Trapasso.
Q: Where do you live, Father?
A: One Park Avenue, Mount Arlington, New Jersey.
Q: What is your profession?
A: I'm the pastor of the local Catholic church.
Q: And when were you ordained?
A: June 11, 1949.
Q: And in what order?
A: Diocesan priest.
(Further questions to establish the identity and training of the priest.)
Q: Father, as pastor of Our Lady of the Lake, have the Quinlans had occasion to seek your advice concerning the plight of Karen?
A: Yes, they have.
Q: And could you please explain the circumstances?
MR COBURN: Excuse me, Judge. If the circumstances are what he knows from his own sense, I have no objection. If he's going to testify what somebody else told him or what their position was, I would object. I would just like that objection noted in advance.
MR ARMSTRONG: I'll withdraw that question and ask another question.
BY MR ARMSTRONG   (*resuming*):
Q: Could you tell us the nature of the advice that you gave to the Quinlan family?
A: In general terms, the advice that I gave them is that in Catholic teaching we see no moral imperative —
MR COBURN: Excuse me, Judge. I object again. *I don't think Father, in all due respect to him, is qualified to state what the Catholic*

Church's position might be as far as teaching. I think he can state the actual opinion of the Catholic Church as it exists and as it's a written document, or at least a transcription of it. But I don't think he can say how it applied to this case, or a personal interpretation on the part of the Quinlans — how they interpret their own religion. I don't know how anyone else can dictate how their religious beliefs should apply.

MR ARMSTRONG: One, I think Father is perfectly able to respond as to the Catholic Church. He is an ordained priest since 1949. The nature of the question is couched as to what was the nature of the advice Father had given them concerning the problem of Karen.

THE COURT: Why can't he testify as to the nature of the advice he gave them? Whether it is the doctrine of the Catholic Church might have to be later established. But it seems to me he can testify as to what he said.

MR COBURN: *As long as that limitation is followed in this case, that he is saying what his understanding is, that it is not official Catholic Church dogma, because he's not a recognized representative of the Pope.* With that limitation, I have no objection.

MR ARMSTRONG: Your Honor, I don't think one has to be an authorized representative of the Pope in order to represent what the position of the Catholic Church is.

THE COURT: Let's take it on the grounds it will be his understanding of what the Catholic Church's teachings are and what he told someone else.

BY MR ARMSTRONG (*resuming*):

Q: Can you work with that?

*(The priest distinguishes ordinary from extraordinary means and begins to report a conversation with Mrs Quinlan.)

MR COBURN: Judge, excuse me. I respectfully object on two grounds: Number one, it is hearsay; and secondly, Mr Quinlan is the plaintiff in this case. His feelings with the plaintiff Mr Quinlan are admissible, but as to Mrs Quinlan and the other members of the family, it is not admissible.

THE COURT: Father Trapasso, would you limit your testimony? Don't include what anyone else said other than —

MR ARMSTRONG: Could I address myself to Mr Coburn's objection, perhaps concurring in reference to the hearsay nature of the statement of Mrs Quinlan to Father Trapasso? However, with relation-

* Comments supplied by the author.

ship to the inadmissibility of the evidence, as to Mrs Quinlan as a member of the Quinlan family being not involved in the situation, I think, through the vehicle of the constitutional argument, we are setting up before the Court the concept that the family has a right to make this decision, and, as such as to Mrs Quinlan, it is relevant, not admissible at this time, but I think in the future it could be relevant. The way I understand it, you were ruling on Mr Coburn's objection on two planes, one hearsay, and two, that Mrs Quinlan as a member of the family is irrelevant.

THE COURT: All right. To make it clear, hearsay evidence in this framework is not admissible. That's the basis of the ruling.

MR ARMSTRONG: Thank you.

BY MR ARMSTRONG (*resuming*):

Q: Could you go on with the nature of the advice you have given, Father, not the conversation that Mrs Quinlan would have had with you?

A: Well, it's hard to state the advice that I gave on that occasion without giving the framework in which I made the statement.

Q: This is one of those circumstances, Father, where you're going to have to do that.

A: I said to Mrs Quinlan, at that time, that it's always been the teaching, *my interpretation of the teaching of the Church*, that people's lives do not have to be prolonged by extraordinary means.

Q: Can you tell us when the Quinlan family ultimately made their decision to seek the aid of the Court?

A: This was kind of a progressive thing, and although Mr and Mrs Quinlan talked about it, I think their decision was arrived at by — at a different rate, and so that in — my impression is that Mrs Quinlan was reconciled to the idea that her daughter ought to be taken off the machine —

MR COBURN: Excuse me again. I have to object.

* (After Mr Coburn successfully objects to the Court hearing from Father Trapasso about Mrs Quinlan's decision, Father Trapasso narrates the steps by which Joseph Quinlan began to make his own decision.)

Q: Father, when did you become aware that Joe had made, or Mr Quinlan had made his decision?

A: I don't remember the lapse of time between the first breaking of this kind of concept to Joe. He came in — I believe it was a Saturday morning. Somehow, I'm associating it with a Saturday. He had come in —

Q: Excuse me, Father. Could you put us at least within the month?

A: Oh yes. It would certainly be within the month. I would say that the first conversation took place in mid-July, and the second one perhaps two weeks later. So that would bring it towards the end of July. *Now, again, I would stand corrected on that. But that's my recollection.* Joe came in and said that he had made up his mind.

Q: Excuse me, Father. This was at the second meeting in July?

A: This was at the second meeting in July, that he had made up his mind, neither of us realizing the legal implications that would eventually emerge. And again, he wanted a reassurance and an affirmation. And we were able to speak, at that point, on a much higher level. I, at that point, now that Joe had arrived at the decision, I didn't feel the need to — I felt that I could speak freely now. I didn't want to influence Joe, at any point, because obviously it had to be his decision and not mine. He was in no way seeking my "permission." I was his spiritual advisor and very dear friend. At this point, though, when he came in with a very clear understanding of himself, his ability to make the decision, not only in terms of a kind of intellectual acceptance of Church teaching, but that emotionally and humanely he could make this decision and not worry about feeling guilty about it later.

   In any event, we did talk about it on that level, and I can remember saying to him that, you know, *our faith teaches us that death is not the end of all being.* I remember saying very clearly to him. And enduring, I was able to say to him, "This would liberate Karen, this would free her so that she could enter into God's presence, and hopefully enjoy the fullness of life."

MR ARMSTRONG: Thank you, Father.

CROSS-EXAMINATION

BY MR COBURN:

Q: Father, you also told him this is *an optional tenet* of the Catholic Church?

A: Yes.

Q: Certainly nothing required on his part.

A: Right.

Q: It also had to be a *personal decision* on his part in the sense, you might say, it's morally acceptable; if he felt it was immoral, he should not do it.

A: Yes. He would ultimately have to follow some conscience, yes, sir.

Q: You told him, I'm sure, that in the event that *your understanding of the Catholic Church's position* was different from as you've described this, he'd still be bound by that, wouldn't he?

A: Yes, I had no doubt about my position. But if it were to be different, so would I be bound by it.

Q: But you wouldn't have to make any decisions?

A: No.

Q: You say you graduated from the seminary in 1949?

A: Yes.

Q: Certainly, the Pope's encyclical wasn't in existence at that time, was it?

A: MR CROWLEY: I object that it wasn't in existence.

MR COBURN: I'll withdraw it.

BY MR COBURN   (*resuming*):

Q: The Church's position in 1949 was not as you described it to Mr Quinlan, was it?

A: Yes, it was. It was very much a part of my moral training and theology.

Q: Describe the Church's position *as you understood it* in 1949 concerning the use of extraordinary devices.

A: My understanding, and the training that I received in my seminary training — which began, my theological training began in 1945 — was that ordinary means must be used to sustain life, and that extraordinary means are not required, are not obligatory to prolong life, that there is an elective, an option in which a person may choose not to use extraordinary means to prolong life. This was taught to me in the seminary in '45, '46, '47.

Q: And what was that based on, *some sort of Papal statement*?

A: No. It's based on Catholic tradition, Catholic morality, and Catholic theology.

Q: What was the significance of the 1957 or '58 statement?

A: I think the significance of that statement, it consists in this, that a group of anesthesiologists, in an audience with Pope Pius XII, posed the question to the Pope for a clarification as to what their role would be in the use of respirators and resuscitators and what have you. So the *allocutio* on November 24th of '57 was a response to a group of doctors who were asking for moral guidance with regard to their specific field of medicine.

Q: So then, *it wasn't even a clarification* of the Church's position?

A: No, I would not see it as a clarification. I've read the document. *I would see it as a declaration.*

Q: You mean before that it had been unwritten, just understood?

A: No, no. There are many moral principles, and some of them are very abstract. And then we have decreasing levels of abstractness to practical cases. And I think that the way I would read the document was that the principle of ordinary and extraordinary means to prolong life was a very basic principle, and I wouldn't be able to trace the history of it back through the evolution of Catholic moral thinking. But very often, you have a moral principle, and the question can arise: How do you apply that now to some situation? I would see the *allocutio* of Pope Pius XII precisely in that vein. The principle of ordinary and extraordinary was always enunciated as a part of Catholic moral teaching. And now the doctors are saying: We have got a new mechanism. We have this type of medical situation; how does that principle apply to this concrete circumstance?

Q: *What you are saying, then,* is that the principle has existed, but its application varies from case to case. Is that right?

A: Obviously, yes.

Q: And the significance of the 1957 statement was at least there when we were talking about use of artificial means of respiration?

A: Right.

Q: That would be the pertinence of this particular case?

A: Yes.

Q: But even in the absence of that statement, I don't know what else might be considered extraordinary; whether it be a brain transplant or something else, the Catholic theology would have considered that situation at least in principle. Is that right?

A: In principle, yes.

Q: When you first spoke to Mr Quinlan concerning what *your understanding of the Catholic Church's position* was, had he solicited it, or can you say? Did he solicit it? Did he instigate the conversation, or did it just sort of come up?

A: No, I would have to say, with Mr Quinlan, that I brought up the question.

Q: When you told him what the *"Catholic Church's position"* was, as best you could, did it come as a surprise to him?

* (It is interesting to note that these quotation marks, not an audible part of oral speech, are nevertheless inserted by the court reporter. Presumably the court reporter is here capturing a gesture or an inflection of the lawyer's speech.)

* (Father Trapasso then speaks of the difficulty which Joseph Quinlan experienced in accepting the hopelessness of his daughter's condition.)

Q: You are aware, I am sure, at least since the beginning of this case, of a variety of *statements alleged to be attributable to the Vatican,* to a variety of other people that have occurred. Is that correct?

A: Yes, very much so.

Q: Would it be safe for me to say that *statements such as that, unless they are authorized by the Vatican, are people's opinions, and that's all it is?*

A: Yes, certainly, particularly in references to yesterday's story.

Q: Yes, I understand there was a statement by a physician that the press —

MR COLLESTER: I object. I don't think Mr Coburn's understanding of what was in the press is relevant.

MR ARMSTRONG: I would echo the sentiments of Mr Collester.

MR COBURN: My understanding is accurate, but it is whether that is what was meant.

MR COLLESTER: I object to his understanding.

MR ARMSTRONG: In addition to the entry of the statement itself. It is hearsay.

THE COURT: Rephrase the question.

BY MR COBURN   *(resuming)*:

Q: Is there any doubt in your mind that, unless a statement is made by a representative of the Pope, either through the Vatican or whatever the source of information may be from the Vatican, *that statement is nothing more than an opinion?*

A: Yes. If I understand your question correctly, that's right; it is nothing more than opinion.

MR COBURN: Thank you.

CROSS-EXAMINATION

BY MR BAIME:

Q: Just a few questions. Are you familiar with the Pope's address in 1945 to the Army Medical Corps?

A: No, I am not.

Q: The Catholic Church does not require termination of extraordinary means?

A: That is correct.

Q: You say it does?

A: No, no. The Catholic Church does not require the termination of the use of extraordinary means.

Conclusion

In examining even these limited excerpts from the proceedings of a single court, it is evident that the process of secularization is far from smooth or the result of merely abstract social processes. Peter Berger (1967) has argued that the reduction of authoritative religious belief to the status of mere opinion is the result of ethnic and religious pluralism and also of widespread and complex social changes that divide societies into various institutional sectors, such as work, the family, education, and politics. But here we find the compelling vision of Joseph Quinlan, supported by the witness of the Catholic Church, slowly reduced to the status of mere personal opinion by means of a political ritual that attempts to dramatize and speak for widespread collective sentiments and for the interests of the larger society. The process is one of severe, however polite and institutionalized, conflict between the believer and the church, on the one hand, and the official agencies of the larger society, on the other.

The first step in the control of potentially divisive or subversive religious witness, therefore, is for a society to provide ritualistic settings in which the rules for witness are governed by the state. Religious witness therefore occurs under the auspices, and usually within the limitations, of the political community. Religious witness is thereby transformed when it takes place in the secular context of what Lukes (1975) has helped us to see as a political ritual.

Social scientists are coming to a renewed awareness of the ritualistic or symbolic aspects of many activities that otherwise serve only casual, entertaining, utilitarian, or political purposes. In a brilliant criticism of what might be called vulgar Durkheimian assumptions on the sociology of such political rituals as Memorial Day celebrations and the Coronation, Steven Lukes (1975) argues that these rituals not only serve dramatic or expressive functions but political and cognitive ones. He notes that a political ritual:

helps to define as authoritative certain ways of seeing society: it serves to specify what in society is of special significance, it draws people's attention to certain forms of relationships and activity — and at the same time, therefore, it deflects their attention from other forms, since every way of seeing is also a way of not seeing. (ibid.: 301)

Ritual thus has a "cognitive dimension" that structures perceptions according to the specific interests of groups or classes in a pluralistic and conflictual society (ibid.: 301).

Political rituals may be found elsewhere. Lukes finds ritual in the theatrical aspects of legislative activities, which arouse respect for the deliberations of certain august bodies. Political ritual may be found outside of a narrowly conceived "politics," as in the administrative regulation of business that gives *the appearance* of ensuring fair practices despite the obvious inequities in the balance of power between corporations and the individual worker or consumer. Ritual thus exists wherever activities have a "cognitive" function that shapes and confines the individual's perception within a certain perspective.

Of course, the powerful have no monopoly on ritual, but, as Lukes implies, the rituals of the discontented are more often called demonstrations. These demonstrations may be ways of acting out a symbolic invasion or the capture of a city in order to dramatize (unseen) sources of collective strength, to gain a symbolic advantage in competition with other groups for public attention and social esteem, and to open up hitherto unseen or untold possibilities for social change. If they result in permanent innovations in a society's or group's way of seeing things, these demonstrations may become liturgical: public symbolic action that is repeated to dramatize the original version and to renew its power to change what people are willing and able to envisage as possible forms of social life. But most demonstrations do not become incorporated in regular symbolic actions. There are few memorials or re-enactments of the demonstrations of the 1960s except for those in which a few individuals died, as at Kent State. Rituals and demonstrations without sacrifice have a relatively short life.

While the individual may choose how to give witness, religious witness is never given in a vacuum. The legal context, for example, a trial or judicial hearing, provides a particularly clear and formal set of contextual constraints on religious and other forms of testimony. Societies, through their legal systems, also claim authority to determine which religious beliefs to take seriously, the topics that may be considered relevant to religion, the extent to which meanings are required to be elaborated, and whether the speaker (witness) must assent to questioning and interruptions. Courts may vary in the degree to which they permit individual witnesses freedom in this regard, but they seek, as much as do religious witnesses themselves, to control the conditions under which testimony will be given. It is the courts' rules which determine the content, relevance, and procedures which transform religious witness into legal testimony, the promptings of the Spirit notwithstanding.

In examining judicial proceedings, I am suggesting that we are in a good position to observe the conflict between the witness of an individual to a vision of the sacred and the official interest of the state and the larger society in limiting such visions to expressions of merely personal or idiosyncratic belief. The proceedings of the Superior Court of New Jersey record at length the moving testimony of Joseph Quinlan to his desire to place his daughter in the hands of a God whose will can only be discerned in the absence of certain artificial and extraordinary means for her life-support. In the subsequent testimony of Joseph Quinlan's priest, spiritual advisor, and friend, Father Thomas J. Trapasso, the church attempted to provide a framework for Joseph's personal witness that would make it conform to Catholic teaching and therefore not lightly to be dismissed as merely idiosyncratic personal belief. But the state, through a court-appointed guardian and the office of the state's attorney, succeeded in reducing that testimony to the statement of personal opinion. The examining attorneys also attempted to reduce the Pope's official declarations on the topic of extra-ordinary measures for life-support in hopeless cases to mere "clarifications" that lack the authority and force of judgments.

Speech-act theory, when applied to religious witnessing in

secular contexts such as the courtroom, thus opens several avenues for the sociological study of secularization. On the one hand, a plaintiff is allowed to "pray" for relief to the court, and witnesses are required to take an oath based on a religious text: clear signs that the origins of much courtroom procedure are to be found in a religious past. Indeed judges have been known, as in the Quinlan case, to refer to their deliberations as an act of "divining" the transcendent nature of justice. But, on the other hand, the constraints of a courtroom are such as to suppress any religious testimony that tries to make the world conform to the reality of the spoken word. Witnesses do not declare (judge, decide, evaluate, pronounce, announce, proclaim); only judges do. Nor can witnesses direct the responses of others, unlike the religious witness who calls for acts of commitment from the hearer. The rationalized nature of discourse in the courtroom severely limits any expression of feeling and requires that all statements satisfy rigorous rules of evidence. Constraints imposed by the context require witnesses to speak to questions addressed to them, to avoid statements unrelated to such directed testimony, and to connect logically their later statements with earlier ones, at the risk of being discredited if they fail to meet these constraints. The speech-acts of a courtroom fragment the unitary event of religious witness, allow witnesses to engage only in one specialized form of testimony, and entirely determine "who can say what" according to the person's occupancy of specific roles within the courtroom and judicial system. Bishops and laymen are required to observe the same restrictions on their speech-acts, so determined are the forms of speech permitted by the court.

In these proceedings, the judicial system weighs the traditional authority of the church and the charismatic authority of devoted laymen against the legal and more highly rationalized authority of the medical profession and of the state. The court, without citing the slightest shred of evidence in support of its final opinion, ultimately decided to leave the matter "to the common moral judgment of the community at large" as this would emerge from the deliberations of an "ethics committee." Only that common moral judgment will supply a justice that resolves the contradictions among these competing sources of legitimate control. Although the court itself could not articulate that common moral judgment, it continued to act as though it believed that widespread moral values and beliefs do, in fact, exist in the larger society. Indeed the court's belief that such a moral community continues to exist is an essential foundation in its attack on idiosyncratic religious belief.

The court's assertion that the larger society represents an authoritative moral community justifies the judicial constraints imposed on religious witness and preserves the ritual function of the court intact. But that ritual function acquires substance only if the courts can articulate the moral sentiments of the larger society: a step that the Supreme Court of New Jersey in this case left to the determinations of an "ethics committee" that would be called together for that purpose. The public ritual here lacks ethical substance while claiming the authority to reduce religious testimony to representations of personal opinion and conviction. Rituals that lack the substance of transcendent justice may eventually lose their function as well. In the long run, I suggest, the process of secularization undermines not only the credibility and authority of religion but of those institutions responsible for resolving the contradictory bases of legitimacy in the larger society.

Chapter 7

In the Matter of Maria Cueto and Raisa Nemikin: The Church's Lost Boundary

In a secularizing society that is marked with conflict over where to draw the boundary between the sacred and the secular, an exceptional burden is placed on the ritualistic aspects of the law to dramatize and mediate what Carl Friedrichs aptly calls "transcendent justice" (1970). Beyond the statement of facts and points of law, the court judiciously balances the visions vouchsafed to individuals and carried by particular groups or institutions with the vision that justifies the authority of the larger society. But the state's "clear and compelling interests" sometimes collide with certain values held sacred, such as life or property, or with certain rules of law, such as the Constitution, that enshrine sacred values, as sacred as liberty itself. A successful ritual will therefore dramatize certain values as sacred in such a way as to incorporate the best interests of the state with the deviant visions of recalcitrant witnesses, conscientious objectors, religious organizations, and communities whose social and economic life is inseparable from their religious beliefs.

In the case before us in this chapter, however, the court's ritual failed to articulate the principles that could reconcile personal convictions, communal loyalties, ecclesiastical interests, and the state's overriding interests in preserving life and property. The breakdown of the ritual was not manifest only in demonstrations by activists within and outside the courtroom. The prophetic silence of the two women was itself symbolic of ritual failure, as was an unprecedented personal statement of their attorney, moments before Judge Frankel signed the order for incarceration. When ritual fails, individuals and groups break the usual roles for testimony and speak for themselves outside the context of their institutional roles (Geertz 1973).

There is some evidence already to suggest that the failure of this judicial ritual to define and express transcendent justice in this case will stimulate the church to take up more seriously the difficult theological tasks of self-definition. One group within the Episcopal Church has already called upon the presiding bishop to support the necessary work of theological and ecclesiological interpretation of the church's nature and mission in what is admittedly a complex and difficult society. The church has yet to define its limits when these limits are indefinitely ramified through bureaucratic agencies and the lay ministry. The state, conversely, has yet to move beyond an *ad hoc* use of definitions of religion and functionalist perspectives to a clear legal theory of the First Amendment. What the state and church now do will serve to define their relationship to each other as one of hostility or of antagonistic co-operation in the work of defining the boundary of the sacred in a secularizing society. There are few boundaries more fateful for human dignity and social order.

The case that I will explore here concerns the right of the government to subpoena employees of the Episcopal Church. The government was seeking information on the whereabouts of Carlos Alberto Torres, a sometime member of the Episcopal Church's National Commission on Hispanic Affairs. Torres, along with the Puerto Rican National Liberation Front (FALN), had claimed credit for a bombing in New York City in which four customers of the Fraunces Tavern were killed and many others wounded. The two employees of the Episcopal Church, Maria Cueto and Raisa Nemikin, argued that they could not testify without violating the trust of the persons to whom they were ministering in the name of Christ and under the auspices of the Protestant Episcopal Church as lay ministers. The court, however, said that their right to the free exercise of religion was *not* being infringed by the government's desire to ask them three simple questions about Carlos Torres. The women went to jail for contempt of court rather than testify, but in going to jail they left a bitter trail of accusation within the Episcopal Church and of suspicion between church and state. The defendants accused the government of not acting in good faith, and of using the Grand Jury to harass the entire Spanish-speaking community. The government, in turn, argued that claims to religious freedom were irrelevant in this case, an argument that directly contradicted statements from a wide range of bishops, priests, and lay persons concerning these women's work. The case dramatizes the inadequacy of any judicial, commonsense, theological, or ecclesiastical definition of religion when the state wishes to draw for itself the line between the sacred and the secular.

In considering some of the details of this case, I will focus primarily on the problem of relevance. When, in fact, is religion relevant to the claims made by any plaintiff or defendant that the government should not intrude in his or her life? But *relevance* is only one of several questions that arise whenever the courts seek to draw the line between religion and the secular world. Even when religious claims are deemed judicially relevant, the courts must decide a second question. Who is *eligible* to make such a claim? In the case we will be discussing here (*In re Maria R. Cueto and Raisa Nemikin*), the two women were both employees of the Episcopal Church and officers of a National Commission chartered by the Episcopal Church to extend its ministry to Spanish-speaking communities. The dozens of letters and affidavits, submitted by church officials on behalf of these two women at various points in the litigation, all argued that the women were eligible to claim the protections of religion offered by the First Amendment because, in fact, they were officers of the church, engaged in "lay ministry," and required to hold in absolute confidence all information about their associations. Had the courts decided the question of contempt on the basis of these women's eligibility to assert First Amendment rights to the free exercise of religion, the courts would have had difficulty in finding the women ineligible.

The courts did not take these assertions seriously in this case because they defined *relevance*, rather than eligibility, as the primary issue. There was some disagreement even among the judges as to whether the women were engaged in social work or ministry, but the disagreement was less over whether they were eligible to claim constitutional protections of religion than whether religion was a relevant issue. Had the courts decided that religion was indeed at issue, the judges' internal differences over the definition of these women's activities as "social work" or church work would have required further adjudication. But the court eventually decided, when releasing the women from jail, that no "religious principles" were at stake. Besides being a judicial opinion, that decision was also a theological statement, and in the eyes of many church leaders the judges in this case were doing "bad theology."

There is a third question that arises once the courts have decided that religion is relevant or that the parties claiming First Amendment protections of religion are eligible to do so as believers, members, or officials of a particular religious body. That is the question of sincerity or authenticity. There was no question in the proceedings over Karen Quinlan's fate that her father, Joseph, was devoutly religious and sincere in expressing his beliefs to the court. In the recent case of the two Episcopalian church workers, however, there was evidently some question in the minds of at least one judge whether Cueto and Nemikin were acting in "good faith." The question is not surprising, since the courtroom was also the scene of dramatic sounds and gestures, and demonstrations were "orchestrated" on the courthouse steps. Judge Frankel, who cited the women for contempt, clearly found the legal testimony offered through their attorneys to be a Trojan horse for religious witnessing and political demonstrations. In the case of Cueto and Nemikin, arguments for their eventual release from custody emphasized the sincerity of the two women in this commitment to silence, despite the fact that their refusal to testify would justify further incarceration. It was an argument that may have expedited their release, although it did not prevent their incarceration for contempt of court.

There is still one other question that inevitably arises, once it is established that religion is relevant in a particular case, that a particular person or group is eligible to claim constitutional guarantees of the free exercise of religion and that these groups or persons are authentic. The fourth question is whether the state has a "clear and compelling" interest that overrides the most sincere and appropriate demands for religious freedom by persons entitled to make such demands. In the Quinlan case, for instance, the state found no such overriding interest, but in the case of a Jehovah's Witness who had refused a blood transfuction, the same court once had found the state's interest to be far clearer and more compelling. The Jehovah's Witness, however, was not irreversibly comatose and could look forward after treatment to a fruitful life. On the other hand, Karen Quinlan's tragedy minimized the state's interest in protecting life and allowed other interests to come into play. Thus the courts could authorize an "ethics committee" to make the decision that the courts found themselves unable to make. In the case that concerns us here, the state claimed an overriding interest in protecting life and property.

The case of the two employees of the Episcopal Church, Maria Cueto and Raisa Nemikin, revolves around the problem of the relevance of religious freedom. The litigation, the briefs, opinions, proceedings, affidavits, and exhibits illustrate and dramatize how the state may define the *relevance* of constitutional guarantees of religious freedom and therefore also the location of the wall separating church and state. Judge Frankel makes relevance, not eligibility, the issue in this statement to the lawyer for Mss Cueto and Nemikin:

Well look, I have indicated to you, Ms Fink that the position in this troublesome position that I thought I was required to take would have been the same if Ms Nemikin had been a Bishop of the Church. So the fact that Ms Cueto's position is thought to move closer to those who profess the religion does not seem to be of material significance.

But I could be wrong and I think you are entitled to make that record. (*In the Matter of Maria Cueto*, before Hon. Marvin E. Frankel, District Judge, New York, NY, 4, March 1977, 9.30 a.m., 77 Ct. Mis., p. 17)

Outside the context of the liturgy, I have been arguing, it is difficult for individuals to make claims that Caesar must take relatively seriously. Certainly Caesar can claim the authority to override even the promises and commands given in the context of the liturgy. But it is easier for the state to gainsay liturgical utterances when they occur in secular contexts, as they did in the case of the Berrigans' prophetic statements outside the Catonsville Selective Service Board. It is easier still for Caesar to remain unimpressed by the promises and understandings of family, however reinforced they are by the doctrine and discipline of the church; the plight of the Quinlan family comes obviously to mind. In this case (Cueto—Nemikin), the state chose not to take seriously the claims that the two employees of the church were defending confidences as sacred as those confided to the priest within the confessional. The employees' utterances were safeguarded, not by the liturgy or even the doctrine and discipline of the church, but only by the organizational self-understanding of a bureaucratized church recorded in memos, letters, and affidavits to the court. Utterances of this order, unfortunately, lack the resonance and authority of the liturgy and of the communicants' confession of a true faith.

The arguments for Mss Cueto and Nemikin display a pervasive confusion within the church concerning its own boundaries, and the same confusion reigns in the courts' several opinions concerning the work and ministry of the church's two employees. The Episcopal Church was alternately hospitable to the FBI and militant in defending its boundaries against federal inquisition. The church claimed that its agency, the National Commission on Hispanic Affairs, was bureaucratic in name only. According to one bishop, that agency was his right arm: as much an extension of the essence of the church, in other words, as the bishop's own office and ministry. The judges regarded the women as employees, however, noting that only one was an Episcopalian, although they could not state univocally that the women were employed in the work of the church rather than in social work. The court also seemed to waver between describing the women as sincere, though misguided in refusing to co-operate with the Grand Jury investigating FALN terrorism, or describing the two women as cloaking purely ethnic loyalties with a veneer of religious enthusiasm. Indeed outside the context of the liturgy, the character of the actors becomes problematical. It is especially problematical whether they are acting on their own or with the mind of the church, and whether therefore they speak with authority or only with personal convictions. What the liturgy makes unequivocally clear concerning the identity of corporate and individual actors remains to be established in the secular ritual of the court.

The secular ritual of the court, however, can fail as surely as any other ritual when the boundary between the religious and the political is not defined to the satisfaction of the participants. Geertz (1973: 161) tells the story of a "ritual that failed" precisely because the celebrant embodied both a political and religious identity. The ritual, a burial for a young boy, could not be performed during an impasse in which the father, obligated by civil law to accept the ministrations of the local magistrate, was hindered from doing so by his religious loyalties because the magistrate was a member of an opposing religious community. The impasse called for a resolution that was delayed until the father engaged in a personal testimony to his quandary: testimony quite uncharacteristic for that society. In the Cueto–Nemikin trial, the two women also maintained a long silence that remained unbroken, but at the end of the proceedings their lawyer called on the prosecuting attorney to speak out concerning his own Christian faith. It was, as the prosecuting attorney noted, a demand quite uncharacteristic of a judicial setting. When rituals do reach an impasse, however, individuals are likely to leave the protection of their roles in order to speak personally and to resolve the impasse with their own voice and vision.

The Case: A Brief Summary

The main source of contention in this case thus has to do with the vague boundary between the sacred and the secular. The question is whether the First Amendment guarantees of religious freedom are relevant to the defendants' case. One judge, Judge Pierce, had argued that the religious issue was not relevant, since the women were doing social work rather than acting as priests, and were not engaged in confidential, priest—penitent relationships either with their bishops or with their Spanish-speaking constituents. Even if they were doing religious work, Judge Pierce stated, the government's actions "do not appear to place any recognizable burden on the free exercise of any religious rights" (opinion of the Honorable Lawrence W. Pierce, US District Judge, 4 February 1977). Of course, the bishops (other than Presiding Bishop Allin) who came to the defense of these women's lay ministry thought that the freedom of religion was indeed relevant because of the women's position and function in the program of the church. But Judge Frankel argued that, regardless of whether these particular women are entitled to constitutional protections by virtue of their ministries, the protections of the free exercise of religion were not relevant because that exercise was not imperilled by a few simple questions regarding the whereabouts of an alleged terrorist.

Even the judge who eventually ordered the release of these two women from jail shortly before the end of the Grand Jury's session reiterated the courts' notion that religion is irrelevant to their claim. Judge Carter puts it bluntly:

Here we are being asked to accept movants' view that to force them to give what seems to be innocuous enough testimony is to require them to breach their religious vows, whereas Judge Pierce's decision makes clear, there are in actuality no religious principles at stake. Perhaps all that is being articulated and acted upon by the contemnors is a commonplace view among the 'outs' in a social system — here the Hispanic poor among whom the movants work — that one is being a traitor to one's group if she co-operates with law enforcement officials. (Opinion, District Judge Carter, *In re Maria Cueto and Raisa Nemikin*, New York, NY, 23 January 1978, pp. 15—16)

It is worth dwelling on this point for a moment to discern the way in which a district judge is acting both from theological and sociological perspectives to determine the relevance of religious issues to a point of law.

The judge had before him affidavits signed by a wide range of church officials who claimed that the work done by Cueto and Nemikin is indeed the work of the church, that trust and privacy are essential to that work, and that constitutional guarantees to the free exercise of religion apply in this case without question. The issue is therefore not initially whether Nemikin and Cueto are sincere in their beliefs or eligible for constitutional protection by virtue of their ecclesiastical membership or employment (although at various points the assistant US attorney raised questions about their eligibility). The court's primary concern was with the relevance of religion *per se* to the "movants' " several motions to quash subpoenae, to avoid contempt citations and imprisonment, and to be released from jail. Judge Pierce's notion of their activities as social workers, and Judge Frankel's analogy between the terrorist's bombing and a murder in a cathedral that the two women may have noticed, clearly set religion aside as a possible basis for defense. But to make this decision stick in the face of affidavits and of less authoritative, but no less convinced, letters from various individuals on the issue is to involve the courts in determining — as Judge Carter put it — that "no religious principles are at stake." That is a theological, as well as a judicial opinion.

Oddly enough, Judge Carter's opinion is very much like a sociological perspective in reducing religious ideas or values to the expression of merely social realities and experience. In this case the judicial reduction of religion occurs when Judge Carter finds ethnic loyalties underlying the religious views and commitments of Cueto and Nemikin. But there is ample disagreement among sociologists on *how far* one can reduce religion to a mere expression or projection of "underlying" social realities. Some sociologists would argue that these communal loyalties are themselves sacred, in a strict sense of that term, so that religious symbols are the proper expression of them. Other sociologists would appear to agree with Judge Carter that religion in a secular society often provides a "halo" effect for traditional, communal relationships. Religion is therefore "ersatz," merely a substitute for the real thing. Judge Carter was not accepting any substitutes. Nor was Judge Carter impressed by the authority of the church to define the boundary between the sacred and the secular.

THE COURT: The unfortunate thing is that the judges make the decision, not the bishops, about where the line [between the religious and the secular . . .] is drawn, and several judges in this court have made that decision.

(*In re Maria Cueto and Raisa Nemikin*, before Hon. Robert L. Carter, District Court Judge, New York, NY, 5 December 1977, M11—188 transcript, p. 42, 1111—25)

The process of secularization occurs in such unheralded events as judges assign responsibility for separating the sacred and the secular. Judge Carter heard a number of arguments for releasing the women from jail prior to the end of the Grand Jury. The arguments began by saying that the lawyers would not again raise the issue of First Amendment protections for the free expression of religion, but that religious issues underlay the women's sustained refusal to testify. Judge Carter then proceeded to try to make distinctions that would enable the court to discern where the religious issues entered in and where secular concerns took over. For instance, he asked whether the women's belief that they represent the church is "personal" or "religious." He went on to ask whether that belief would lead them to withhold *all* information from a Grand Jury or only certain information. Finally he tried to determine whether the argument applied to all persons under religious orders or only to certain echelons in the churches. The arguments *for* the women clearly tended to include the widest category of lay ministers and of information under the rubric "religion." In the following passage the judge begins to boggle at extending the coverage of the law to so broad a segment of the church and to such a wide range of information.

THE COURT: I find it hard to really assess, unless you are contending, and I gather that the amicus curiae are, that because of their mission any information in regard to any matter in regard to this — what is the name?

MISS FINK: The National Commission on Hispanic Affairs.

THE COURT: — that any matter in regard to the National Commission on Hispanic Affairs is within the realm of their belief. Is that what you are arguing?

MISS FINK: We are contending that anything that has to do with the National Commission on Hispanic Affairs —

THE COURT: Anything?

MISS FINK: Anything within their work in the church, right, they refuse to testify about.

As a sociologist interested in tracing the process of secularization, I find these court records illuminating precisely because they document the actions by which the problematic boundary between the sacred and the secular is defined, obscured, and clarified once again in a three-sided conflict between various groups, the state, and the church. Here we see a fragment of a much more complex series of exchanges between the state and the Spanish-speaking community, in which the church attempts to set up sacred barriers between the state and the Spanish-speaking community beyond which the state cannot legitimately cross in its pursuit of Puerto Rican liberationists. At first, the FBI asked Mss Cueto and Nemikin relatively narrow questions, to which they responded with some relevant information. But when the Grand Jury subpoena demanded far more information about associations within the Hispanic Commission, the two women refused to testify further and sought the protections afforded the exercise of religion by the First Amendment. As the state widened its inquiry, so the women broadened their definition of what is included within religious ministry, in order to protect their relationship to the Spanish-speaking community. Various judges in the case tried to reassure Cueto and Nemikin that the assistant US attorney was conducting a narrowly focussed inquiry into the facts associated with a terrorist bombing, but the women feared a broad intrusion into their community. The church put its body on the line between the state and a vulnerable ethnic group in the hope that its extended body would define the location of the constitutional barrier between state and church. But the church was risking a bureaucratic extension of its ministry that seemed to some actors and to the state itself less like the church's body than, say, the church's footprints. The church, in the eyes of the state, had at least overextended itself, with the result that neither the ethnic group nor the religious organization in this case succeeded in defining its boundaries as sacred.

In this case the courts acted as agents of secularization in several ways. They defined religion narrowly enough to exclude both the stores of information filed in church bureaucracies and also many of the actions of its employees. The court listened to arguments that the sincerity of Cueto's and Nemikin's religious convictions reinforced their refusal to testify in order for the court to assess the utility of further incarceration, but in so doing the court reduced religion to a manifestation of sincerity: a reduction which makes religion "personal" rather than authoritative and hence less pertinent to determining the range of freedoms protected by the Constitution. As we have seen, furthermore, the courts reduced religion to a symbolic expression of ethnic sentiments and loyalties after the fashion of some sociologists who have argued that religion in a secular world only provides a halo for these traditional social ties.

The Church's Confusion Concerning its own Boundaries

The church failed to define its boundaries as sacred partly because it was not entirely clear or consistent about where those boundaries lie. Presiding Bishop Allin noted that he, at least, was not refusing to comply with the Grand Jury, while another bishop, Paul Moore of New York, argued that the state was tampering with the arm of his episcopate: an arm reaching out through the Hispanic Commission to the Spanish-speaking community. The church does not seem to know how seriously to take its own forms of bureaucracy: one bishop saying that it has nothing to hide and welcoming official inspection of church files, another bishop saying that the divulging of information would be just as damaging to the church's ministry as would be the sharing of confidences confessed to a priest. The sharing of such confidences thus would cut the heart out of the Body of Christ, whether they were originally entrusted to lay ministers or to the ordained clergy.

The imprecision in the church's thinking about its boundaries may be due in part to the church's language, which makes heavy use of "natural symbols" of the body (cf. Douglas 1970). Bishop Robert DeWitt, in an editorial in *The Witness* (March 1977), uses such imagery when he speaks of "the penetration" into a diocese (New York) made possible when the presiding bishop or his agents gave the FBI "such unwarranted free access to the private files of one of its program units." Indeed, as Bishop DeWitt notes, there are other church "bodies" that might find their integrity similarly threatened by an administration willing "to collaborate with the FBI." Church members and officers all over the country, who knew of the Hispanic Commission's work, agreed that the church surrendered, along with the files, its claim to the trust of a frightened and desperate minority that had begun to believe that the Episcopal Church was willing to cast its earthly lot with them. The Episcopal Church was thus in conflict not only with a state, which it saw abusing its powers in order to intimidate an ethnic minority, but with its highest officers who had allowed the "body" of the church to be penetrated and to lose its life-blood, that is, the trust that enables its several structures to function in ministry. But is an administrative unit identical to an organ of the body in such a literal sense? Or is this churchly literalism only a defense against the letter of the law?

There seems to have been no question *within the church* regarding the personal integrity of the two jailed women who had been employed by the church to build up the Spanish-speaking community's strength and hope. There seems to be no question that these women were engaged in the ministry of the church, that the ministry requires confidentiality and freedom from political intrusion, that the women themselves were officials of the church as well as "employees," and that the church therefore has a right to see *in them* an embodiment of the church's ministry. Sometimes natural symbols, drawn from the body, make sense even when applied to administrative units created by legislative action within the church. But the bureaucratic extension of the church at least makes the use of natural symbols problematical in specific cases. In sociological terms, the problem is to determine how far the charisma of the institutional church can be diffused throughout its organizational units and functions.

The letters from clergy and laity to the prisoners or the affidavits to the court on their behalf from church workers throughout the country exhibited the church's own vagueness about its boundaries. For instance, a letter from an Episcopal clergyman to the two women when they were in jail for contempt was placed as an exhibit to support a plea to the court to end their imprisonment. He wrote:

I do feel some special closeness to your imprisonment, in that I have been jailed for much briefer periods for *essentially political activity* on two previous occasions.

The first paragraph of the letter had placed their imprisonment in a theological context, whereas the second paragraph referred to political activity, the third paragraph to a prisoner in World War II, and the fourth paragraph to the women's "struggle for freedom." A judge would be entitled to wonder about where the author of that letter himself drew the line between religion and the secular or even whether that clergyman could draw the line at all. In another exhibit, designed to document the women's unswerving commitment to remain silent before a Grand Jury, appears Raisa Nemikin's final statement before going to jail. The only reference to religious matters is a critical comment on "Bishop Allin and his administration (who) have allowed the Church to become an unwitting pawn in the FBI's illegal investigation of the Puerto Rican Independence Movement and the Hispanic Community" (*The Witness* no date). In the eyes of one Episcopal observer, however, the women were on the *via dolorosa*. According to a quotation in the same excerpt from *The Witness* on exhibit to the court, that observer saw the women's story as a passion narrative. From the point of view of Raisa Nemikin, however, the story narrates the odyssey of the Puerto Rican Independence Movement. It is not surprising that a judge would therefore reduce the women's religious convictions to a symbolic expression of ethnic loyalties. That judge could find support for this reductionism in another exhibit — a letter from a supervising officer of the Episcopal Church that states:

. . . they will never do anything that they see as in anyway a threat to their loyalty to their people, or, and perhaps more important, anything that might raise questions among the Hispanic people about that loyalty. (Carman St J. Hunter, 29 October, 1977)

It is clear that when the church speaks about the sacredness of its precincts, activities, and commitments, it uses language that is often ambiguous and open to contrary interpretation. The church, it appears, does not itself draw a clear boundary between the sacred and the secular.

The church's boundaries are understandably vague in view of the historic ambiguity of the church as both a sacred and secular reality. It is not enough simply to say that the state in this case was acting out an invitation extended to the FBI by an overly compliant presiding bishop or that the Grand Jury is simply a tool used by law enforcement agencies to pry open the unwilling mouths of potential witnesses. Indeed the presiding bishop may have betrayed the confidences and trust of those to whom the church ministers, just as the Grand Jury may indeed have been subverted by official interests. But surely the church is aware of similar patterns of disagreement between the state and a wide range of groups, organizations, and individuals over where to locate the boundary between the sacred and the secular. Never entirely clear, that boundary has been probed ever since Jesus was asked to decide whether a particular coin belonged to God or to Caesar. Although often intentionally obscured by Christians, that boundary has seldom been more problematical in American society than at the present time. The problem cannot be solved by finding villains in high places, so long as the church itself knows no boundaries.

In view of the churches' vagueness regarding their boundaries, it is not surprising that the judges in the case tended to oversimplify the situation. One rather neat oversimplification appears in an analogy drawn by Judge Frankel of the US (Southern) District Court, who ordered Mss Cueto and Nemikin incarcerated following his finding that they were in contempt of court for refusing to testify before the Grand Jury. He argued:

. . . if a priest were asked did he see a murder in his cathedral and this was asked wildly and irresponsibly it might be an invasion of First Amendment freedoms that a judge ought to be sensitive to, but if a judge then looked at the materials on which the prosecutor swore he was asking the questions and it looked as though somebody had indeed killed somebody in the cathedral and the priest had indeed possibly seen it, then I don't think anybody's religion is hurt or anybody's freedom is impaired if the priest under oath says yes or no, he did or did not see the murder. (Quoted in Government's Memordanum of Law, Robert Fiske, Jr, by Thomas E. Engle, Assistant US Attorney, *In re Maria T. Cueto and Raisa Nemikin*, Contemnors, Cr. Misc., p. 4)

Judge Frankel here clearly has in mind the narrow focus of a limited judicial inquiry that safeguards the religious liberties of all concerned. He oversimplifies, however, since he fails to note the symbolic and strategic importance to the church of turning over *anything* from the church's sacred precincts to the state. A few centuries ago certain heretics were so named precisely because they "gave over" sacred symbols to the state. What goes on in the cathedral, or in the confessional, or a private conversation cannot be surrendered without turning sacraments into something profane because they are open to inspection.

The question is where to locate the cathedral: that is, where to draw the boundaries around the sacred precincts. It is a question the churches must answer for themselves, regardless of the willingness of the courts to help them locate their boundaries. Remembering that the Sabbath was made for man, and that all human concerns therefore belong to the Sabbath day of the Lord, the church refuses to draw a line that excludes from the sacred any basic human concern. But the Christian faith does not hold unduly sacred even the office of the bishop, let alone the office of the church's administrative agencies. In the eyes of the Christian faith neither bishops nor ethnic groups need to be taken more seriously than the widows or orphans of bombing victims. Even the representatives of the state, on occasion, may be doing the work of the Lord. The church recognizes as Lord a person who was the victim of official terrorism by the state and of churchly cowardice: no doubt about that. But the same person also rejected the terrorist proclivities of some of his own disciples and cleanly broke off with the ethnic loyalties of his own community. That is transcendence.

The church accused the courts of doing "bad theology" in stating that Mss Cueto and Nemikin were social workers rather than ministers of the church, but the church itself lacks a theology adequate to its ramification through extensive offices and agencies. One of the clergy, for instance, argued that the sacred veil (guarding the secrets of the temple) had been torn by the intrusion of the FBI into the records of the church pertaining to the National Commission on Hispanic Affairs. The same person spoke of that agency as an "organ" of the church: a metaphor clearly derived from the symbolism of the body. But there was little official comment to suggest that the Puerto Rican liberationists and their terrorist activities also broke the veil of the church. Is the intrusion of the FBI in the pursuit of terrorists morally more repugnant than the covert terrorism of the FALN carried out under the partial shield of a quasi-ecclesiastical agency? If the church had stated without hesitation that it grieved over its indirect and tenuous responsibility for the deaths of four persons, and the wounding of many others, in a bombing attack on Fraunces Tavern, its effort to draw sacred boundaries around the work and membership of the Hispanic Commission might have been more convincing.

The church uses organicist imagery to define the boundaries of the sacred in a highly bureaucratized religious organization. Bishop Moore's statement, that the Commission is his arm and must therefore be treated with the same respect as the person and ministry of the bishop himself, identifies the center of the church, located symbolically in the office of the bishop, with its organizational periphery. In the liturgy, center and periphery are united in one corporate act. But on the church's periphery are a wide range of activities and an assortment of agencies that mix the church's ideals with the interests of particular constituents. In the Hispanic Commission the church's ideals were thoroughly mixed with the secular concerns of an ethnic community and with the political concerns of a liberation movement. If the church does not draw the line between the sacred and the secular in such situations the state will take the responsibility for doing so. Where the liturgy fails to define boundaries, secular rituals will intervene.

The church's theology, then, must determine how far the charisma of office and sacrament can be dispersed through the complex organizational apparatus of a modern and bureaucratized denomination. Reformation efforts to define the boundaries between the visible and the invisible church may be either of little use or of great interest in the church's current situation. In any event the church does not lack theological resources for defining its situation or for deciding, in the last analysis, to refuse to define its boundaries even if such ambiguity forces the hand of the state. It is clear, in any event, that the churches will not be able to have it both ways: to rejoice in an ambiguous boundary between the sacred and the secular while insisting that the state keep its hands off ecclesiastical agencies. If the church's theology does not help to define its boundaries, surely the state will write its own "bad" theology.

The church's argument that literally "anything" in its files pertaining to the Hispanic Commission is privileged with the protections accorded the exercise of religion reflects what some social anthropologists call a "totalistic" orientation. Totalism takes an "all or nothing" stance toward the social world. Either everything makes sense or nothing is meaningful. All the Commission's activities are sacred, according to the totalist, or none of them are. Totalism also tends to draw overly sharp boundaries and so tends to make what appear to be arbitrary exclusions. On the one hand, the church argues that anything in its files pertaining to the Hispanic Commission is privileged because it carries on the work of the church through lay ministry. On the other hand, the church fails to give the same recognition as a lay minister to an adult Episcopalian who happens in this case to be the prosecuting attorney. The paradox was not lost on the assistant US attorney, who found that many, perhaps most, of the members of the Hispanic Commission were not members of the church, although the church closely defended any information regarding their identity and activities. Some coins, as the early church once understood, belong clearly neither to God nor to Caesar. If the church is to be effective in the world it will need to move beyond totalism to a stance in which some of its possessions are permeated with both sacred and secular significance and are therefore legitimately the media for exchange with the world. But the church is not likely to define these areas of ambiguous significance until it is far clearer on where its essential boundaries lie. What does it mean that Maria Cueto and Thomas Engel, the "contemnor" and the "prosecuting attorney" in this case, have shared a common sacramental cup? When the church lives out the implications of this central fact in its life, it will have something clear to say to its own members and to the state concerning their respective responsibilities.

The Confusion of the State: Broad Views and Narrow Constructions

The state, all things considered, shares many of the church's dilemmas and can afford to be tolerant of considerable ambiguity even when the state has a "clear and compelling" interest at stake. If the church lacks thorough knowledge and control over the actions of persons associated with its many agencies, so also does the Department of Justice. A consistent theme in the case involving Mss Cueto and Nemikin focussed on the threatening interrogation by the FBI, in which the FBI used the possibility of a subpoena from the Grand Jury to persuade the women to talk. Having been alarmed by the threat of a Grand Jury subpoena that might demand the widest possible range of information about the Hispanic Commission, it is understandable that the church's employees were unwilling to believe that the Grand Jury would ask only the three carefully worded and narrowly focussed questions offered by the assistant US attorney. In this particular case, Judge Frankel, an expert on the history of grand juries and the need for their reform, was convinced that the Grand Jury was a responsible extension of the court, but the worst damage to the church's confidence in the court had already been done before the case came before him as a question of civil contempt. The Episcopal Church has now joined the groups pressing for reform of the Grand Jury, and there is some evidence already that effective reform is in progress for some federal jurisdictions.

The state lacks a definition of religion as clear and compelling as the state's awareness of its own interests. In some cases, the state appears to borrow a social scientific perspective, "functionalism," to determine when an individual or group is legitimately claiming constitutional protections for the free exercise of religion. The US Supreme Court has protected the secondary educational practice of the Amish as a functional necessity to the Amish who in this way train the young to take on responsible adult roles in their religious community. The same court has found that philosophical or ethical beliefs, that have the same centrality and functional importance in the life of an individual as more conventional or orthodox religious beliefs, can legitimate a person's claim to be a conscientious objector. Although these beliefs would lack the traditional substance of religion, they possess the functions of religion and thus entitle the individual to the protections offered by the Constitution to the free exercise of religion.

Like sociologists who work with functionalist notions of religion, the courts have adopted rather inclusive definitions in accepting such individualistic belief-systems as the functional equivalents of religion. But when the courts have wished to apply a stricter construction of First Amendment protections they have relied on a less inclusive, substantive notion of religion. Thus in its prosecution of Mss Cueto and Nemikin the state argued that the women were not part of the priestly or sacerdotal aspect of the church, just as Judge Frankel relied on the analogy of a priest who might have noticed some extraneous homicidal activity in his cathedral. Narrow constructions of the First Amendment are more easily based on relatively narrow definitions of religion. It appears that the state abandons the more generous perspectives of functionalism when it perceives a danger to its own clear and compelling interests.

The courts are fostering the process of secularization when they further restrict the activities and areas of social life that carry religious significance. In prosecuting the two female employees of the Episcopal Church, the courts adopted a restrictive view of religion that removed the aura of sanctity from ethnic loyalties, from the trust and privacy established through the alliance of the church with the Spanish-speaking community, and from the conception of lay ministry as the functional equivalent of priesthood. Of course, the Episcopal Church may yet succeed in sacralizing these activities and relationships, but in the meantime they have been deprived of the halo that sets them apart from ordinary community organization and social action. While the opinion of the court may not yet represent the consensus or common sense of the society at large, it will doubtless have an effect on common-sense notions of the substance and function of religion in American society.

In addition to fostering the process of secularization, of course, the courts may simply be recognizing that certain areas of social life have already been "disenchanted." Social action is social action, regardless of the motives and principles of the persons engaging in it, just as ethnic loyalties are just that, regardless of how sacred they are to Spanish-speaking persons and integral to the church's expanded notion of its own boundaries and role in American society. In periods like the 1950s, in which religion is recognized to have had a major role in defining and supporting an American consensus on basic values, the courts were inclined to define Americans as a "religious people" and to take a sympathetic view of functional equivalents to conventional or orthodox religion. But in the current period, in which fissures in American society have cracked the surface of consensus, the courts may be far less inclined to entertain functionalist arguments and to use broad notions of religion.

From a sociological viewpoint, then, it is understandable but ironic that the National Council of Churches would use functionalist arguments in its *amicus curiae* brief urging the court to release the two church workers from prison. The National Council of Churches argues, first of all, that the mission of the churches is to bring to the disadvantaged "the word of Christ and, at the same time, the knowledge and skills necessary to cope with an increasingly difficult and complex society" (motion and memorandum of the National Council of the Churches of Christ in the United States of America in support of contemnors' motion for release, Cahill Gordon and Reindel, p. 4). It is understandable that the church would use this functionalist defense in view of the long-standing Protestant belief that faith is conducive to democratic institutions and that these institutions in turn edify the individual and exemplify the fundamental beliefs and values of the Christian faith. This religious functionalism underlies the National Council's further assertion that interference by the state with the social ministry of the churches will be "to the detriment of both the spiritual and the temporal well-being of the Nation" (ibid.: 4). This statement reflects the functionalist argument that religion generally serves to undergird the social fabric, to develop and sustain at least minimal levels of social trust, and to encourage the faith of potentially dissident minorities in the society's basic institutions.

It is inevitable that sociologists have had difficulty in testing these broad functionalist tenets, since the tenets are seldom stated in a way that permits direct comparative or historical testing. Functionalist arguments still support the ideologies of the churches, of intellectuals interested in religion, and of a dominant minority claiming to represent a consensus of American values. But ironically, these ideological claims do not seem to fit the facts of a "difficult and complex society." Those facts make it impossible to say with any precision where the functions of religion end and those of the secular world begin. The more complex the society, furthermore, the less indispensable are the functions of religion, as other institutions provide education, welfare, and wisdom to the population. The more difficult the society, indeed, the less confidence one can have that the consequences of religious action will be the ones intended. It is doubtful, to say the least, that the Episcopal Church intended to aid and abet a terrorist organization in developing its own ties to the Spanish-speaking community. Only within the confines of the liturgy, in fact, can one say with authority what is intended and what indeed has been concluded. Outside the liturgy, there is no guarantee that what is said will be done, and that what is done will be properly understood. It is therefore left to secular rituals to establish the motives and assign responsibility for actions undertaken from a religious motive outside the confines of the liturgy. Where the actors choose silence rather than to speak within the constraints of a secular Grand Jury, they face inquiry not only from the Grand Jury then in session but from any other that should be constituted to pursue the facts in the case. In that sense, this "trial" is not yet over.

Chapter 8

From Signs to Symbols: The Inner Secularization of Prophetic Speech within the Religious Community

Secularization, Metaphor, and Literalism

In the process of secularization churches are often defeated by their own success. In the span of almost two thousand years, Christian culture has succeeded in convincing the West to take speech very seriously indeed. For instance, the political system in Western democracies is legitimated by words: perhaps by a constitutional text, or by promises and pledges, or simply by citizens who vote "yea" or "nay." Scientists similarly gain credit because they know what they are talking about and because their predictions can be verified. Judges are taken seriously because their words elaborate and specify the meaning of other words that provide a body of precedent in the judiciary. Academics give and receive academic credit for following the rules for speech in a given field. Scientists must provide clear measures for words and follow the rules for logical speech, whereas poets have license to follow somewhat less rigid rules for language. Individuals are given and receive financial credit largely on the basis of their word, which among certain socio-economic classes is as good as gold. There is no doubt that the dynamism of Western societies owes much to the process in which the church's seriousness about words has been generalized to such other spheres as science, education, politics, and the law. In the process "the word" is "established" in ways that are reminiscent of these early Christian instructions to believers: ". . . in the mouth of

two or three witnesses, every word shall be established"
(Matthew: 18:16).

The success of the Christian tradition has been bought
with a price, however, that limits the capacity of religious
language to transform institutions and everyday life. The
transforming capacity of religious language is still evident in
a liturgical context, where single people are pronounced
married, children are given new names and a new community,
and sinners are called to repentence. But outside the liturgical
context the vocabulary of the church often falls on skeptical
ears. In academic or judicial contexts, we have seen that
religious langauge is subjected to tests of logical rigor and
empirical accuracy. Academics test the relation of religious
symbols to actual facts, to events, or to other words: a test
often applied by Christian scholars as well as by secular
academics.

When religious words are taken out of their sacred context,
they seem to be metaphors for something else. When Jimmy
Carter, for instance, speaks of himself as a born-again Christian,
a phrase that has the power to draw people together within a
community of shared hope and faith, it is received with less
charity than suspicion in the larger society. Religious language
tends to slip outside the careful institutional boundaries that
have been created after several centuries of violent, political,
or merely judicial conflict. But in secular contexts such as
the court, religious language is subjected to rules that make
sharp distinctions between literal and metaphorical truth, as
we have seen in the trials of the Catonsville Nine and in the
court's treatment of Joseph Quinlan's testimony. Those rules
are both made and applied by secular elites that have learned
much from the clergy about how to credit and discredit a
person's speech.

The process of secularization therefore dissolves the powerful speech of the religious community, in which the same
words are both sign and symbol, into two distinct vocabularies
and rules for speaking. One, in which words are taken literally,
is a vocabulary of symbols that obeys rules of relevance and
reliability in secular courts and classrooms. The other is a

liturgical language that creates, as I have already argued in earlier chapters, a community of common faith and hope. Between the two lie metaphors that may evoke common loyalties and hopes on occasions, but metaphors are often slippery, however evocative they may be of human emotions, and they often appear to the critical eye as outworn and in need of refreshment. Whether it is a literary critic refurbishing a metaphor from a sermon by John Donne (cf. Smith 1974), or a judge who dispenses with the metaphors of a devout Christian, religious speech in secular contexts is vulnerable to secular rules for language. It is hardly surprising that religious movements, at least in their early and most vulnerable periods, have strict rules against casting verbal pearls before swine. The New Testament community was reminded that their founder chose to speak so that outsiders might hear without understanding, while those with faith might hear and also learn to see what was happening in their midst. But the founder of the community, like Mss Cueto and Nemikin, also employed silence in order to avoid verbal traps and secular translations.

I do not mean to imply, however, that the churches themselves transcend the secularizing split between signs and symbols: quite the opposite, in fact, is the thesis of this chapter. The Protestant clergy range over a long continuum from the literalists to those who allow themselves several degrees of freedom in interpreting Christian tenets in modern contexts (cf. Hadden 1976). Many fundamentalists insist on a strict literalism in interpreting biblical texts. Their critics, however, might well accuse the literalists of reducing the Bible to a fetish: a linguistic substitute for the authentic speech that conveys both sign and symbol in a single proclamation, pronouncement, or liturgical utterance.

Mary Douglas, in her anthropological study of language and religion, has found fault with the English Catholic episcopate for reducing liturgical formulae not to literalisms but to mere metaphors for "togetherness": "The mystery of the Eucharist is too dazzlingly magical for their impoverished symbolic perception" (1970; 1973: 72). When language fails to unite symbols with signs those with a more secularized view of the tradition turn its signs into metaphoric symbols for social experience. Relatively few insist with Mary Douglas on the original, prophetic, and therefore transforming powers of religious speech. It is perhaps surprising that even theologians will explain the meaning of theology and ritual in metaphoric terms: but I suspect that even a superficial glance at contemporary American theology will discover several instances of theological reasoning in which specific theological positions are justified as metaphors for the complexities of an urban world or for the open-ended aspects of social life. But symbols and signs, when used together, form a code that "unites speakers to kin and community" (ibid.).

Once words or phrases that combine the functions of symbol and sign in one expression are used out of their sacred context, they are vulnerable to criticism as *"mere metaphor,"* and they are vulnerable to powerful contrary assertions as to what words really mean. Take, for example, Charles Williams's statement about grace: "The thing we call 'grace' is here and there and gone and back . . . It is a kind of life, and in that life *we are for a moment no more ourselves"* (1956: 101; emphasis added). How easy it would be for a critical sociologist to note the resemblance between grace and alienation and to claim that here again religion makes a virtue of self-estrangement through metaphors. The conflict between religion and a critical perspective is quite clear at this point. Outside a sacred context the term "grace" may simply seem to be a metaphor for self-estrangement. (Whether it is merely such a metaphor depends on one's commitments to a religious or secular community and to their respective world-views.) But the difference is not merely verbal. The state in this country as well as in Russia is not above deciding that a political dissident is "alienated" rather than genuinely religious. The tyranny of the state is one clear alternative, therefore, to living openly with the ambiguities raised by sacred words in secular contexts.

The use of religious metaphor gives several degrees of freedom to the user: a point not lost on Caesar and his representatives. Like Joseph Quinlan, the father whose daughter lay in an irreversible coma, one may go to court to demonstrate that, in a metaphorical sense that is intelligible within the Catholic tradition, one's daughter is dead, but one may also be required to change one's pleas to conform to the more stringent terminologies of the legal and medical professions. In the passage from which I quoted Charles Williams on grace, he also notes that grace may "redeem us from a too specialized imprisonment in a terminology," and from "the tyranny of special forms of words" (1956: 101). Of course, these verbal tyrannies are imposed not only by the state and by secular occupations, but by religious communities that seek to constrain the freedom of individuals to make their own sense of things. Not all the literalists who attack metaphorical uses of religious language are therefore members of fundamentalist churches. Some literalists engage in the revision of prayer books and in contemporary translations of Scripture. But here we are concerned with the justices who occupy important seats on federal benches, from which they define with authority such terms as religion, the sacred, and ministry. The judicial system has an apparent antipathy to metaphors that allow individuals, on the basis of their sacred commitments, to step outside limited degrees of secular freedom.

Prophetic Speech in the Religious Community: The Roots of Secularization

The distinction between signs and symbols is, of course, vague and troublesome. I have been unable to locate a single, binding form of the distinction to which most writers will adhere. But I will start by assuming that signs are far more "condensed" than symbols, and that symbols are a kind of sign whose meaning is relatively clear, explicit, and limited. For instance, Perrin (1976: 30ff) notes that "not all signs are symbols," although, in his view, all symbols are signs. His distinction between the two focusses on the multiplicity, opaqueness, and openness of the "symbol." If a sign has one, and usually only one meaning, if that meaning is clear, and if that meaning can usually be exhausted, I will therefore call that sign a symbol. If that sign has several meanings that are not clear and are open to progressive interpretation through analogy or experience, I will call that sign simply a "sign." This usage, according to Perrin (1976: 29ff), resembles Wheelwright's distinction between steno-symbols and tensive symbols (the *latter* being equivalent to what I am here calling "signs"), and it is the reverse of Ricoeur's usage. Our usage also departs from the conventional English translation of the New Testament. When Jesus said that "an evil and adulterous generation seeketh after a sign," he meant that people wanted the clear, unambiguous, and easily understood indicators of meaning that I am here calling symbols. It is easier to trust symbols than to have faith in open-ended, ambiguous, and multi-faceted signs.

The distinction between signs and symbols is especially important if we are to understand how "prophetic" religious language loses its eventfulness in becoming secularized not only in contact with secular authorities but within the religious community itself. To begin with, prophetic religious language evokes a myth, a complex set of ideas and beliefs, rather than a clear and testable proposition. I will argue that, precisely because of its openness, ambiguity, and suggestiveness, prophetic religious language may speak the mind of a community of people: a mind that also speaks in common prayer, in creed, or even in liturgical exclamations of joy and praise. It is this communal dimension that contributes to the authority of the individual prophet. Prophetic language may be uttered in classrooms and courts, where it will be inappropriate and disruptive, or it may be segmented from everyday life and concentrated in moments of appropriate ceremony. In these liturgical contexts, the eventfulness of prophetic language depends on the responses of the faithful community. Liturgy guarantees the eventfulness of prophetic speech by limiting it to certain times and occasions. In secular contexts, however, prophetic speech may be extraordinarily disruptive. That is why, of course, classrooms and courts set stringent limits on the use of metaphor and the more powerful acts of speech.

In an eloquent passage from Perrin's discussion of the "Kingdom of God" in biblical literature, we can easily identify these fundamental characteristics of religious language. Speaking of the use of the "Kingdom of God" in Jewish and early Christian prayer, Perrin states:

. . . this is the use of the symbol in a prayer used regularly by the community *as a community.* The very fact that the symbol is being used in prayer by a whole group of people means that while it will always have evoked the myth of God active as king on behalf of his people, the form of the expectation expressed by the petition, "May he establish his Kingdom" will have varied from individual to individual, and no doubt that for many Jews living between the period of Pompey's "settlement" of them in 63 BC and the beginning of the Jewish revolt against Rome in 66 AD the prayer will have expressed the hope for the kind of dramatic irruption of God into human history that is the central theme of ancient Jewish (and Christian) apocalyptic. (1976: 29)

Here are two central characteristics of prophetic religious language. One is that individual understandings, hopes, fears, and perceptions are incorporated into the language of an entire community's faith. As corporate and personal testimony are fused in the act of witnessing to religious faith, witness becomes authoritative. The second is that the individual's faith tends to reduce the vague expectations of the myth of the Kingdom to expectations for events at specific times and places. An inner secularization of religion therefore begins in the reduction of corporate faith to individual expectations of "Lo, here" or "Lo, there."

Prophetic testimony is politically more seditious when it occurs in relatively less segmented and concentrated contexts than religious rituals. Perrin notes the similarities between the Kaddish prayer for the Kingdom of God and the two lines of the Lord's Prayer taught by Jesus to his disciples. The Kaddish prayer, after magnifying the divine name, states: "May he establish his kingdom in your lifetime . . ." whereas the prayer taught by Jesus states: "Hallowed be thy name; thy kingdom

come . . ." The latter is an immediate form of address to God
instead of to one's fellow believers in a ritual context. It is a
prayer to be uttered by the laity at any time; and it *can* be
uttered in any place. The age of prophecy, as the New Testament notices, is thus opened when religious testimony breaks
out of its confinement in ritual contexts, erupts into the
secular, and yet continues to lay hold of corporate faith and
an authoritative myth or theory.

We are now in a position to understand how prophetic
religious speech becomes secularized not only in the court or
classroom but within the religious community itself. Signs, as
I use the term, are particularly ambiguous. They have more
than one meaning, refer to a myth or theory, and can sym-
bolize an open-ended range of ideas or objects in the real
world. But with symbols the situation is entirely different.
One knows what is meant, no theory is necessarily involved,
and the relationship to an idea or thing is unique and one-to-
one. Now Perrin reminds us that religious language, and particularly signs such as the "Kingdom of God," can be used
either as symbols or signs (as steno- or tensive symbols, in his
usage). Properly understood as signs, Jesus's preaching and
instruction concerning the Kingdom are words that evoke
the entire myth of a divine King, active in the world for the
sake of His people: so active, in fact, that ordinary responses
and judgments no longer make sense. The only response
commensurate to such a proclamation is to stand in radical
judgment on all one's commonsense notions, to abandon the
effort to make sense of one's life as a whole, and to be ready
indeed for anything: even for the total disruption of what has
hitherto stood for personal or social reality. As symbols,
however, Jesus's statements are subject to several types of
misunderstanding that cause his sayings and proclamations to
pass the way of most secular utterances, that is, to become
irrelevant or to be transcended by more recent insights and
understandings.

One or two examples may help in understanding the transformation from prophetic sign to ordinary symbol. Perrin
notes that the New Testament records precisely such a shift

in usage. Jesus's own preaching of the Kingdom of God employs the usage of signs: an emphasis on words that evoke a myth, even convey the experience of the Kingdom in the telling of it, without permitting any exact interpretation of a *concept* of the Kingdom or any clear reference to persons or events as *examples* of the Kingdom in everyday life. The Kingdom is always at hand, and so enters the everyday world, but the Kingdom is never quite yet and so continually disrupts efforts to identify the Kingdom with particular times, places, persons, or events. Jesus himself apparently warned against efforts to reduce His preaching of this Kingdom to a quest for simple symbols:

The kingdom of God is not coming with signs to be observed; nor will they say, "Lo here it is!" or "There!" for behold, the kingdom of God is in the midst of you. (Luke 17:20–1; cf. Perrin 1976: 57–8)

But the early church apparently translated the preaching of the Kingdom-myth into a prophecy of the coming of the Son of Man and identified the historical Jesus as that saving figure. The preaching thus invited attention to specific occasions for the return of a specific person, that is, invited the very search for clear, univocal, and easily interpreted symbols that Jesus's own preaching sought to prevent. As such, this translation shared with Jewish apocalyptic a tendency to seek for such specific, clear, historical symbols as Enoch, the archangel Michael, or the abomination (Perrin 1976: 59).

When the ambiguous and multi-faceted meanings of the Kingdom-myth took on the more symbolic and therefore transparent and unambiguous meanings of early Christian apocalyptic, it was relatively easy for the Christian message to become fixed on specific times and places, to refer either positively or negatively to certain practices as consistent with a Christian's response to God's activity, and so to limit the uncertainty and disruption called for by Jesus's own preaching. Communal meals, such as the agape feast, became the exact expressions of divine presence in history: the sacramental meal itself being a way of saying successfully "Lo here, lo there" to the Kingdom, despite the early injunctions against such clear and exact references. The only remaining mystery is therefore one that focusses attention on the divine presence within the sacrament, but the major uncertainty concerning the active presence of God in history is removed as certainty derives from sacramental times and occasions. Sacraments, the church, and specific practices become part of the world. Their meanings and significance are established, sometimes in literal rather than metaphorical usage. The openness of the Scripture to new revelation is closed with the closing of the canon. The age of prophetic religious language, the revelatory speech of the early preaching, is over for the time being.

The early church "established the word" by specifying the religious meaning of practices, institutions, sacraments, and the allegorical interpretations of Jesus's sayings. The church thus reduced the uncertainty of the message at a relatively high cost — *the partial secularizing of the Gospel even within the religious community.* By "secularizing" I refer to the identifying of ambiguous and open-ended terms with referents and meanings that are so specific as to become outmoded and irrelevant in other contexts and at later times and occasions. Later times and occasions, for instance, have found the apocalyptic interpretations of the early preaching lacking in the dynamic and disruptive character of the original message, although biblical literalists continually try to update the interpretations of key passages to fit modern empires and emperors rather than Rome and the Caesars. But the updating is itself a sign of the irrelevance of a secularized Gospel too clearly and closely related to specific persons and events. The search for a specific secular context so changes the ambiguous and open-ended sign into a limited symbol as to create a need for new versions or at least for a repetition of the sacramental act. But, as I argued earlier in connection with liturgical changes (chapter 2), the demand for renewal cannot be met by improving on a liturgical text when prophetic speech has lost its original force and ambiguity. Texts, like allegorical interpretations, are secular in the sense that they pass away with the world because of devout efforts to fix their meaning and to close the otherwise open-ended character of prophetic religious speech.

To summarize, the paradox is simple enough. Efforts to establish the meaning of prophetic religious speech have the opposite effect from the one intended. Instead of making the meaning of a message permanent, that meaning takes on the specific interpretation and local references of everyday linguistic usage and so shares the transient nature of everyday life. Efforts to fix meaning in this way make it precarious.

Until signs become wholly separate from symbols, the choice between literal and metaphorical usage remains problematical. In prophetic religious speech, of course, it is not clear whether the sign in question should be taken literally or metaphorically. When Jesus preached the Kingdom, some of his hearers may have understood him to be speaking literally of a Kingdom that would come in fact: a literal truth about a new King on the old throne of David. Some of his hearers did take him literally and began planning accordingly for the overthrow of the Roman state. Others took him to be speaking metaphorically of a divine sovereignty whose presence, like the Spirit, is incalculable, powerful, and unavoidable: of a kingdom that may come, like a bridegroom, at any time, so that one can only be faithful who is always ready to respond. In that interpretation, the preaching of the Kingdom calls for a non-political response that suspends judgment indefinitely on all virtues and failings (as Jesus noted in cautioning his disciples not to separate too soon the weeds from the chaff in his Kingdom-parables). But the point is that the sign of the Kingdom, precisely because it *is* a sign rather than a symbol, is ambiguous and open-ended. It is therefore open to a variety of interpretations, some of which are literal. These literal interpretations, however, in turn make it possible to reduce the ambiguity of the sign by pointing to certain clear events or objects in the world as evidence of the fulfillment of the preaching, for example, to someone riding on a colt (as it was indeed prophesied the King would one day come to claim his throne). If literal interpretations prevail in a certain context, as they did in the early Christian community's sacramental and apocalyptic theologies, the separation of sign from symbol may become institutionalized. The word thus becomes established in a literal sense within a particular context. But in this development lies the first step of secularization, in which the open-ended, ambiguous, and powerful religious sign becomes of limited relevance and authority outside its proper context. In this sense those commentators are right who suggest that Christianity, like other religions, is in the long term defeated by its apparent secular successes.

Perrin provides an especially helpful example of this transformation in his essay on the interpretation of parables. Speaking of the parable of the Good Samaritan, he notes that it has a clear and telling point: that true acts of compassion are more likely to be found among heretics than among the clergy. The parable is meant to be "applied," not "interpreted" (Perrin 1976: 94): the telling of the parable being eventful in the sense of calling hearers to responsibility. But Perrin notes that in the early church, and later in the work of Augustine, the metaphor of the parable was transformed into an allegorical usage, in which the traveler is Adam, the priest and Levite are the "ministry of the Old Testament," and Jesus is the Good Samaritan (ibid.: 93). The open-endedness of the parable, in which the Good Samaritan is the one who, hearing the parable, responds by showing compassion and by being a neighbor, is reduced to a static text calling only for an allegorical interpretation in which each person in the narrative stands for one external entity, as the traveler — in Augustine's view — stands for Adam. The parable is no longer so condensed, because it is elaborated in terms of the myth of original sin and of the second Adam who brings healing. The allegorical elaboration of the parable here suggests that the context is no longer corporate or communal but esoteric and intellectual, although the framework is still mythological. Ambiguity and open-endedness, characteristic of signs, require the context of a religious community who intuitively understand the meaning of a sign and give it application in a variety of individual acts and decisions.

Table 8.1   Secularization of Religious Meaning

| | Mythical framework | |
Corporate beliefs and values	Present	Absent
Present	1 Prophecy	2 Metaphor
Absent	3 Allegory	4 Literalism

In table 8.1 I have illustrated these transformations of meaning in religious language. Prophetic utterance, which combines literal and metaphoric usage without distinguishing them, is replaced by other rules of religious discourse. In tracing the shift in the interpretation of the parables, I have moved downward from entry 1 to entry 3 in the table. This movement indicates that a parable becomes allegory after metaphoric usage reduces the force of the original utterance, and eventually the transformation makes a purely literal usage possible in the interpretation of parables. Of the two major background variables, one remains constant while the other changes in the transition from prophecy to allegory: the mythic framework staying intact while the corporate context is replaced by the personal context of the religious intellectual. We may now examine another shift in the rules governing the interpretation of religious language as we move from entry 1 horizontally to entry 2 on the right. In this part of the table (entry 2) parables become metaphors for discipleship: primarily texts to be used for the instruction of the faithful. They may have allegorical passages, but these allegorical passages are supplied as partial additions to the text, as in the case of the parables of the Sower and of the Good Samaritan. Perrin (1976: 102) notes that biblical critics largely argee in finding these allegorical verses in the parables to be later additions. The purpose of the allegorical additions, he notes (ibid.: 95ff), is largely "pedagogical." We may infer that the additions to the Sower reminded Christian disciples of the

impediments to Christian discipleship (thickets and hard rocks
in everyday life), while the additions to the parable of the
Good Samaritan inculcate neighborliness as a Christian virtue.
As I have noted, furthermore, the pedagogical purpose interprets the text as *a metaphor* rather than as a text with
allegorical or literal truths (cf. ibid.: 100—1). The transition
probably reflects the institutionalization of religious social-
ization for a second or third generation of members of the
Christian community.

The parables, as they are to be understood in entry 2 of
the table, are close to the original version in the preaching of
Jesus. In the original, the parable calls for an immediate
response from the hearer: not for discourse or discussion as
would befit a text in the Jewish wisdom literature or for
moralistic and allegorical interpretations, developing later
in the church, as I have pointed out in the discussion of entry
3. Perrin argues that the parables, at least by the time that
they have moved from oral to written format, are not myths,
fables, or popular folklore; hence I have located them outside
the range of myth in the table. But the parables do "assume a
whole spectrum of history, culture, and collective experience
shared by the parabolist and his hearers" (Perrin 1976: 104).
Thus I have included metaphoric parables within the corporate
framework of the self-understanding of a people. The corporate context accounts, as many have noted, for the realistic
aspect of the parables that draw primarily from scenes of
everyday Palestinian social life among peasants and the "petit
bourgeoisie" (cf. ibid.).

To summarize: I have been describing a process by which
prophetic utterances undergo changes that make them vulnerable to secularization. At the outset are utterances that are
powerful both because they evoke a myth and because they
express the corporate understanding of an entire people or
religious community. Certainly the exegetes are correct in
identifying the Kingdom of God as expressive of such a corporate understanding and of a powerful myth. The symbol of
the Kingdom has no single meaning, no clear referent, and
can be endlessly elaborated. Indeed it is still being clarified

and elaborated by contemporary exegetes after nearly two thousand years. But in that time, the condensed sign of the Kingdom of God, expressed first in parables, has been elaborated in several ways as the social context expands to include a second generation and, later, to add religious intellectuals not rooted in a single, local community. First, I have speculated, it is elaborated as a metaphor for something else. The parables of the Kingdom have been separated from their original context in the eschatological preaching of Jesus and have been elaborated as metaphors for general conceptions or values. The parable of the Good Samaritan is therefore interpreted by the early church as a moral lesson in neighborliness for disciples and converts or as a commentary on the law (cf. Perrin 1976: 10): not as a compelling sign that presents a claim on hearers to respond to the presence of the Kingdom in their midst, as the Samaritan once upon a time responded to the injured traveler. In the hands of later exegetes in the early church, the same parable became an allegory. Thus in the fourth century Augustine takes the parable from metaphor to an allegory for the original myth of Adam and for the Kingdom of the New Adam, the Son of Man. To borrow a useful distinction from Owen Barfield (1977: 34), the exegesis has moved from the "concomitant" meanings of metaphor (entry 2) to the "substituted" meanings of allegory (entry 3).

Barfield helps us to understand the transition from the original prophetic utterance to the final stage in the table, viz. the stage of literalism. As Barfield puts it: "We call a sentence 'literal' when it means what it affirms on the face of it, and nothing else" (1977: 32). It may surprise many observers to find in modern societies a flourishing movement of biblical literalism. But on this view such literalism is precisely what one would expect of a religious language that has lost its roots in a compelling myth or in the corporate values of an entire people. The words thus mean only what they say: no more and no less. The Kingdom of God is thus only a kingdom, just as the words say, and the parable becomes a story that tells how to be a "Good Samaritan."

The scheme that I have developed here touches on a problem that has periodically preoccupied historians of language and notably Owen Barfield. The last stage of this process is, so far as this speculative scheme is concerned, one of relatively literal meanings. I agree with Barfield (1977: 43) that "literalism is a late stage in a long-drawn-out historical process." Barfield's concern is to refute a positivist notion of language that sees a word like "wind" slowly adding spiritual connotations and meanings to its original and simple reference to movements of the air. One starts out with a corporate sense of the divine breath only to discover later that the winds of God may be just wind. But since I have not started with such notions of primal literalness or with materialist conceptions of history, I have no need here to engage in the polemic. It is nonetheless worthwhile to note in passing that my scheme agrees with Barfield's: that language originates in an ambiguous and open-ended mixture of mythic and communal meanings rather than in the simple grunts of the human animal or with everyday notions of matter.

In this brief discussion, of course, I have only opened the window on a landscape littered with the remains of controversies over the interpretations of symbols. In the foreground are the disagreements among partisans of an "old" and "new" hermeneutics over the possibility of understanding from within the allegorizing and eschatological habits of mind of the early Christians. How can modern interpreters really understand the world of the first Christian century if, as Barfield suggests, the mind of earlier man enjoys a smaller ratio of intellect to imagination than obtains in the "modern" mind? Barfield argues the same point, in fact, as those New Testament critics who insist on the intimate connection of the parables with the myth of the Kingdom of God. The apparently \ realistic and everyday images of the parables can only thus be understood within a framework of belief in a Kingdom whose arrival is unpredictable and imminent. While interpreting early allegorizing tendencies in the New Testament or among later theological reflections (like Augustine's), it is therefore important to appreciate the development as a separation of symbols from signs. If Barfield is right, in fact, the lack of proportion and synthesis in the modern mind between intellect and imagination is the result of a steady separation of the two in a history which, from a crude scientific viewpoint, is an "ascent." The decline comes precisely in the proportion of imagination to intellect and in the capacity to harmonize the two visionary faculties in symbols that are also evocative signs. Thus the facts of a parable become separated slowly from their imaginative, mythic framework, and the relation between the two becomes strained and artificial rather than dynamic. If Barfield is right, the steady progress toward images that are clear, complete, and of a single meaning is a fall rather than a triumph (1977: 108–9). If he is wrong, Barfield may simply be uniting imagination and intellect in order to take the hope for redemption out of the hands of the positivists and away from those of a literal cast of mind and speech.

Setting the rules for speech has been the focus of most religious conflict in the West over the last two millennia. Even in the first three Christian centuries, the early church entertained a number of heresies which developed several grammars and styles for expressing fundamental Christian beliefs. But J. A. T. Robinson (1952) notes that it was the issue of metaphor that divided even two groups of early churches in the *first* century. One group, associated with the leadership of Paul, claimed that the church *is* the Body of Christ. The notion that Christians are "members" of that body was therefore not a metaphor for organic relationships among believers. On the contrary, the phrase "you are the Body of Christ" was, and still is, to be taken "literally," Robinson argues, if we are to understand the basis of Pauline theology.

Some splinter groups in the early church, however, argued that the relationship of the individual believer to other believers and to Christ was more fluid and inexact than is implied in a literal usage of the term "Body of Christ." The believer could have direct access to Christ without membership in certain Christian groups and without participating in the rituals of that Body (cf. Pagels 1979). By the same argument, they could also engage in non-Christian practices and associate with non-Christian friends on an intimate basis. Such claims are defensible, of course, if membership in the Body of Christ is a metaphor for intimacy or for a type of interdependence in which each person has a useful function to fulfill within the church. Such a metaphor allows relatively higher degrees of freedom for interpreting and acting out the meaning of that membership. But for others more concerned with order and control in the church, the notion of the Body was not a metaphor: not merely a way of speaking about functional interdependence or intimacy and freedom. Taken literally, the idea of the Body of Christ locates each member in an explicit, irreducible relationship to other Christians and to Christ. On this latter view, the likeness is not the inexact likeness of a metaphor or an equivalence of some sort, but is due to their sameness. A later interpretation of the Body of Christ, then, reduces the freedom of each member to think and to act independently of the others.

Out of the metaphor's Trojan-horse belly come the soldiers of deviant interpretation and rival claims to the holy city. The conflict over the rules for interpreting Scripture is thus a conflict over who will control the sacred mysteries and define a hierarchy of control within the churches. In the same way the rules of style and grammar determine who is a member of the Christian community and who indeed is not. I have already noted that many believers would insist that to consider biblical truth as metaphor is to kill that truth in one's own heart. The fundamentalists and biblical literalists indeed have a point. If we treat certain biblical phrases as metaphors, we can then free them from their original context. In claiming the right and ability to expand and improve on the metaphor in our own context, however, we are placing ourselves in a position which transcends the original words. In the same way the literary critic finds that he is able to understand, explain, and even to expand the metaphors, say, of John Donne (cf. Smith 1974: 35). But in doing so the sermon of Donne is not preached to him; rather he transcends that original utterance and plays with its words with self-conscious expertise. To approach another's words as metaphor is to set the rules for speech in such a way that the words of one speaker can more easily be transformed by the words of another. It is an approach particularly suited to the needs of religious intellectuals who prefer their religious truths to be free from the constraints of a particular "parochial" context.

Conclusion

The first chapter focussed briefly on the particular fate of a single prophetic act that originated in the secular context of a local draft board office. In examining the courtroom testimony that interpreted the meaning of that prophetic act, it became clear that prophets claim for themselves rather high levels of credibility, of authority, and of authenticity. They claim to speak from long and intense personal experience and so to be credible; they know whereof they speak. Prophets claim to speak with authority as exponents of a sacred tradition that, in the case of Christianity, makes civil disobedience legitimate, at times even obligatory, to the conscience. Prophets also claim to be authentic, because their words reflect their deeds; and so prophets claim to be trustworthy. With these claims, it is small wonder that prophets find so little honor, especially in their own countries.

Action that disrupts everyday life is likely to be misunderstood. Prophetic action is most likely to be disruptive and to break through the limiting context of ritual. It is therefore also liable to misinterpretation by those outside the religious community. Although prophets claim traditional authority for their messages, their testimony is often discredited as being the expression of idiosyncratic persuasions. Prophets intend to speak a final word, but courts often demand further explanation and question whether the prophets' words are consistent with their deeds. Prophets speak in words that are intended to speak for themselves, but in other contexts, such as the courtroom, their words are reinterpreted as "mere" metaphors or even forced into the limits of literal usage. That is the fate of prophecy: to break out of safe, limited contexts and therefore to be open to misunderstanding. But here I have argued that the fate of prophecy is in part determined *before* religious speech ever leaves a religious context. The prophet is in a sense most likely to be misunderstood among his own countrymen.

There is a development to be traced here, from words that evoke commitment because they speak powerfully and at the same time of common values and of a historic myth, to words that are merely the literal equivalents of objects, events, people, and organizations in "real life." That development begins within the religious community long before the prophet's words are taken out of context. Secularization begins, so to speak, in the household of God.

We have focussed on the shift from prophecy to metaphor as contexts separate the original speaker or initial speech from those who later hear and interpret the prophetic word. The shift from prophecy to metaphor takes time, although it may not take much time. We have also seen how the church's commitment to serious speech has over time made the church's own testimony subject to the rigorous demands of secular authorities who claim high levels of credibility and authority for themselves. These demands are most tangible in contexts where secular authorities control the rules for discourse, as in the courtroom. I have argued that prophetic language undergoes a process of differentiation as it passes from liturgical to secular contexts over time. At the outset of that process signs, which initially stand within a community of shared belief, are still inseparable from the symbols which express reality in the form of a myth about a people's history or of a theory about the universe. But over the course of that process communal signs become separate from symbols for reality. Those signs thus lose their authority and become more context-bound, while the symbols gain credibility only to the extent that they become literally true as symbols of an external and relatively discernible reality.

Somewhere in the open space between prophetic words,

where sign and symbol are indistinguishable from each other, and the courtroom or classroom, where the two are rigorously separated, individuals are given a limited credit and authority for speaking in metaphors. One has a limited freedom from the rigors of a legal or scientific language if one is allowed to speak in metaphor, just as religious intellectuals claim the freedom of metaphor in interpreting the Scriptures of church doctrine. But metaphor is not as credible or authoritative as prophetic speech. Metaphors are replaceable, especially when they are tired or ancient. Moreover, while metaphors may have a certain communal reputation, they do not speak with the clear authority of a myth or theory because they are a bit too vague and slippery. Metaphors score low on a hypothetical scale of symbolic closure; one never has a metaphorical last word. Relatively autonomous and communal but over time becoming idiosyncratic, relatively condensed but over time too easily elaborated, metaphors are the speech for what Auden once called "the time being": the time between the moment of revelation and the eventual transformation of everyday life.

Chapter 9

The Liturgical Spirit versus The Literalism of the Law

At the heart of Western religious culture is the tension between the spirit and the letter of the law. In each case that we have discussed in these pages individuals with religious convictions give testimony that is constrained by the literalism of the courtroom. The Berrigans used metaphor to break the literalistic constraints of the secular law. The Quinlans defined life and death in terms that went well beyond the literal meaning permitted by expert witnesses trained in medical measurement and diagnosis. To break through the literal meaning of specialized terms they invoked the authority of Christian beliefs and the corporate understandings of their religious communities. In each case the court insisted that their witness be understood as merely personal and even idiosyncratic rather than corporate and authoritative; otherwise the witnesses would have had the right to declare, to pronounce, and command, rather than the obligation to conform their testimony to the limits imposed on witnesses in the courtroom. Witnesses are required to be literally exact in their recall of what has been intended or said and done. A mother's memory of what her daughter meant, rather than what her daughter said, is not taken as literally accurate within the courtroom. Judges take a narrow, literalistic view of terms such as ministry and religion against the expanded meanings for those terms employed by individuals seeking the protections accorded religion by the First Amendment. In this final chapter we will see a judge reminding a priest that only a literally exact statement of his earlier intentions will be acceptable testimony. The letter of the law constrains testimony to be literally true and leaves no room for prophetic speech. But in the terms of the Western religious tradition, the letter kills and the spirit alone is life-giving.

It is ironic that religion through the liturgy should strive to fit language to reality in a way that no one can deny, so that words and deeds speak for each other with no residues of unexpressed meaning or intention, whereas it is secular professions that claim the ability to achieve the best goodness-of-fit between words and reality in the classroom or in the court. Concepts have measures, and statements have supporting observations whether in the laboratory or the courtroom; otherwise the secular trial could not go on. The irony is that the secular world should establish the rules for pursuing what is essentially the goal of the Christian tradition: the incarnate and therefore indissoluble connection of word and reality. Like the incarnation of Christian doctrine, the secular connection between word and reality is indissoluble, but the distinction between word and reality is never lost in the nominalism of the classroom and in the insistence of the court that witnesses can at best "represent" that their statements reflect an actual state of mind or occurrence in the world. Unlike the representations of the liturgy, however, these representations in the court do not carry their own conviction and re-present what is being recalled in words. The secular testing of words with reality never reaches the finality of the liturgy. In this sense the trial that accompanies the goal of incarnating language and reality is never over within the secular constraints on the speech of all except the few who are permitted to declare and pronounce. Even they may have their judgments reviewed in higher courts or by the force of new law that must, in turn, be taken literally.

Liturgy is marked by what Luckmann (1975) would call freedom from "literalism." For instance, the Eucharistic liturgy celebrates the transformation of bread and wine into the "body and blood" of Jesus. But literalism misunderstands the transformation: a misunderstanding that the Roman Catholic Church has been at some pains to correct through the doctrine of transubstantiation. That doctrine insists that the devout need not expect any literal characteristics of flesh and blood in the sacrament to believe that the proper trans- formation has occurred. In examining the transcripts of the trial of the Catonsville Nine, however, we will see that a demand for limited, literal usage tends to reduce the prophetic, effective speech of individuals, on trial for their religious beliefs, to virtual nonsense. Literal usage is simply devoid of operative as well as of liturgical force.

The liturgy also exhibits another characteristic of religious ritual which Luckmann (1975) would probably identify as a strong connection between the sounds of speech and the social organizations of speaking. In the liturgy, for instance, only certain people are allowed to make certain sounds: the priest alone to utter prayers of consecration or blessing, and the cantor to sing certain phrases. Anyone, however, can make any sound by speaking in tongues: a fact that suggests the radical implications of glossolalia and charismatic utter- ances for religious or secular social organizations. Although I will not in this discussion make explicit use of this (phono- logical) aspect of liturgical speech, it might help here to note that when Allen Ginsberg was chanting Hare Krishna or Om in the trial of the "Chicago Seven," he was showing a profound disregard for the social organization of the court. The radical implications were not lost on the defendants, the gallery, or the trial judge, who insisted on the observance of judicial rules of discourse.

On 17 May 1968, the protesters were clearly engaging in liturgical action when they burned the files of Local Board No. 33 in Catonsville, Maryland. Most of the defense of the protesters, once they stood trial, revolved around the religious, liturgical nature of that symbolic action. The prosecution, and on occasion even the judge, sought to question the spirit of the action and the intention of the actors. To the extent that the prosecution could find other intentions in the actors than their stated ones, other meanings in their words, and other interpretations for their words and deeds, the more easily the defendants could be found guilty. A critical moment in the testimony occurred when the judge questioned Daniel Berrigan's testimony:

DEFENSE: Could you state to the court what your intent was in burning the draft files?

D. BERRIGAN: I did not want the children or the grandchildren of the jury or of the judge to be burned with napalm.

JUDGE: You say your intention was to save these children, of the jury, of myself, when you burned the records? That is what I heard you say. I ask if you meant that.

D. BERRIGAN: I meant that. Of course I mean that or I would not say it. The great sinfulness of modern way is that it renders concrete things abstract. I do not want to talk about Americans in general.

JUDGE: You cannot think up arguments now that you would like to have had in your mind then.

(Berrigan 1970: 82; punctuation supplied)

A truly liturgical action is, of course, action for all times and places, although it occurs at particular times and places. The intentions of celebrant and faithful alike include all mankind in the general celebration of universal redemption. In the liturgical spirit of their act, it is therefore reasonable for the Berrigans to assert that they had in mind the children of the judge and jury. But the judge's intervention reminds the jury that the liturgical nature of the action here is entirely questionable. The spirit of the act is not discernible in rules of discourse that insist that statements of intention be literally true, especially when witnesses are representing prior states of mind and intent. What liturgical action puts together, judicial rules of discourse tend to put asunder. But to separate religious intentions from particular actions is to give the latter an entirely meaningless construction from the point of view of the actor. Daniel Berrigan put it succinctly enough:

DEFENSE: Was your action at Catonsville a way of carrying out your religious beliefs?

D. BERRIGAN: Of course it was. May I say if my religious belief is not accepted as a substantial part of my action, then the action is eviscerated of all meaning and I should be committed for insanity.

(Berrigan 1970: 83, punctuation supplied)

Liturgical speech is readily discredited according to judicial rules of discourse precisely because the courts insist on a degree of literalism that is absent from the liturgy. During the trial of the Catonsville Nine there were several occasions on which the court or the prosecution sought to impose a higher degree of literalism on the defendants' testimony. Two such occasions are given below as examples.

In the first example Thomas Lewis, a defendant, is making the point that the anti-war activists had met only "apathy," "hostility," and a "lack of concern" in their visits to government and military officials:

LEWIS: We engaged in conversations with the military hierarchy. They accepted no responsibility for the direction of the war. The responsibility was not theirs. They were just taking orders.

JUDGE: You said "No response." You mean they did not do what you asked them to do, is that it?

LEWIS: No response, Your Honor. We were standing there . . . We were saying to the military, "This is wrong. This is immoral. This is illegal." And their response to this was they were only obeying orders.

(Berrigan 1970: 42; punctuation supplied)

The judge first transforms the statement of the defendant from an assertion that the military took *no responsibility* on themselves for the "direction of the war" to an assertion that the military did *not respond* according to the defendant's wishes: a clear transformation and reduction of meaning from a prophetic accusation to a presumably mistaken representation of facts. "Response" is a word in this context that has a relatively clear, easily tested, and literal meaning, whereas "responsibility" lacks such clarity. The defendant then tried to retrieve the situation by reiterating his earlier statement about "just taking orders," but the judge insists on the transformation:

JUDGE: But they did respond to you, did they not?

LEWIS: It was an atrocious response.

(Berrigan 1970: 42; punctuation supplied)

In this last exchange, the judge has forced the defendant to leave his original point concerning "irresponsibility" and to describe the military's inaction as a response, however "atrocious" it might be in the eyes of the defendant. It would then have been a simple matter for the court to argue, as it did on other occasions, that the military were not on trial.

A second reduction to the literal level of meaning occurred when the prosecution gave its final summary:

> But this prosecution is the government's response, the law's response, the people's response, to what the defendants did. And what they did was to take government property and throw flammable material upon it and burn it beyond recognition. And that is what this case is about. (Berrigan 1970: 100)

The defense argued the opposite point: that, while the defendants did seek "to impede and interfere with the operation of a system" which they felt to be "immoral" as well as destructive and "illegal," they were engaged in a "symbolic act" of free speech presumably within their constitutionally guaranteed rights. "The defendants weren't burning files for the sake of burning files" (ibid.: 103). The jury were not convinced, however, for they found the defendants all quite literally guilty of the acts the defendants had admitted at the outset of the trial. Judicial rules of discourse, by introducing opportunities to reduce testimony to literal usage, tend to discredit individual witnesses' claims to credibility.

You may have noted that, in quoting the Berrigan volume of the transcripts, I have on several occasions felt it necessary to supply punctuation. In editing the transcripts, Berrigan has transformed the bare, legal text into the typographical setting of blank verse, with a corresponding effect on the apparent structure of the language spoken by the defendants in the trial. (The prosecution and the judge apparently spoke only in prosaic syntax and grammar.) To speak in poetic form is to transcend the limitations of any social context and to claim considerable autonomy for one's own words: to claim freedom from the literalism of the classroom or the court. The issue came to the attention of the judge on several occasions, for instance:

D. BERRIGAN: . . . But our moral passion is banished from this court. It is as though the legal process were an autopsy.

JUDGE: Well, I cannot match your poetic language. [Applause from the audience.]

Any further demonstration and the court will be cleared. And I mean that, the whole crowd.

Father Berrigan, you have made your points on the stand, very persuasively. I admire you as a poet. But I think you simply do not understand the function of a court.

D. BERRIGAN: I am sure that is true.

(Berrigan 1970: 114)

The use of metaphor by Berrigan is exceedingly important in the effort to establish autonomy for the speaker's own usage and meaning. In the passage above we find Berrigan using the metaphor of an autopsy to describe the legal process: a metaphor that also calls to mind the "dead" letter of the law and the need, as Berrigan later put it, "to bring the tradition to life again for the sake of the people" (1970: 114–15). It is as if Berrigan were reminding the court that the letter of the law kills, while the spirit alone gives life: a biblical reminder, which, if taken seriously by the court, would force a change in the judicial rules for discourse.

The autonomy of religious speech requires us to focus on what is perhaps the most costly reduction of religious testimony in secular judicial context. It is clear from many sources that the Berrigan brothers and the other defendants sought a dramatic, liturgical action on which to issue a prophetic condemnation of the war in Vietnam. That was the meaning of the burning of the draft board's files in a sacrificial offering that symbolized as well the prayers of the faithful for peace and the lives literally and figuratively burned beyond recognition in the war itself. Because they felt the war to be illegal, they sought to place the war on trial. Because the war was immoral in their view, they wished also to issue a prophetic denunciation in the courtroom as well as in the open air out-side the draft board. In a larger sense it was not only "war crimes" but an unjust social order at home and abroad that became the object of their accusation:

BERRIGAN: Some ten or twelve of us will, if all goes well (ill?) take our religious bodies during this week to a draft center in or near Baltimore. There we shall remove the 1–A files, sprinkle them in the public street with homemade napalm, and set them afire. For which act we shall beyond doubt be placed behind bars for some portion of our natural lives, in consequence of our inability to live and die content in the plagued city, to say "peace, peace" when there is no peace, to keep the poor poor . . .

(Berrigan 1970: 93)

Berrigan (Daniel) has made it very clear that he did not wish the moral question put to the society as a whole to be lost in "the routine of the trial itself" or in "the wrangling and paper shuffling which threatened to obscure the *firmness and clarity of the original deed*" (ibid.: viii). I have italicized certain words here to emphasize the ritual nature of that symbolic act, its autonomy in Berrigan's eyes, his wish for it to be free from the judgment of other contexts or from limi-tation to its physical context, his belief in its prophetic power, and in its symbolic completeness. That is why Daniel Berrigan welcomed the "rigors" of the court's literalism and wished to avoid a polite agreement that would blunt the conflict between prophet and judge (ibid.: 119).

Like all formal language, liturgical acts depend for their effectiveness on their ability to isolate purely personal or idiosyncratic factors. Liturgists do not permit the private, religious, or moral heresies of the faithful to interfere with the elegance and serenity of the ritual as a whole. But in the courtroom the judge made frequent reference to the personal and the idiosyncratic on a number of occasions. The effect of those references was to discredit the moral persuasiveness of the defendants' arguments.

A few examples may suggest the ways in which the judge

or the prosecution re-introduced personal or idiosyncratic elements into the corporate witness of the protesters. The judge noted that he, on personal grounds, could agreed with the defendants' protest, but as a judge he had an oath of office to uphold. That oath required him to administer the law rather than to act upon personal viewpoints, no matter how cogent the latter might be. Thus the judge reminded Daniel Berrigan that the priest was probably ignorant of the principles on which both the court and the judicial system in general are organized. In that judicial context, his views would indeed be idiosyncratic. On occasion Daniel Berrigan would refer to expert and authoritative testimony in order to buttress his own opinions, but on these occasions the judge would again remind Berrigan of the personal or idiosyncratic nature of his testimony. For instance, Daniel Berrigan once cited an international panel:

> French, English, Swedish experts, doctors testified. These were actually the bodies whose pictures accompanied the exhibits (referring to "parts of human bodies preserved in alcohol" — Fenn). The evidence was unassailable. The bombings were a massive crime against man . . .
> JUDGE: We are not trying the air war in North Vietnam.
> D. BERRIGAN: I must protest the effort to discredit me on the stand. I am speaking of what I saw. There is a consistent effort to say I did not see it.
> JUDGE: The best evidence of what some "crime commission" found is not a summary you give.
> (Berrigan 1970: 90, punctuation supplied)

In an effort to put the war on trial, the defendants chose a social context, the courtroom, where the rules of evidence and of discourse favor those who, as the judge put it, understand the organization of the court and the principles of the American judicial system. Those speak with authority in that context who speak according to judicial rules of discourse. Those achieve credibility as expert witnesses who are certified as expert by the court. In the courtroom, the priestly celebrant who offered in the ritual outside the draft board a sacrifice for the sins of the whole world finds that in the courtroom he is merely a lay person without special qualifications to give testimony. By definition, in that context his principles are idiosyncratic. The same process of secularization reduced the force of another priest's testimony (Father Trapasso on behalf of the Quinlan family), just as it limited the credibility of Mss Cueto and Nemikin in their claim to represent the official ministry of the Episcopal Church in America.

The defense thus lost a major point when the government, through the prosecution, acknowledged that a reasonable person might agree with the defendants on the illegality and immorality of the war. When the prosecutor said that "a reasonable man could have the defendant's views" (in referring to Philip Berrigan), the defending attorney exulted that they have "scored a capital point" (Berrigan 1970: 28). But the defense had, in fact, lost a capital point. In being hospitable to a wide range of differing views on the war, the government was saying that the views of Philip Berrigan were simply his own, personal, and idiosyncratic standpoint: no less reasonable than the views of those who uphold the war, but no more reasonable at that. Their reasonableness was in any event not at issue, since the defendants were on trial for acts that were quite separate from the larger issues of the war itself. The defendants joined their personal views to a corporate condemnation of the war on behalf of the Christian faithful, and vicariously on behalf of all those who suffered directly and indirectly from American foreign policy. The prosecution intended to show that their action was personal rather than corporate. Thus their punishment would not vicariously atone for anyone's guilt other than their own. To summarize, an additional proposation can be stated thus: by stressing the idiosyncratic and personal aspects of a witness's testimony, judicial rules of discourse limit the *credibility* of that witness. A corollary of this proposition would state: by stressing the idiosyncratic and personal aspects of a witness's reported values and beliefs judicial rules of discourse limit the *authority* of the witness's testimony in the court. In the same way, it will be remembered, the court refused to acknowledge as sacred the corporate shift and testimony of the Quinlan family in order to treat each member separately as individuals whose views and testimony varied in reliability and weight before the court.

Early in this discussion I distinguished between operative and non-operative rules for discourse. That distinction is particularly useful in understanding the effect of constraints placed on the witnesses' testimony within the courtroom and in accounting for the transformations in meaning that their testimony undergoes as it is interpreted by the prosecution and by the judge. The rules of judicial discourse severely limit the defendants' operative speech as well as their ability successfully to claim credibility, authenticity, and justification. Judicial rules of discourse, to use Habermas's term, limit witnesses' illocutionary force: the ability of the witness to gain assent to the truthfulness of what is said, or trust, or accord concerning the rightness of what the witness says and does. Where the speaker steps outside a particular institutional context, the standards for taking a speaker seriously and for reaching such agreements are problematical. Habermas (1979: 82) puts it this way:

> When it is a question of institutionally bound speech actions, he [the hearer] can perhaps rely on the binding force of an established norm of action. In the case of institutionally unbound [non-segmented] speech acts, however illocutionary force cannot be traced back directly to the binding force of the normative context.

In other words, the rules for understanding, trusting, and taking seriously a speaker who acts outside any taken-for-granted context, as did the protesters at Catonsville, must be drawn from somewhere if not from the nearest available institution. For the protesters, the grounds for the validity of what they had said and done were to be drawn from themselves and their own acts of speech. For the court, however, the grounds for validity concerned, as we have seen, a rather literal interpretation of the law and of the functions of the judiciary.

The defendants' claim to validity rested on their testimony that the war was illegal, that the deaths of women and children violated every important canon or morality, and that the resources devoted to war could otherwise have prevented starvation and destruction in the Third World or in the United States itself. But again, we have seen the court insist that the witnesses were not the most expert or reliable sources of evidence regarding, say, the war "crimes" in Vietnam. The judge insisted that Daniel Berrigan and others employed poetic license rather than more exact usage. On the grounds of truth as well as of truthfulness, the court contested the defendants' claims. Credibility in court depends partly on the degree to which the court accepts witnesses' right to a usage other than the most literal in giving testimony. The right to be taken seriously lies, as Habermas (1979: 64) might put it, in choosing successfully "the *normative context* that gives the speaker the *conviction* that this utterance is right" (ibid.). For Daniel Berrigan, his experience as priest and author provided such a context, whereas another's work as a nurse or an artist provided the normative context. But the court consistently refused to allow the speakers to claim to be taken seriously as speaking from such contexts. As the prosecution asked concerning Daniel Berrigan, "What difference does it make how many books he has written?" (Berrigan 1970: 87). The authority of a witness therefore depends partly on the court's willingness to respect the origin of a witness's testimony in other contexts. Without a clear institutional context for one's beliefs and actions, testimony in court to one's religious convictions is likely to fall on barren ground. The less clearly it is grounded in a context where intentions and beliefs are elaborated and action is clearly concentrated in solemn, symbolic acts, witness in court to religious beliefs and motives will more likely appear to the court as idiosyncratic and lacking in the authority of corporate or official, institutional creed and standard. To segment liturgical action apart from all other activities and loyalties may make liturgies seem irrelevant to everyday life and to the hard politics of modern societies, but symbolic acts without any liturgical context run the risk in court of being interpreted as more strategic than solemn, more idiosyncratic than authoritative, and not unmixed with mundane motives.

Testimony that lacks the support of the liturgy will be interpreted in judicial context as lacking in literal truth what it enjoys in poetic or other license, and witnesses' beliefs will appear to be merely personal and hence suspect of idiosyncratic perversions of authoritative religious beliefs. Secular symbolic actions lack the closure which would otherwise enable a witness to claim that at a given time and place all relevant motives were stated, and all relevant action taken: no residues being left over for later addition to the defendant's testimony, and nothing left unstated at the time for the prosecution later to discover and develop. Religious ritual, to use a legal phrase, "establishes a record" that is complete, authoritative, and that guarantees the authenticity of the witness given at a certain time and place. A secular symbolic action such as the ceremonious burning of files from a draft board cannot establish a record that will resist the scrutiny of the court and escape revision of judicial rules of discourse. Indeed judicial proceedings establish their own institutional standards for authoritative, credible, and authentic testimony. The only balance to an authoritative secular ritual appears to be an equally authoritative religious ritual.

It is precisely because religious rituals are concentrated and segmented in specific institutional contexts, however, that they lack any direct effect on the normal course of events. Prayers for peace at the Eucharist do not normally stop the Selective Service system, for instance, from inducting young men for service in the armed forces. The cost of liturgical freedom is widespread literalism outside the sanctuary of the church. What originally is public action, in which individuals define the nature of their citizenship on earth and in heaven, is reduced liturgically to a private sphere which does not impede Caesar's progress. On occasion the clergy or courageous laity have shown themselves impatient with the constraints imposed either by the church or the state on symbolic acts in public spheres and have chosen to demonstrate publicly the spirit and force of the liturgy. On these occasions, they have testified to their right to terminate extraordinary measures for keeping the body alive long after the spirit has departed or have prophesied against a war that kills both body and spirit in endless and senseless human sacrifice. It is not the first time that individuals have challenged or broken the letter of the law in order to make fresh room for the spirit. It is not the first time that individuals have been discredited for breaking the rules of secular discourse in order to give testimony to their religious convictions. When, however, the meaning and force of liturgical actions are taken into contexts as secular as the classroom and the court, the authority of secular elites is challenged and the letter of the law is sometimes opened to new meanings and applications.

Not all challenges to secular rules of discourse are successful, and the letter of the law is not easily opened to reveal gaps in the administration of justice. On the contrary, social change of the order attempted in the cases we have recounted here is not won easily or without sacrifice. These interruptions of religious testimony into secular contexts will have various outcomes according to a wide range of factors that we have not begun to consider in these pages: the personal characteristics of the persons involved, the strategic importance of the specific issues at stake, and differences of social class and power among the litigants, to name only a few of those to be considered in a more inclusive analysis than the one attempted here. But I will venture a single, and highly speculative, generalization about the process of secularization on the basis of these simple sketches. Secular contexts may well find their rules for discourse broken more frequently in the future than in the past as individuals demand the right to testify to their religious convictions in the classroom, in the court, on the political campaign trail, and even in the hospital where matters of life and death have been the prerogative of only one profession to decide. Reflecting on the secularization of institutions in modern societies, Max Weber once argued that the spirit had left them and survived only in the private world of friendship and devotion. It is possible that Weber was premature in announcing the end of the Reformation, and instead we may expect to see the secularity and literalness of seminars and courtrooms increasingly interrupted by testimony concerning the things of the spirit.

Summary of Karen Ann Quinlan's Story

An understanding of the issues in their basic perspective suggests a brief review of the factual base developed in the testimony and documented in greater detail in the opinion of the trial judge. *In re Quinlan, 137 N.J. Super. 227* (Ch. Div. 1975).

On the night of April 15, 1975, for reasons still unclear, Karen Quinlan ceased breathing for at least two 15 minute periods. She received some ineffectual mouth-to-mouth resuscitation from friends. She was taken by ambulance to Newton Memorial Hospital. There she had a temperature of 100 degrees, her pupils were unreactive and she was unresponsive even to deep pain. The history at the time of her admission to the hospital was essentially incomplete and uninformative.

Three days later, Dr Morse examined Karen at the request of the Newton admitting physician, Dr McGee. He found her comatose with evidence of decortication, a condition relating to derangement of the cortex of the brain causing a physical posture in which the upper extremities are flexed and the lower extremities are extended. She required a respirator to assist her breathing. Dr Morse was unable to obtain an adequate account of the circumstances and events leading up to Karen's admission to the Newton Hospital. Such initial history or etiology is crucial in neurological diagnosis. Relying as he did upon the Newton Memorial records and his own examination, he concluded that prolonged lack of oxygen in the bloodstream, anoxia, was identified with her condition as he saw it upon first observation. When she was later transferred to Saint Clare's Hospital she was still unconscious, still on a respirator and a tracheotomy had been performed. On her arrival Dr Morse conducted extensive and detailed examinations. An electroencephalogram (EEG) measuring electrical rhythm of the brain was performed and Dr Morse characterized the result as "abnormal but it showed some activity and was consistent with her clinical state." Other significant neurological tests, including a brain scan, an angiogram, and a lumbar puncture were normal in result. Dr Morse testified that Karen has been in a state of coma, lack of consciousness, since he began treating her. He explained that there are basically two types of coma, sleeplike unresponsiveness and awake unresponsiveness. Karen was originally in a sleep-like unresponsive condition but soon developed "sleep-wake" cycles, apparently a normal improvement for comatose patients occurring within three to four weeks. In the awake cycle she blinks, cries out and does things of that sort but is still totally unaware of anyone or anything around her.

Dr Morse and other expert physicians who examined her characterized Karen as being in a "chronic persistent vegetative state." Dr Fred Plum, one of such expert witnesses, defined this as a "subject who remains with the capacity to maintain the vegetative parts of neurological function but who . . . no longer has any cognitive function."

Dr Morse, as well as the several other medical and neurological experts who testified in this case, believed with certainty that Karen Quinlan is not "brain dead." They identified the Ad Hoc Committee of Harvard Medical School report (*infra*) as the ordinary medical standard for determining brain death, and all of them were satisfied that Karen met none of the criteria specified in that report and was therefore not "brain dead" within its contemplation.

In this respect it was indicated by Dr Plum that the brain works in essentially two ways, the vegetative and the sapient. He testified:

> We have an internal vegetative regulation which controls body temperature which controls breathing, which controls to a considerable degree blood pressure, which controls to some degree heart rate, which controls chewing, swallowing and which controls sleeping and waking. We have a more highly developed brain which is uniquely human which controls our relation to the outside world, our capacity to talk, to see, to feel, to sing, to think. Brain death necessarily must mean the death of both of these functions of the brain, vegetative and the sapient. Therefore, the presence of any function which is regulated or governed or controlled by the deeper parts of the brain which in laymen's terms might be considered purely vegetative would mean that the brain is not biologically dead.

Because Karen's neurological condition affects her respiratory ability (the respiratory systems being a brain stem function) she requires a respirator to assist her breathing. From the time of her admission to Saint Clare's Hospital Karen has been assisted by an MA—1 respirator, a sophisticated machine which delivers a given volume of air at a certain rate and periodically provides a "sigh" volume, a relatively large measured volume of air designed to purge the lungs of excretions. Attempts to "wean" her from the respirator were unsuccessful and have been abandoned.

The experts believe that Karen cannot now survive without the assistance of the respirator; that exactly how long she would live without it is unknown; that the strong likelihood is that death would follow soon after its removal, and that removal would also risk further brain damage and would curtail the assistance the respirator presently provides in warding off infection.

It seemed to be the consensus not only of the treating physicians but also of the several qualified experts who testified in the case, that removal from the respirator would not conform to medical practices, standards and traditions.

The further medical consensus was that Karen in addition to being comatose is in a chronic and persistent "vegetative" state, having no awareness of anything or anyone around her and existing at a primitive reflex level. Although she does have some brain stem function (ineffective for respiration) and has other reactions one normally associates with being alive, such as moving, reacting to light, sound and noxious stimuli, blinking her eyes, and the like, the quality of her feeling impulses is unknown. She grimaces, makes stereotyped cries and sounds and has chewing motions. Her blood pressure is normal.

Karen remains in the intensive care unit at Saint Clare's Hospital, receiving 24-hour care by a team of four nurses characterized, as was the medical attention, as "excellent." She is nourished by feeding by way of a nasal-gastro tube and is routinely examined for infection, which under these circumstances is a serious life threat. The result is that her condition is considered remarkable under the unhappy circumstances involved.

Karen is described as emaciated, having suffered a weight loss of at least 40 pounds, and undergoing a continuing deteriorative process. Her posture is described as fetal-like and grotesque; there is extreme flexion-rigidity of the arms, legs and related muscles and her joints are severely rigid and deformed.

From all this evidence, and including the whole testimonial record, several basic findings in the physical area are mandated. Severe brain and associated damage, albeit of uncertain etiology, has left Karen in a chronic and persistent vegetative state. No form of treatment which can cure or improve that condition is known or available. As nearly as may be determined, considering the guarded area of remote uncertainties characteristic of most medical science predictions, she can *never* be restored to cognitive or sapient life. Even with regard to the vegetative level and improvement therein (if such it may be called) the prognosis is extremely poor and the extent unknown if it should in fact occur.

She is debilitated and moribund and although fairly stable at the time of argument before us (no new information having been filed in the meanwhile in expansion of the record), no physician risked the opinion that she could live more than a year and indeed she may die much earlier. Excellent medical and nursing care so far has been able to ward off the constant threat of infection, to which she is peculiarly susceptible because of the respirator, the tracheal tube and other incidents of care in her vulnerable condition. Her life accordingly is sustained by the respirator and tubal feeding, and removal from the respirator would cause her death soon, although the time cannot be stated with more precision.

Source: In the Supreme Court of New Jersey, September term, 1975, docket no. A—116. *In the Matter of Karen Ann Quinlan, an Alleged Incompetent*; on Certification to the Superior Court, Chancery Division, whose Opinion is Reported at *137 N.J. Super. 227* (1975). Opinion argued 26 January 1976 — decided 31 March 1976.

Coburn's Testimony

The court made an amazing statement. They concluded that the over-whelming majority of people would make the choice that they were allowing the father to make on behalf of Karen. That conclusion just came out of no place. It's written in the opinion. They said: "We recognized that the overwhelming majority of people would choose to have the respirator discontinued." Obviously they cited no authority for that conclusion. They are the supreme court, they can say what they want. At the oral argument before the supreme court, one of the Justices asked me: "Can we say this?" And I said frankly, "You are the supreme court, you can say whatever you want." They don't need authority. By the way, I think the court is absolutely correct. The overwhelming majority of the people in Karen Quinlan's position would probably make that decision. Whether they would in other cases such as that of a cancer patient, I really couldn't say . . .

Basically the case was tried — totally absent any medical issues — was tried on the family's right of privacy which they prevailed on by the way. The overtones of the case were religious all the way through, that the Catholic Church's position, which was optional, the father had determined to exercise one of the options, the option being that extra-ordinary means of life support should be discontinued. There was just no cross-examination at all on medical issues. Even on the right of privacy the determination in this case, which is as far reaching on right of privacy as can be determined, Mr Quinlan's answer to my question on, "Could you please explain your argument on right of privacy," was, "I think I have the right to do it." That was the extent of it, which is why in the opinion there is no discussion of how he felt this would be exercised.

Another thing that was interesting is the right of privacy cases talk about financial burden. One of the factors which I think is a significant factor is, I wouldn't want to see my family bankrupt after I've killed myself — well, not literally killed myself, but worked hard to establish some estate for my [sic] family, and in this case it never got played up at all, but the family never spent any money. The hospital ate their bill, which is about a quarter of a million dollars, the doctors 70—80 thousand dollars. I ate my bill — my bill was easy. At least I can deduct it. I don't think they can even deduct theirs. There is now some reason that Medicare or Medicaid is involved in the case prospective, not retro-active. But that was a significant factor that wasn't even in the case. It was tried primarily on the father's right as a Catholic to exercise the religious beliefs of his daughter.

Source: Columbia Journal of Law and Social Problems, Vol. 12, no. 4 (1976), pp. 518—25.

Bruner's Monologue

I need to express a puzzlement here. It seems to me that two possibly complementary modes of approach to language are constantly being discussed. In the first, in linguistics proper, as it were, we look at language opaquely, to see the structure. In the second, the transparent way, we look at language to see what it is used for. And of course there are many sad accounts of teachers converting in their teaching from the second to the first so that children are suddenly asked to study a verb conjugation and vow they will never go to another Latin class. Clearly in language learning we simply cannot use the formal approach of the structural linguist. So what needs to be done, I suggest, is to look at kinds of situation of use in which there are the maximum opportunities for learning the structures that are to be converted for use. Let me give some examples:

1   Writing — there is no naturalistic account of what people use writing for. I would bet my bottom dollar that most of the writing people do is of the "Don't leave milk today" kind of message to the milkman. Either simple commands of this kind or sequence instructions like "Turn left to get to George Street and then turn right."

2   Tutor theory — I was delighted to hear Clark tell us about her study of "successful" mothers of early readers. I recently tried to find something on the theory of the tutor — when there is any assisted instruction at all. There are lots of theories about it but I could not find a single paper that dealt in detail with the different kinds of assistance given by adults to children. I am afraid that whoever is going to finance this kind of work has to accept that it will be very low-level research. But very necessary.

3   Language and culture — Halliday made the point that the main thing we do with language is to transmit culture. I think that is only very partially true. I want to argue that one of the main things we are doing

when we transmit is to attempt disambiguation. In other words the point of communication very often is to try to reach argeement on a common referent, on which people can join together. We know very little about techniques of disambiguation in other than face-to-face discourse.

4 Transmission and acquisition — what is really needed here, I think, is to get on with the task of studying the acquisition of transmission. Do not, that is, stop your study of Adam and Eve when they have mastered the acquisition. Go on as they now learn to acquire transmission. We are trying to do something of this kind, to build up a code that has in it something I should like to call "vicarious functioning." It tries to look at the different codes people work with that may be substitutable for one another and asks the question whether there is not some way in which in effect we carry around different code books.

So to come back to Bernstein's initial point, how can Halliday talk only about transmission and Bruner only about acquisition? How indeed! I think it comes from the fact that we have gone far enough in our respective enterprises for each to know that he cannot deal with the nature of the transmission or the acquisition aspect until he finds out more about the nature of the formal code. And I certainly cannot move on to the question of how the code is learned unless I put things into a much more sociolinguistic context, in which I find out why they are transmitting, to what end, and what permits correction between people.

Source: Alan Davies, *Problems of Language and Learning* (1975), pp. 137—9.

References

Austin, J.L. (1962), *How to Do Things with Words*, Oxford University Press, Oxford.

Barfield, Owen (1967), *Speaker's Meaning*. London: Rudolf Steiner Press.

───── (1977), *The Rediscovery of Meaning, and other essays*, Wesleyan University Press, Middletown, Connecticut.

Bell, Daniel (1962), *The End of Ideology: On the Exhaustion of Political Ideas in the Fifties*. Free Press, New York.

Bellah, Robert (1964), "Religious Evolution," reprinted in Bellah, Robert N. (1970), *Beyond Belief, Essays on Religion in a Post-Traditional World*, Harper & Brothers.

Berger, Peter (1967), *The Sacred Canopy: Elements of a Sociological Theory of Religion*, Doubleday & Company, Inc., Garden City, New York.

───── (1972), *Sociology: A Biographical Approach*, Basic Books, New York.

Bernstein, Basil (1974), *Class, Codes, and Control*, Routledge & Kegan Paul, London.

Berrigan, Daniel (1970), *The Trial of the Catonsville Nine*, Beacon Press, Boston, Mass.

Bloch, M. (ed.) (1979), *Political Language and Oratory in Traditional Society*, Academic Press, London, New York, San Francisco.

Boman, Thorlief (1960), *Hebrew Thought compared with Greek*, translated by Jules L. Moreau, Norton, New York.

Buckner, H. Taylor (1978), "Transformations of Reality in the Legal Process," in Luckmann, Thomas (ed.), *Phenomenology and Sociology*, Penguin Books, New York, pp. 311–23.

Coleman, James (1974), *Power and the Structure of Society*, Norton, New York.

Cox, Harvey (1977), *Turning East*, Simon & Schuster, New York.

Cuddihy, John Murray (1978), *No Offense: Civil Religion and Protestant Taste*, Seabury Press, New York.

Davies, Alan (ed.) (1975), *Problems of Language and Learning*, Heinemann, London.

Douglas, Mary T. (1970; 1973), *Natural Symbols: Explorations in Cosmology*, Barrie & Rockliffe, London.

Foucault, Michel (1970; 1973), *The Order of Things: An Archaeology of the Human Sciences*, Vintage Books, New York.

———(1974), *The Archaeology of Knowledge*, Pantheon Books, New York.

Friedrichs, Robert W. (1970), *A Sociology of Sociology*, Free Press, New York.

Frye, Northrop (1976), *Spiritus Mundi: Essays on Literature, Myth, and Society*, Indiana University Press, Bloomington and London.

Geertz, Clifford (1973), *The Interpretation of Cultures*, Basic Books, New York.

Goldstein, Doris S. (1975), *Trial by Faith: Religion and Politics in Tocqueville's Thought*, Elsevier, New York.

Goodin, Robert E. (1978), "Rites of Rulers," *British Journal of Sociology*, Vol. 29, No. 3, pp. 281–299.

Gouldner, Alvin W. (1976), *The Dialectic of Sociology and Technology. The Origins, Grammar and Future of Ideology*, Seabury Press, New York.

Habermas, Jurgen (1979), *Communication and the Evolution of Society*, translated and with an introduction by Thomas McCarthy, Beacon Press, Boston, Mass.

Hadden, Jeffrey (1976), "Dimensionality of Belief among Mainstream Protestant Clergy," with C.F. Longino, *Social Forces* 56: 1 (Sept): 30–42.

Holzner, Burkart (1978), "The Construction of Social Actors: An Essay on Social Identities," in Luckmann Thomas (ed.), *Phenomenology and Sociology*, Penguin Books, New York, pp. 291–310.

Labov, William (1969), "The Logic of Non-standard English," *Georgetown Monographs on Language and Linguistics*, Vol. 22, pp. 1–31.

Luckmann, Thomas (1973), "Philosophy, Sciences and Everyday Life," in Natanson, M. (ed.), *Phenomenology and the Social Sciences*, Northwestern University Press, Evanston.

——— (1975), *The Sociology of Language*, Bobbs-Merrill Company Inc., Indianapolis.

——— (1979), "Hermeneutics as a Paradigm for Social Science," in Brammer, Michael (ed.), *Social Method and Social Life*, Academic Press, Oxford.

References   209

Lukes, Steven (1975), "Political Ritual and Social Integration," *Sociology*, Vol. 9, No. 2, pp. 289–308.

Martin, David (1978a) *The Dilemmas of Contemporary Religion*, Basil Blackwell, Oxford & St Martin's Press, New York.

—— (1978b), *A General Theory of Secularization*, Basil Blackwell, Oxford.

Merleau-Ponty, Maurice (1974), *Phenomenology, Language, and Sociology*, selected essays edited by John O'Neill, Heinemann, London.

Merton, Thomas (1950; 1965), *New Seeds of Contemplation*, New Directions, New York.

Nisbet, Robert (1976), *Sociology as an Art Form*, Oxford University Press, New York.

O'Neill, John (1978), "Can Phenomenology be Critical?" in Luckmann, Thomas (ed.), *Phenomenology and Sociology*, Penguin Books, New York, pp. 200–16.

Ong, Walter (1970), *The Presence of the Word: Some Prolegomen for Cultural and Religious History*, Simon & Schuster, New York.

Pagels, Elaine (1979), "The Suppressed Gnostic Feminism," in *New York Review of Books*, Vol. XXVI, No. 18, pp. 42ff.

Parsons, Talcott and Platt, Gerald M. (1973), *The American University*, Harvard University Press, Cambridge, Mass.

Perrin, Norman (1976), *Jesus and the Language of the Kingdom*, Fortress Press, Philadelphia, Pa.

Poirier, Richard (1971), *The Performing Self: Compositions and Decompositions in the Languages of Contemporary Life*, Oxford University Press, New York.

Ricoeur, Paul (1977), "La structure symbolique de l'action," *Aetes*, 14ème Conférence Internationale de Sociologie des Religions, Strasbourg, Lille, France.

Robertson, Roland (1979), "The Sociology of Religious Movements: Shifts in Analytical and Empirical Foci," paper presented at the annual meeting of the American Sociological Association, Boston, Mass.

Robinson, J. A. T. (1952), *The Body: A Study in Pauline Theology*, SCM Press, London (reprinted in 1977 by Westminister Press, Philadelphia).

Rosenstock-Huessy, Eugen (1970), *Speech and Reality*, introduction by Clinton C. Gardner, Argo Books, Norwich, Vt.

Schur, Edwin (1976), *The Awareness Trap: Self-Absorption instead of Social Change*, McGraw-Hill, New York.

Scott, John P. (1978), "Critical Social Theory: An Introduction and Critique," *British Journal of Sociology*, Vol. 29, No. 1, pp. 1–21.

Searle, John (1969), *Speech Acts: An Essay in the Philosophy of Language*, Cambridge University Press, Cambridge.

——(1979), *Expression and Meaning. Studies in the Theory of Speech-Acts*, Cambridge University Press, Cambridge.

Sennett, Richard and Cobb, Jonathan (1972), *The Hidden Injuries of Class*, Knopf, New York.

Smith, Charles Kay (1974), *Styles and Structures: Alternative Approaches to College Writing*, Norton, New York.

Troeltsch, Eugene (1931; 1960), *The Social Teaching of the Christian Churches*, translated by Olive Wyon, Harper Torchbooks, New York.

Von Rad, Gerhard, (1961), *Genesis: A Commentary*, translated by John H. Marks, Westminster Press, Philadelphia. Pa.

Wald, Kenneth (1979), "Religion and Mass Political Behavior: A Conceptual Analysis with Applications to British Voting Since 1885," paper presented to the Workshop on Religion and Politics, European Consortium for Political Research, Brussels.

Ward, J. R. (1979), "The Poem's Defiance of Sociology," *Sociology*, Vol. 13, No. 1, pp. 89–102

Weber, Max (1958), *The Protestant Ethic and the Spirit of Capitalism*, translated by Talcott Parsons, Charles Scribner & Sons, New York.

Williams, Charles (1956), *He Came down from Heaven*, and *The Forgiveness of Sins*, Faber & Faber, London.

Wilson, Bryan (1976), *Contemporary Transformations of Religion*, Oxford University Press, Oxford.

Wooden, Ken (1976), *Weeping in the Playtime of Others: America's Incarcerated Children*, New York, McGraw-Hill.

Wootton, Anthony (1975), *Dilemmas of Discourse: Controversies about the Sociological Interpretation of Language*, George Allen & Unwin, London.

Ziolkowski, Theodore (1977), *Disenchanted Images: A Literary Iconology*, Princeton University Press, Princeton, New Jersey.

Index